Courtroom Survival for Traffic Officers

By

Martin C. Brhel, Jr., Esq.
Retired Prosecutor

Dedication

Experiencing success in the courtroom is a team effort: law enforcement officer and prosecutor, working as one. Same deal here with *Courtroom Survival for Traffic Officers*.

In court, you need a DA, or whatever else you call them, in your own jurisdiction, leading interference. And, you need a cop, doing the heavy lifting. So, you need the LEO, both on the street and in the courtroom.

Prosecutor, in court, preferably also seeing the world through the windshields of police cars, sharing your unit's front seat. Why ride-alongs? Three reasons: Education. Build rapport. E-ticket rides.

As a corollary, I endorse DA walk 'n talks for cops. They teach you what prosecutors do for a paycheck. How are filing decisions made? How do they prepare for court? And, how do they know the right questions to ask witnesses, especially you?

Now, it's time to introduce some rock stars, with badges, scattered throughout the USA. They made this book the bomb it has turned out to be. I brag up them, not myself. I remain the humble piano player.

First and foremost? From California, two lads I've known seemingly forever. Riverside County Sheriff's Sgt. Dan E. Devinny. Cathedral City Police Department's Sr. Officer Michael J. Van Gorder.

Without Dan and Mike, this book would lack two critically important chapters, **Radar**, and **Traffic Collision Investigation & Reconstruction**.

I thank these longtime friends, from the bottom of my heart, and cannot crow enough about them. I still recall, with great fondness, the quality of the reports they wrote, and their high wire acts on the witness stand. Dan-Dan, the Traffic Man, and Mike the Bike. Kudos, bros!

In addition to these proven California traffic enforcement gurus, praise of the following LEOs, from Arizona through Texas, Arkansas, Missouri, and Michigan, all the way northeast, to Maryland, and New Jersey, on our Atlantic coast, for insightful contributions, concerning traffic issues, in their own states.

It's obvious our out-of-state brethren are as knowledgeable about the own state's traffic enforcement as Dan and Mike are, with our state. You will find their information scattered throughout this book.

Such information is important enough to also have its own chapter, titled **Foundational Requirements-California vs. Other States**. Alphabetically, by name, rank, department, and state, I am privileged to introduce the traffic cops who gave this book the additional depth and breadth it would otherwise lack.

Dep. Sharon Beltz, Oakland County Sheriff (*MI*)

Officer Mark Grant, U of Arkansas-Monticello PD (*AR*)

**Sgt. John H. Groh, Annapolis PD (*MD*)

*Lt. Russell R. Hall, Annapolis PD (*MD*)

*Sgt. Mark W. Howes, Anne Arundel PD (*MD*), Attorney at Law

*Cpl. Gary J. Hughes, Passaic County Sheriff (*NJ*)

*Chief Dennis E. Postel, Crystal Lakes PD (*MO*)

Lt. Mark W. Reynolds, Comal County Sheriff (*TX*)

Sgt. Jeffrey Sprong, Maricopa County Sheriff (*AZ*)

As with any books I write, whether it's a Courtroom Survival tome, a *Joshua Travers DA, Adventure Series* novel, or a biography, I'd be devoid of any manners, if I didn't salute Captain Bill Kasal for his involvement.

Sans, my **Copper Bible Book Company** Executive Editor, this book would lack a great cover, proper formatting, and Bill's predictable tutorial, showing me how to upload to **CreateSpace** and **KDP**, in order for **CBBC** to publish it.

Lastly, in order to prevail, you must enter any courtroom, prepared for battle. Know the facts. Know the law. In my humble opinion, this book will help you do just that, if you apply what you learn. Be well, stay safe, and happy hunting, my stalwart brethren.

Marty

*retired from active duty

**deceased (*RIP, Johnny. We'll meet again, my brother, and hoist a couple!*)

Table of Contents

Chapter 1
An Introduction

This chapter introduces you to many issues you will likely face in the courtroom, but probably will not learn about elsewhere. It does not matter which state you are in. The basics are pretty much the same. They include the following:

1. overcoming defense tactics
2. interviewing witnesses
3. reasonable suspicion vs. probable cause
4. importance of foundation
5. use of radar
6. traffic collision investigation and reconstruction
7. proper preparation
8. alternatives to trial *(aka selling the citation)*
9. possible administrative actions
10. the importance of good notes
11. corpus delicti
12. trial preparation
13. courthouse etiquette
14. trial strategy
15. calibration evidence
16. burden of proof
17. meeting and overcoming objections
18. examination of witnesses

Additionally, chapters, at the book's end, provide you with helpful information, including:

1. a glossary of terms you may deal with, in traffic court and administrative hearings

2. miscellaneous state and federal laws, including both statutes and appellate cases
3. state-by-state information will assist you, when contacting your own state's driver's licensing and vehicle registration office, including its website.

You will observe, I rely on statutes, from several states, in this book, including ones from California. There is a very simple reason why I do this. I'm a California lawyer. These are the tools I've been using for decades.

But this book is not purely about legal research. And, this is not a Criminal Law class. This is how you take care of business. Know your own state's laws. Apply them to the facts you've gathered for each case.

Courtroom Survival for Traffic Officers combines my courtroom experience, with research and information, from peace officers in several states, including California. Its purpose is to provide you with as broad a professional viewpoint as possible.

Frankly, you will never find every relevant law from every state in this or any other Courtroom Survival book I write. There are too many laws and not enough pages to include them. Instead, I use appropriate examples to show you how to function properly.

Several law enforcement officer (*LEO*) buddies from other states have provided information about their own jurisdictions. This allows me to offer a more balanced approach. This was done by relying on both federal and state appellate cases and state statutory law. You will find them throughout this book. You will also learn the difference between mandatory and persuasive authority and its impact on state and federal jurisdictions.

Appellate cases in your own jurisdiction are mandatory for your own courts. They must be followed. Those from other jurisdictions are merely persuasive. While lower courts may follow persuasive authority, they must follow mandatory cases. And if a persuasive case is in conflict with a mandatory one, the latter must be followed by that jurisdiction's courts, whether the ruling is from a federal or state court.

The legal concept controlling this issue is called *comity*, aka legal reciprocity. Each state is expected to deal with the same types of issues, reciprocally, as other states would similarly do. Each state has a high court. Its rulings must be followed by its own inferior courts.

U.S. Supreme Court cases must be followed by every state and federal American jurisdiction. If you are a constitutional devotee you already know authority, found in Article III, Section 1 of the U.S. Constitution is as good as it gets. From it, springs all other American law.

Three levels of federal courts exist for criminal and civil matters: the U.S. Supreme Court, the Circuit Courts of Appeal, and the U.S. District Courts. The Circuit Courts of Appeal are the first level of federal appellate court. They answer only to the Supremes. District Courts are federal trial courts. Separate from them are specialty courts dealing with issues, such as bankruptcy, admiralty, taxes, international trade, and so on.

Within each circuit are a set number of district courts, based on population. For example, in a populous state like California, there are several districts within its boundaries, such as Northern, Central, Southern, and Eastern. States like Alaska or Arizona, by comparison, have one district for their entire geographical area.

Circuit Courts of Appeal are separated into thirteen distinct geographical areas, throughout the entire United States, ranging numerically, from the First to the Eleventh circuits, plus the District of Columbia (*DC*), and the Federal Circuit. Any more details are not relevant to the purpose of this book.

In researching needed material for this book, however, I rely on California law to illustrate issues. This is the law I have practiced since 1977. But I also rely on input from officers in other states, from east coast to west coast, and relevant law from those other jurisdictions.

In my opinion, in addition to this being the place where the rubber meets the road, we also rely on first-hand experience. This results in shared knowledge, by the boys and girls who patrol the highways and byways of their own communities.

How do basic traffic laws function? From a practical standpoint, we must do more than merely know what we lawyers call the *black letter law*. In order to keep the length of this book manageable, rather than list entire code sections verbatim, my intention herein is to simply list some statutes, including relevant language.

Each court tends to function a bit differently from other courts. In addition to relying on the uniqueness of their own state's laws, each jurisdiction also writes its own rules of court which set forth procedures that must be followed. That is true whether we are talking about neighboring counties within the same state, counties within neighboring states or courts on opposite sides of the country. Courts have their own way of functioning. This is known as habit or custom.

Judges are about as individualistic a group of people as you will probably ever deal with. And even though they are each duty bound to follow the law, they still have their own way of doing things.

You must learn, by trial and error, how judges you will deal with conduct business. I cannot tell you that. Frankly, I do not know any other author who can do that either. Therefore, the best way I know for you to learn the day-to-day nuts and bolts of what your own traffic courts require? Talk to the more experienced officers in your area. The guys who go to court a lot because they write citations.

As noted, cases from your own state courts will take precedence over the cases from other states' courts, including my state. And if federal cases are in conflict with state court cases, federal takes precedence over any state.

As noted earlier, U.S. Supreme Court cases outrank those from other courts. Case law will either be from state or federal courts. Should you review appellate cases, you will find them in sets of books called *Reporters*, aka appellate case books. Each federal and state court will have its own; each with different names.

The easiest way to familiarize yourself with appellate cases is to read your own state's annotated statutes. They list appellate case citations. Legislators write statutes. Courts interpret them. These judicial interpretations are in appellate rulings, found in Reporters.

Here is a quick cram course in legal research. Take the time to go to your local law library. Ask librarians for assistance. They will be more than happy to help. The way the Internet is replacing everything, they will probably be only too happy to assist. Tell them you are doing legal research. Start with something easy, such as your own state's basic speed laws. Ask them to locate both statutes and appellate cases. Once you begin reading your traffic statutes, next read the appellate cases in the annotations. In addition to learning what the courts say, you will also learn names of the various Reporters, and how they are cited in the annotations. It will be an eye opener. I guarantee it.

One more point before we move on. There's a valid reason why lawmakers frown on the use of hearsay in the courtroom. Hearsay can be unreliable. Therefore, if an author refers to any source of outside authority, such as an appellate case, do not get lazy and take our word for it. Read the case yourself. Once you learn how to research, the old-fashioned way, you can begin taking shortcuts and do it online.

Findlaw.com is an excellent resource. Many lawyers, including me, use it to read statutes, cases, and constitutional verbiage. You can also just Google sought after information.

Lawmakers tend to not be a terribly original bunch. Irrespective of what state they serve, they tend to do essentially the same thing their brethren, in other states, do, even if they say it differently. But please remember, you cannot have a better resource than your local prosecuting attorney's office, when you need to know current relevant law. They are on your team. Use them.

If you have not already done so, get acquainted with a couple of their more seasoned trial lawyers. Get to know them well enough, you can contact them. Pick their brains, as you need to, for practical guidance. Simply knowing the black letter law is not good enough. You need to know how things work in your own area's courtrooms. No one is going to guide you better than they will. This should also show you how to become acquainted with statutes and cases you need to know, to do your job.

In short, akin to the old expression, *parts is parts*? Evidence is evidence is evidence. Evidence codes are not terribly distinct from one state to another, mainly because their basis is the old *British common law*. The United States is based on this legal concept, with the exception of some aspects of the Louisiana system, which many people refer to as a *civil law* jurisdiction.

Civil law springs from Roman law, as in the former Roman Empire. Over time it has also gained influence from both Spain and France, ergo the name *Napoleonic Code*, when Napoleon was the leader of France. If you need a civil law tour guide ask your local Pelican State prosecutor.

In real estate, an age old mantra proclaims *Location. Location. Location.* Perhaps we should begin this exercise by creating our own mantra. Let's call this one *preparation...preparation...preparation*. As we discussed previously, the key to winning? Be better prepared, than your opponent. This is not rocket science. But it is hard work. If you do not mind working hard, you will succeed. If you do not work hard, you will not succeed.

Traffic is a unique area of law enforcement. In addition to focusing exclusively on the laws of your state, dealing with the operation of motor vehicles, any trials you experience will normally be before a judge or a commissioner, rather than a jury, because most of these crimes are infractions, not misdemeanors or felonies. Depending on your jurisdiction such tribunals may be known by a variety of names, including court or bench trials. Crimes are infractions, misdemeanors, or felonies.

Infractions are normally punished by fines only. In fact, the only time I am aware of defendants going to jail following such a conviction? If they request custody, in lieu of paying their fines. Misdemeanor convictions may result in grants of probation, with fines and/or county jail. Felony convictions may result in state prison. Violating any federal felony statute may result in commitment to federal prison.

Another common difference between traffic court, and other courts? Most people who receive traffic citations are not represented by a lawyer. In such instances, after all potential witnesses have been sworn to an oath by the clerk, when your case is called, the presiding jurist will ask you to recite, narratively, what you observed. Unless a lawyer insists otherwise, traffic court rules of evidence are fairly informal. They are in my courtroom.

States do things differently than other states. For example, in Arizona and elsewhere, unlike California, officers can issue citations from unmarked vehicles, and do so, in plain clothes. Let me give you an example of such an officer in court for a speeding citation. If radar was used to determine speed, the officer may only need a card to show the radar unit, in question, was calibrated, unlike required machinations in my own state.

Below is an example of what such an officer's testimony might be:

"My name is John Doe. I have been a deputy with the Maricopa County Sheriff's Office for 11 years. On 07/11/11, at approximately 0745 hours, I was on routine patrol, in the area of 111th Avenue and Olive, within the jurisdiction of the West Valley Justice Court. I observed a white van, bearing AZ license plate AZD-111, traveling westbound on Olive. The van appeared to be moving at a higher rate of speed than the posted 45 mph speed limit. I visually estimated the speed of 65 mph; verified by my radar unit, to be 65 mph. I stopped the vehicle, which pulled over properly on Olive. I contacted the male driver, sitting to my right side here in court, wearing a red shirt and tan slacks. He identified himself, with his valid AZ driver's license, as Jose Williams. I asked Williams if he knew why I stopped him. He replied, 'Yeah, I was speeding.' I then issued him a citation for ARS 28-701.A, commonly called speed greater than posted."

Irrespective of what state you are in, following your testimony, the court will next allow the defendant to cross-examine you. Once that is completed, assuming the defendant chooses to question you, they next have the right to call their own defense witnesses, and testify in their own behalf, if they choose to do that.

Do not blithely assume you will not have to contend with a lawyer. Why do I say this? Lawyers provide a service, in return for a fee. Clients, in turn, pay a fee, for an agreed upon service, by the lawyer. Lawyers like to get paid. Do the math.

Always out-prepare your opposition, irrespective of whether defendants represent themselves, or are represented by counsel. Self-representation is known as *In Propria Persona*, aka *In Pro Per,* as is the case with many traffic court defendants.

Just like LEOs, or lawyers, defendants are people who come from many different walks of life. Some are impecunious. Others have money to burn. Some opt to hire lawyers, even when doing so is a financial strain.

Sometimes they do this because they cannot afford another traffic conviction.

People who hire lawyers may hire them for reasons, having nothing to do with the strength of the case against them. In every class where I've taught police officers, irrespective of state, I always remind officers, if they are going to err, always err on the side of caution. Therefore, any time you issue a traffic citation, assume the motorist has just hired the most competent trial lawyer available to represent them. In prior times, that might be the author.

Believe it or not, the professional experience that motivates me to write books for police officers, has more to do with what I learned, during my tour of duty on the so-called *dark side*, than it does from my role as a prosecutor. That's because I found weaknesses I likely would not have discovered, as a prosecutor.

How did I get into traffic ticket defense? Early in my career, another lawyer referred a guy, with a very fast BMW, to me. He kept getting speeding tickets. The other lawyer believed nothing could be done for him. Actually, he was wrong. In fact, my research was rather illuminating. It led me to believe I had an actual chance of winning, *if the judge followed the law*.

Unfortunately, I based my assessment, on little more than speculation, because no authoritative books existed on this subject. And, I had not done this before. You don't leave law school saying your career will be traffic ticket defense. One of my favorite law school classes was Evidence. My knowledge of it told me I was correct. However, I still had no actual traffic court lawyering experience to confirm my beliefs. Needless to say, I was concerned.

Therefore, I had to rely on understanding my own state's Evidence Code. As I readied for court, I prepared, by relying on foundation, the hearsay rule, and the Best Evidence Rule. We will talk about this in a bit.

I knew I could not allow the officer to present any evidence of my client's speed. As soon as the judge heard how fast he was going, my client was convicted. But if I could choreograph all this properly I would win. If I failed, my client would lose. It was that simple.

My likelihood of winning could not depend on any evidence gathered by the citing officer. Instead, the possible outcome had to rely entirely on the rules of evidence, primarily the rules dealing with foundational issues. It all boiled down to whether I could properly control the flow of evidence.

Let's take a brief moment and discuss *foundation*. In the courtroom, foundation is nothing more, than presenting some preliminary evidence. You do that to convince the judge, you can present additional evidence.

That's why it's called foundation. Conversely, it means you must convince the judge your opponent has not presented enough preliminary evidence, in order to present additional evidence. Translation: the real damaging stuff for the defendant.

This may include a variety of subjects, such as:

1. establishing an arresting officer's qualifications, as an expert, in order for them to present their opinion, on the issue why they are court, in the first place.
    a. In a narcotics case this may include:
        i. proving a controlled substance was possessed for sale, rather than mere personal use, solely via an officer's opinion.
        ii. proving a suspected controlled substance was, in fact, a controlled substance, solely from an officer's opinion.

Foundation also deals with presenting evidence about *things*, including mechanical things. This may include items, such as the speedometer in your patrol vehicle. Or, radar devices. Obviously, if you determine a motorist's speed, by bumper-pacing his vehicle, it is critical to the integrity of your testimony, competent evidence be presented, the speedometer in your patrol vehicle was properly calibrated. Same is true with calibrating and testing radar.

Otherwise, neither has any value to your pending case. Examples?

1. Establish an arresting officer's qualifications, as an expert, to present their opinion on the testimonial issues. In a narcotics case this may include:

    1. proving a controlled substance was possessed for sale, rather than mere personal use, solely via an officer's opinion.
    2. proving a suspected controlled substance was, in fact, a controlled substance, solely from an officer's opinion.

There are a number of ways a traffic officer can determine a motorist's speed. These may include:

1. radar
2. devices such as stop watches, if permitted by your jurisdiction
3. your patrol unit's speedometer

I've heard officers claim they can accurately estimate speed. The problem with this route? It's vulnerable to be called too subjective. If you do not lay enough foundation to satisfy the court you have adequate training and experience to really do this, forget about it. If judges let you testify to this, without first obtaining an adequate foundation, they are not doing their job. And I mean very adequate. Hint: successful completion of a POST 24-hour Radar class works.

As for bumper-pacing, if the court is doing its job you will first need to present evidence your unit's speedometer was properly calibrated. Not doing this would be akin to permitting results of a breathalyzer without first establishing it was working properly.

Your state's lawmakers determine how many tools, you can use to do your job. Or, they erect obstacles, hindering you from doing it properly. California is obstacle-rich. Our legislature prohibits stop watches, requires uniforms and marked units, and until fairly recent years, did not even allow CHP to use radar. I do not know why. I respectfully suggest you ask a local assembly member, or state senator, if you need the answer.

Are you really surprised? These lawmakers have the constitutional tools to eradicate gangs, but don't. This same crowd believes dope possession should be a misdemeanor. Yet, every hearing I conducted for Board of Parole Hearings? Each parole violator or lifer was an addict. They also removed 40,000 felons from state prison and formal parole. Removed. Gone. Do the math. I know I did. It's called Penal Code 3000.03, aka Non Revocable parole. Lasts one year. Our Strike Team implemented that public safety stain. We oversaw prison and parole reductions, for the same basic crowd, I worked hard, as a DA, to send to prison. Even gang-bangers made the cut, unless they were *validated prison gang members*. Hello? The street crowd hadn't completed their apprenticeship yet.

With, or without a defense attorney's involvement, be prepared to present such foundational evidence. Otherwise, the speed shown by the device you are relying on, is irrelevant. So who presents such evidence? Assuming he is qualified to so testify, it is the person who did the calibration. If he is not qualified, it is a total waste of time.

In California, measuring speed by determining elapsed time, and other ways, such as use of radar, but without an Engineering and Traffic Survey that justifies the posted speed limit, is inadmissible *speed trap* evidence, per Vehicle Code §40802.

Back when I was still representing the accused, each CHP traffic officer had to rely solely on their patrol vehicle's speedometer, in order to lawfully prove a motorist was speeding. Fortunately for my then-traffic clients, CHP failed to properly introduce evidence establishing its patrol units' speedometers were competently calibrated. And, on most of my cases, the issuing officer paid the price. Without that tour of duty, I would not have written this book.

Unless your own state's laws permits this, a citing officer is not competent to testify to the calibration of his unit's speedometer. Why? Simple. You did not do the calibration. Some mechanic did. If the officer tried to testify to this it would be inadmissible hearsay. Let me repeat: hearsay.

A typical officer is paid to drive his government car, not calibrate its speedometer. Even if your state permits you to present a document that attests to the calibration, unless it qualifies as a public record, and complies with the Best Evidence Rule, it is still not admissible evidence. Evidence is evidence, irrespective of location.

As an aside, even if the mechanic testifies, evidence must first be presented he is qualified to do the calibration, based on his own training and experience. All this became my plan of attack in traffic court. And it works.

If the lawyer you deal with convinces the judge you failed to present evidence the speedometer was properly calibrated, whatever speed you purportedly measured becomes irrelevant. The lawyer will succeed by making timely and proper objections, when you attempt to introduce any evidence of his client's speed. The defense does not even need to present evidence. The defense will establish reasonable doubt, through your own testimony. Case closed.

There is only one person you can rely *Y-o-u*. If you do not take the time to gather all the evidence you need to prove your case, including knowing what your own statutory laws require, do not expect the judge or prosecutor to bail you out. They will not. That is not their job. Plus, they may not know the law either. Should you fail to perform your duties, the only thing you can expect, *and should* expect, is to hear the judge say *not guilty*.

Some motorists mistakenly believe they have an absolute right to a driver's license. Wrong. A driver's license is a *privilege*, not a constitutionally protected right. By example, California's Vehicle Code calls a driver's license a *privilege to operate a motor vehicle*. So does your own state.

Conduct falls into one of two basic categories. Constitutionally protected rights, include: free speech, and the other rights found in the U.S. Constitution's Bill of Rights, as well as all the Amendments. Other behavior, such as operating a motor vehicle, legally, is a privilege.

That is true for a number of reasons. First, even if someone is deemed competent enough to lawfully obtain a driver's license on a given date, this is always subject to change. Some motorists simply fail to conform their driving conduct, so it comports with the safety owed other motorists, pedestrians, bicyclists, and vehicular passengers, as well as to themselves.

Former U.S. President Thomas Jefferson spoke clearly to this issue many years ago when he declared "*...the only purpose of government is to protect the People...*" Part of that protection is regulating the privilege to operate a motor vehicle. What are some of the assorted reasons a driver's license should be listed as a privilege, rather than a right? Possible safety considerations are:

1. drug abuse
2. alcohol abuse
3. lack of proper mental faculties, due to retardation, or mental illness
4. deterioration of physical functions, due to aging, illness, or disease

As a police officer, you view events through the windshield of your police vehicle, non-participants may not even realize exist. This is why I regularly went on ride-alongs, as a prosecutor. And it is why I still encourage my former colleagues to do that. Seeing the world in this fashion, a person learns, first-hand, how LEOs earn their paychecks. In short, doing this makes a prosecutor a better prosecutor, just as time in court makes you a better law enforcement officer.

Ride-alongs truly opened my eyes. They helped me see things, giving me a completely different perspective, than, otherwise, I would have had. Reading myriad *ivory tower* appellate cases does not improve judgment or common sense. Appellate cases tell you what isolated appellate court judges think about a given topic. That particular view, may or may not be accurate.

Ride-alongs illustrate what the expression *trained observer* really means. These outings educated me, as to the ability of police officers to make helpful public safety observations. I learned firsthand, appellate verbiage criticizing police officer conduct as *mere hunches* is often misguided and unwitting babbling. Some appellate court justices simply do not know what they are talking about on these issues. Sorry, but I speak the truth.

You can make observations others do not make, or even know of, because of your unique *training and experience*, unlike the so-called *hunches* the unlearned have the nerve to wrongly criticize. As we both know, a hunch is not a hunch *if the formed opinion is based on appropriate training and experience*.

That makes you an *expert*, not a *speculator*. If you have not already done so, I also encourage you to open an authentic channel of communication with your local prosecutors. Invite them to go on ride-alongs with you. That's how, and why, I went on ride-alongs. You will give my brethren the same opportunity to see the world through the windshields of police cars, as I did.

As a traffic officer, you may be wondering why you should encourage prosecutors to go on ride-alongs. You may respond most, if not all, of your appearances in traffic court are done, without even having a prosecutor at your side. That may be true. View part of your job, as educating your local prosecutors. Here's why.

Some prosecutors are *career prosecutors*. These are people who chose to spend their entire professional lives as prosecutors. Others may work a few years in the local prosecutor's office, before they bail. Some migrate to the defense side of counsel table. Others become judges.

Routinely, former prosecutors who become judges, begin life on the trial court bench. If they have the opportunity to share your observations, from a police car, they will be more inclined to make better, more objective, decisions about the quality of your work. That's true, irrespective of whether they ride with you, or some other cop. And this is not limited to the evidentiary decisions they must make, in order to determine, if you meet your burden of proving someone's guilt, beyond a reasonable doubt.

It goes even further than that. In other words, some prosecutors grow up to become trial court judges. Some trial court judges grow up to become appellate court jurists. Appellate courts render the decisions. Those impact the validity of the very laws you are sworn to enforce, including determining, if statutory laws even pass constitutional muster. Such decisions must be followed by the trial courts you work in.

This gives you an opportunity to play a role in creating sound public safety appellate decisions by impacting the way a future appellate court justice thinks, on issues such as, whether a hunch is a hunch, as opposed to deciding folks like you made a traffic stop, or pedestrian check, by relying on training and experience, as experts.

But, you argue, what if the guy becomes a defense attorney? Then, by educating them, they'll be hard pressed to ethically challenge your credibility on such issues. It might allow the prosecutor to accuse them of perpetrating a fraud on the court. That sort of misconduct can cost a lawyer their bar license. If you think I'm kidding, ask Bill Clinton what happened to his.

Hot off the presses. On Monday, June 8, 2015, the Judicial Council of California, issued an edict, according to a June 9 *Los Angeles Times* article: **People can fight traffic tickets without paying fine first, Judicial Council says**. Not the way I'd create a title. But, I digress.

The rule-making arm of my state's court system, since 1926, just did the seemingly impossible. In my humble opinion, the decision lets traffic scofflaws off the hook. Here's what they did. The Judicial Council determined traffic court defendants can no longer be forced to post bail, in order to set their cases for trial. Instead, they get a free ride. Why not? In bail hearings, any defendant is presumed guilty, not innocent. Talk to the Legislature.

With all due respect to Chief Justice Tani Cantil-Sakauye who "...said she was proud the council had acted so swiftly," this decision goes against decades of stare decisis. Therefore, I have a respectful suggestion for those who believe traffic court defendants are being mistreated. If you don't want a citation, obey the law. Not that difficult. I do it, as do many other motorists.

Between California lawmakers trying to reduce all felony drug possession to misdemeanors, and ignorant California voters doing just that on November 4, 2014, with Proposition 47, combined with this miscarriage of justice, I weep for the future of what once was the Golden State.

Prop 47 ignores the fact drug addicts commit significant felonies, daily, to get the wherewithal to obtain their chemical body additive of choice. Pick a crime. Any crime. Addicts are committing one, or more, as I type, and as you read this. My 37 months, as Deputy-in-Charge of the Major Narcotic Violator Program for Riverside County's vast Eastern Division, tells me I'm right.

Pool this thoughtlessness, with forbidding the posting of bail on traffic cases? You have a recipe for disaster. Taxpayers are footing the bill, and being abused. Yet, poverty lawyers insist the Council didn't go far enough. Frankly, they should do two things, which may open their eyes: (a) go on copious police ride-alongs, as I did, repeatedly, with every agency that sent us cases to prosecute, including any and all city, county, state, and federal agencies, and, (b) sit in traffic court.

Listen carefully to what I've been hearing, in two separate counties, since 1978. Unpaid traffic infraction fines amount to more than $10 billion, according to "...a recent report by the Lawyers Committee for Civil Rights of the San Francisco Bay Area and other groups."

Are these folks serious? They seek to reward motorists who put the rest of us at unnecessary risk of harm? Envision what $10 billion would do to improve public safety? Public education? Eradicate drug addiction? Taking better care of the elderly? The infirm? Our at-risk youth? Better arming our military and repairing those injured, in the line of duty? Better training of law enforcement? Again, I must cry, then sigh, before I seethe. The inmates are running the asylum. Perhaps literally this time.

Ignorance is NOT bliss. It's merely the product of abject laziness.

Chapter 2

Prosecutorial Ethics and Common Defense Tactics

How do you overcome common defense tactics? First, acquaint yourself with the contrasting ethical duties of prosecutors and defense counsel. A prosecutor is paid to dispense justice. Defense counsel is duty bound to zealously represent their client. I will explain.

Both sides must adhere to antagonistic ethical requirements, if they wish to avoid facing professional discipline. Akin to your own job, as noted, the prosecutor's role is to dispense justice. That's because you are both on the law enforcement team, dealing with bad guys and protecting public safety.

Defense lawyers, on the other hand, are in your life to acquit the defendant. That is their sole purpose. If you hate defense counsel, it's not their fault. Blame their mandated ethics. Ironically, justice is irrelevant to them because of their unique professional obligations. What if counsel believes their client is guilty? It does not matter. The very same duty to acquit attaches.

On the other hand, prosecutors must prove guilt, beyond a reasonable doubt, *if and only if*, they have a good faith belief: (a) the defendant is guilty, (b) they believe they can prove it, beyond a reasonable doubt, to a unanimous jury. If not, they are duty bound to not prosecute. And prosecutors must seek a fair disposition in every case

On the other side of counsel table, a defense attorney only has an ethical onus to create reasonable doubt. In a jury trial, they must convince at least one trier of fact the prosecution did not prove its case. In a court trial, they must convince the judge to find the defendant not guilty. If it's a jury trial, they must confuse at least one juror. The only parameter defense counsel must stay within? They cannot suborn perjury. Nor, can they perpetrate a fraud on the court. Translation: they can't allow witnesses to commit perjury. They can't mislead the judge.

Judges have strict boundaries within which they must function. These borders are spelled out by canons of judicial ethics. They define what judges can, and cannot, do in their professional roles. The same is true with lawyers. The American Bar Association formulated canons of ethics, aka a lawyer's code of professional responsibility. Lawyers must unfailingly abide by this, if we wish to avoid disciplinary action by our state's bar association. Such actions can range from informal reprimands, all the way up to and including disbarment.

I do not seek to create the misimpression lawyers have no other professional concerns. Below is a rather extensive list of no-no's from the **Rules of Professional Conduct** found at the California State Bar Association's website. It ranges from the bar's disciplinary authority, in general, to attorney contact with jurors. I have chosen to list only the general topic headings.

If you are in another state, your own state bar's website should contain the same basic information. Just click on the *Professional Responsibility* or *Ethics* link. They seem never ending and run from Rule 1-100, up through and including, Rule 5-320. Feel free to explore your own state, as well as any of the rest. Remember, it's the Internet. You are not limited to just one state. So feel free to search to your heart's content.

As noted already, standards of ethics vary greatly for prosecutors and defense attorneys. Prosecutors have a far simpler set of rules, within which they are required to perform their duties. The basic mantra is an uncomplicated one. Prosecutors are required to *dispense justice*. In other words, we are paid to do the right thing. In simple language, this means prosecutors must:

1. prosecute only the guilty
2. always acquit the innocent
3. seek a fair disposition in each and every case

How does this impact many filing decisions a prosecutor must make? It means no criminal case can be filed, unless and until two questions can be answered in the affirmative. First, do we believe the suspect is guilty of the crime, for which he stands accused? This is answered, only after reviewing all relevant police reports.

Secondly, do we believe enough evidence exists, to allow us to file the case? In other words, is the evidence sufficient to convince a unanimous jury the defendant is guilty, beyond a reasonable doubt? What, if the answer, to either question, is no? That is most elemental. Ethically, the case cannot be filed. Period. End of conversation. In case, you are wondering why I write as if I am still active duty, since I am now retired, it is because I will always be a prosecutor at heart, just like most of you will remain LEOs, long after you pull the pin too.

There are two ways a prosecutor can commence a criminal case:

1. file a criminal complaint
2. seek a grand jury indictment

As the Supreme Court noted in *Borderkircher v. Hayes* 434 U.S. 357 (1978), "...so long as the prosecutor has probable cause to believe that the accused committed an offense, defined by statute, the decision whether or not to prosecute, and what charge to file or bring before a grand jury generally rests entirely in his discretion."

With all due respect to the court, this makes no sense to me. I believe they set the standard too low. First, what is *probable cause*? Does the officer have a reasonable belief the suspect has committed a crime? Don't confuse this, with the *reasonable suspicion* standard, required for a *temporary detention*.

Proof beyond a reasonable doubt means that state of the case, after the comparison and consideration of all the evidence, you cannot say you have an abiding conviction of the truth of the charges. The latter standard is a much higher one.

If a prosecutor must convince a jury, beyond a reasonable doubt, a defendant has committed whatever crime he stands accused of, why is the court only requiring a standard of probable cause to support a filing? At some point, does a case magically gain strength it previously lacked, if the initial standard is only probable cause? Isn't this akin to a Category 2 hurricane somehow becoming a Category 5 storm? Who waves the magic wand?

Keep something in mind. I do not expect everyone with whom I cross paths to agree with me. I expect some to point out the constitutional standard for arrests or searches is also only *probable cause*. Therefore, a critic would note, why should prosecutors have to adhere to a stricter standard than their armed brethren? However, even though prosecutors and LEOs are all on the same law enforcement team, this does not mean we all have the same duties.

When a police officer is making the decision to curtail a person's liberty, with an arrest or a search, the probable cause standard makes sense. Why? The officer must act quickly. They are protecting the public. And, they are also safeguarding themselves from allegations of false arrest, or deprivation of some other constitutionally protected right, enjoyed by the accused.

At this point, in the investigation, incriminating evidence is still being gathered. To require a LEO to meet the much higher standard of beyond a reasonable doubt is unduly burdensome, thus increasing the likelihood of frivolous civil rights lawsuits, on the one hand, or decreased public safety on the other. That's especially true as riots consume Ferguson, NYC, and Baltimore.

By the time any case is reviewed by the prosecutor, however, most of the investigation is complete. In fact, one of the primary reasons cases are rejected for filing purposes is to allow the agency, requesting prosecution, to do further investigation. That answers prosecutorial questions, dealing with whether adequate evidence has been gathered to convince a courtroom jury. Pardon my cynicism, but this particular holding strikes me as yet another example of ivory tower thinking. A ride-along might cure that.

The Supreme Court may have enunciated a lower standard of proof, than beyond a reasonable doubt, as the standard for a filing decision. And I respect that. That's the law. If I were still an active duty DA I would have to do, at least that much. But, from lots of experience on this issue, I am satisfied prosecutors adhere to a much higher practical filing standard. I know I did.

In other words, if proof beyond a reasonable doubt is required to support a conviction, does it make sense a prosecutor would only require probable cause when he files? I did not. And, I suspect any other self-respecting prosecutor would not either.

The bar of each state should set its own standards. For example, the California State Bar deals with this issue in Rule 5-110 (*Performing the Duty of Member in Government Service*): "A member in government service shall not institute or cause to be instituted criminal charges when the member knows or should know that the charges are not supported by probable cause…"

Here's a side thought. My state bar appears to compound the problem by relying on the reasoning of *Borderkircher.* However, I do not expect my reservations, expressed herein, to change the landscape on that issue. Therefore, for illustrative purposes, I will do what any other lawyer does. I'll adhere to the legal standard enunciated by the court. But, acquiescing does not change my opinion, one iota. The mere fact I yield to the Supremes does not impede my free speech rights to disagree.

What if a prosecutor discovers the answer to either of the above-noted questions, concerning belief in guilt, and the ability to prove that, has changed from *yes* to *no*, during the pendency of their prosecution of any defendant? If so, the same ground rules apply.

According to Rule 5-110, "...(i)f, after the institution of criminal charges, the member in government service having responsibility for prosecuting the charges becomes aware that those charges are not supported by probable cause, the member shall promptly so advise the court in which the criminal matter is pending."

A defense attorney's job is to win, i.e., acquit their client. That is not the prosecutor's role, irrespective of what his official title is: deputy district attorney, assistant district attorney, deputy prosecuting attorney, assistant prosecuting attorney, deputy county attorney, assistant county attorney, or any other title. Push the title aside. Geography does not change our ethical duties.

Prosecutors are duty-bound to resolve our cases fairly and justly, both to the defendant, and the People, Commonwealth, State, or whatever other name your jurisdiction carries, on its own charging documents. If the prosecutor learns something has occurred, now exonerating the defendant, he has an affirmative duty to inform the defense, immediately.

U.S. Supreme Court case *Brady v. Maryland* (infra), to be more fully discussed later, is the landmark case on this issue. *Brady* is a judicial mandate. Prosecutors shall promptly, and voluntarily, provide the defense with any exculpatory evidence, as soon as they discover it.

What if opposing counsel tells a prosecutor the case has purported problems? This is not the same as a *Brady* issue. Obtaining such information means the prosecutor should objectively determine, if a reduction of charges, or dismissal, is actually warranted. Remember defense counsel's duty is to acquit. A prosecutor should receive such information objectively. They must make an intelligent decision, consistent with the evidence. This could mean a reduction, a dismissal, or no change.

Canon 7 of the American Bar Association's Code of Professional Responsibility contains clear and convincing language. It reads: "A Lawyer Should Represent a Client Zealously Within the Bounds of the Law." This verbiage gives defense counsel much greater latitude, than a prosecutor, not only in terms of what they can do, but what they must do, if they are to avoid professional discipline. Short of suborning perjury, or perpetrating a fraud on the court, defense attorneys are duty-bound to do anything, and everything, they can to acquit their client of any criminal charges they face.

Subornation of perjury is the act of knowingly providing perjured evidence. This means offering evidence, to a material fact, the lawyer knows to be false. An example of this? A client tells the lawyer he committed the crime. But, the lawyer nonetheless decides to allow the same defendant to take the witness stand, and testify he did not commit the crime, of which he stands accused.

I actually handled a case nearly three decades ago, with a defense witness ready, willing, and able to commit perjury. But for me, he would have done that. My client was a convicted felon, charged with being a felon in possession of a firearm, in violation of California Penal Code §12021.

He told me a witness would testify he was not the guy in possession of the contraband rifle, despite five, on-duty, police officers, who knew him from previous professional encounters, observed him carrying the seized weapon, around midnight. Before I forget, my client was also a gang-banger. Are you connecting the dots yet?

My investigator and I talked to the witness. We asked him where he was, when he made this observation. He claimed he was in the bathroom of his house, across the street. He allegedly saw my client, and all the cops. He also said a bright overhead light was on, in that room. But, he insisted he could clearly sec what was happening outside.

We attempted to duplicate his incredible feat. Neither of us could see anything outside. I reasonably concluded the witness was lying. So did my investigator. Since possession of the rifle, by a convicted felon, was a material element of the crime, I knew I would suborn perjury, if I allowed him to take the witness stand. So he did not testify. I do not know if other counsel would have permitted this. I did not. And, I will always feel quite comfortable with my decision.

Perpetrating a fraud on the court is the other way a criminal defense lawyer can be disciplined. This means attempting to mislead the court about something relevant to the case. What if the lawyer knows his client is guilty? Doesn't he have a responsibility? Plead the client guilty, and not waste taxpayer dollars, on a trial, to avoid being accused of doing this? The answer? No.

Even if the lawyer knows the client is guilty as charged, he is still duty bound to mount a zealous defense, providing he does not suborn perjury, or perpetrate a fraud on the court. Other than these provisos, defense counsel not only has free reign, to create reasonable doubt, Canon 7 mandates they do.

Allow me to share a true story with you, involving a very good defense attorney I have known since the late '70s. To protect privacy rights I will not identify him other than to say this was a death penalty murder case. This lawyer has a lot of experience. He has handled a wide variety of criminal cases. And, he's well respected by those who know him.

He was appointed, by the court, to represent a defendant, charged with a brutal, cold-blooded murder of a convenience store clerk. Against his better judgment, as he stated on the record, his client forbad him to offer any defense, in the penalty phase, after the same jury found him guilty of murder, and found special circumstances, supporting death.

Predictably, the defendant was sentenced to death. But his sentence was overturned, by the California Supreme Court. The Supremes said this very competent lawyer *did not adequately represent this cold-blooded murderer by following his instructions*. True, even though appellate courts have long held, such ultimate decisions, are the sole province of the defendant.

Such rulings tend to affect many decisions lawyers make on behalf of any client they represent who is accused of a crime. As a result, counsel may do many things, with no reasonable basis in fact for doing. That's because they are afraid of being labeled incompetent by an appellate court.

As an analogy, visualize how certain highly visible arrests tend to make you, as a LEO, much more cautious. How about the Rodney King arrest that tossed four LAPD uniforms under the bus? Get my point?

Would such a published opinion make me cautious? You better believe it. Wouldn't that make you wary? Another concern? Being sued by a disgruntled client for malpractice. Please understand something. I am not proposing an abstract concept, or some hypothetical scenario, that will not happen in real life. Clients sue lawyers who have done nothing wrong. Some who do are simply looking for an undeserved pot of gold.

Case in point? I was sued by a client, following our settling his case in federal court, approved in open court by a U.S. Magistrate Judge, on the record. It took forever to get a frivolous suit dismissed. Face it. Stuff happens.

Fortunately, I don't face such decisions anymore. I will never be so challenged either. I do not represent any defendants, I would have sent to prison, during my prosecutorial years. In fact, I do not practice law anymore. When I'm not playing Traffic & Transportation Commissioner or hearing traffic cases as a San Diego Superior Court Judge Pro Tem, I write books. But from first-hand experience I did things, as a defense counsel, because Monday morning quarterbacks might second-guess me.

Defense counsel is duty bound to zealously represent their client, irrespective of their personal feelings about their client, or the charges they face. The only exception to this steadfast rule is when a lawyer is so repulsed by the charges the defendant faces he cannot zealously represent him. I refused to accept appointment to be lead counsel for a double cop killer. I just couldn't do it. Ironically, he had to be retried. Years later, an appellate court found his appointed counsel did not adequately represent him. Had I represented him, he'd probably already be dead. Slam dunk case. No Inadequate Assistance by Counsel (IAC) finding, on appeal. Go figure. That case is why I became a DA.

In such instances counsel is duty bound to *not* represent the defendant. Obviously, the court can also relieve counsel from representing a client, should such information be gained, after counsel commences representing the accused.

Never assume the court, or the prosecution, will automatically do the right thing, just because you believe you have thoroughly prepared your case. In other words, just because you do your job does not mean the judge, or the prosecutor, will do theirs.

Do not expect either to bail you out. If you have not done your job you are on your own. That is why it is so critically important, to take the time to do things right.

Chapter 3
Interviewing Investigative Subjects

Investigative subjects fall into one of three different categories: *witnesses*, *victims*, *suspects*. And, they can actually occupy all three groups, at the same time. It happens. Example? Visualize a two-vehicle collision. The drivers get into a fist fight, with one another. Each asks you to arrest the other driver for battery. Even if you do, the DA should *wisely* choose to not file, due to Fifth Amendment issues. I would certainly reject such a filing request. But this does not mean you will not take all involved parties to jail. Why? Keeping the peace? Maybe? Add probable cause vs. reasonable doubt.

Should something like this occur, do you Mirandize? That depends. Add a final twist. Assume you inventory the vehicles. You find dope. A simple civil matter may now be a felony, except in CA, thanks to legislative incompetence. What if both vehicles have dope? You find yourself with a nice felony two-bagger for your efforts, if not in my state. It's your very first week, without any training wheels. Now this? Dream date or nightmare?

Let's tweak this hypothetical one more time. Even though the prosecutor is not filing the mutual combat counts against anyone, you will soon find yourself preparing to give testimony, at a preliminary hearing, or before a grand jury, for two possible felonies.

What do you do? For starters, always expect the unexpected. If you do not, you may quickly find yourself in, over your head. Therefore, always err on the side of caution. If an investigative subject falls into all three categories, if you treat them like a suspect, you should be okay.

Traffic duty is unique, compared to other areas of law enforcement, such as regular patrol, or investigative work. Some things you do as a traffic cop are pretty much the same as you might experience with any other police duties. This includes methodology you need to follow, when interviewing any investigative subjects.

Why don't we just call them witnesses? Because some of them will not be witnesses, even in the face of our hypothetical, just passed. Let's explore these three categories:

1. witness (*Miranda probably not necessary, but another admonition is required.*)
2. victim (*Miranda probably not necessary, but another admonition is required.*)
3. suspect (*Miranda may be necessary, depending on custodial status.*)

Where an investigative subject fits, into any investigation, will determine how you deal with them. Depending on the nature of the contact, *Miranda* may or, may not, be required. If a subject is *not* a suspect, *not* in custody, and *not* about to be asked questions leading to possible incriminating answers, do not Mirandize. This involves three easy questions you must answer, before you know if, *Miranda* is required:

1. Is the person a criminal suspect (*Yes? Go to [2])*
2. Are they free to leave? (*No? Go to [3*])
3. Is anyone on the law enforcement team going to ask them questions that may lead to incriminating answers? (*Yes? Read them their Miranda rights.*)

Please keep something at your mind's forefront. If anything can go wrong, it probably will. It's called *Murphy's Law*. Just because you have issued a so-called routine traffic citation, do not assume the motorist will appear in court, without counsel. Mentally revisit Chapter Two. Please reacquaint yourself with defense counsel's role.

Remember, defense counsel is not your friend. They aren't supposed to be. In short, defense counsel's job is to prevent you from doing yours. I repeat: *defense counsel's job is to keep you from doing yours*. Commit this mantra to memory. Short of perpetrating a fraud on the court, or suborning perjury, defense counsel is ethically mandated to do anything, and everything, possible to acquit their clients. Does that mean painting you, as a fool or a liar, to the jury? Yes.

Speaking of mantras, here are three, I respectfully ask you commit to memory:

1. If you are going to err always err on the side of caution
2. If anything can go wrong, it will
3. A defense attorney's job: keep you from doing yours

If #3 immediately above, means a lawyer must make you look like a complete and total fool, or a pathological liar, in front of judge or jury? They will do so *if they are doing their job*. Treat every traffic matter, as if the most high-powered attorney, in the known universe, will be gunning for you in court.

Avoid being accused of impermissibly tainting the gathering of evidence. Remember, defense counsel gets paid to make you look bad. To them, the best defense is often a good offense. They do this by slinging mud. Their rationale? Gain an acquittal. Convince the jury to try everybody, but the defendant.

Be sure to separate all parties from one another, prior to interviewing them. Separate them, so they can't hear, or otherwise observe, what you are asking, or any other investigative subjects, are telling you. This includes any identification of the suspect by a victim, any identification of the suspect by witnesses, and any identification of the suspect, by any other suspects. Expect to encounter scenarios where you deal with multiple suspects, even on traffic cases. An example of this is a speed contest, with two or more scofflaws, racing one another.

Aside from this type of scenario creating more than one suspect, the investigative mechanics will be the same, as if with one suspect. Ditto for DUIs. I have actually prosecuted multiple DUIs, in the same case. One DUI was towing another DUI. Their lawyers opted for a court trial. They believed the law did not support my prosecution of both. It did. Each was found guilty.

During any interview, only one subject will speak to you, at the same time, if you are doing your job, following my direction, and controlling your investigation. I gained knowledge of this phenomenon first-hand back when I was in charge of major narcotic prosecution, and did a ten defendant meth lab preliminary hearing, with ten defense lawyers and ten Spanish-English interpreters.

Was I more than a bit anxious, prior to court? Sure I was. We were numerically outgunned. However, I quickly discovered a ten defendant case shares something in common with a one defendant case. *Only one person can speak, at the same time*. Learning this made me far more formidable, than I was five seconds earlier.

Properly controlling your investigation, means you separate investigative subjects, from one another. Why is this necessary? It prevents any of the statements you obtain, from being successfully challenged, by the defense. Impermissible tainting happens, when you allow an investigative subject to hear what any of the others said, what you told them, or what they told you.

Victims are interviewed for a number of pertinent reasons. Each case is going to turn on its own unique set of facts. Therefore, some of the suggestions you read may apply. Or, they may not, depending on the type of case you are investigating.

What if there's not a named victim? This eliminates one person to interview. The generic victim is the state, in which you work. Cases have named victims, whenever someone is injured, or when property is damaged. Such cases may include a variety of citations, for traffic collisions, with property damage, with or without personal injury, such as failing to stop for traffic controls, speeding, or following too closely.

If there is no named victim, be sure to tailor your investigation accordingly. However, for sake of illustration, assume we have a case, with a victim. Once you separate subjects, from one another, it does not matter who you first interview. Obtain the same basic information from each subject, irrespective of whether it is a victim, a suspect, or a witness.

You need to do a number of things, when obtaining information about any investigative subject. First, obtain relevant suspect information. Follow protocol laid out, by your own department. Include height, weight, age, ethnicity, gender, clothing worn, and the suspect's role.

Be sure to list direction of travel, following the event, last known location, type of vehicle operated, if any, including any and all descriptive pertinent information. Variables? License plate number. Vehicle identification number. And, any other relevant information.

CAVEAT: NEVER say *VIN number*. VIN is an acronym for *Vehicle Identification Number*. Saying *VIN number* is redundant, it's wrong; frankly, it just sounds stupid. Don't give defense counsel free ammo. They will use it.

Be sure to obtain registration documents and drivers licenses from everyone. Do not forget to run everyone for wants and warrants. If you are in a state, such as Maryland, and have made a T-stop, while in plain clothes, you have no legal authority to request production of a driver's license. *Taylor v. State* 9 Md. App. 402 (1970), *Cornish v. State* 215 Md. 64 (1957) Stupid ruling?

You can still request a motorist provide their registration. Maryland Vehicle Law §16-112. *Goode v. State* 41 Md. App. 623 (1979). Unlike my state, it appears traffic duties can be performed, while you are operating a vehicle, sans the usual patrol vehicle markings. Maryland Vehicle Law 21-106, *Taylor v. Mayor of Baltimore* 314 Md. 125 (1988).

Run all persons involved. Ascertain, if driving privileges are current. Are all registrations current? Is vehicle insurance current? Does anyone have outstanding arrest warrants? Are any of the vehicles stolen? Do all drivers have proof of insurance?

If the suspect is still present at the scene, does this mean you do not have to waste time, obtaining suspect information from the victim? Of course not. Can you obtain the required information directly from the suspect? If so, do it. Attempt to interview each and every investigative subject. Otherwise, your investigation will be incomplete. More defense ammo.

An important reason to interview suspects? The potential likelihood of obtaining *inconsistent statements* from them. If you have not dealt with this yet, in court, such information is quite useful. You can impeach their credibility, should they take the witness stand. The message it delivers? They lied. Why? Because they did. That is powerful stuff. Catching suspects in lies, means you can neutralize them, as witnesses.

You can prove your entire case from the testimony of victim or witness. But, you cannot rely solely on an admission, from a suspect, to prove it. You need more, in order to establish the *corpus.* We will talk about this, in a bit.

A very important reason why you cannot prove your case, based solely on suspect admissions. First, suspects have an absolute right to refuse to talk to you, even if they are not in custody. Should they utter the magic words *I want a lawyer*? Discussion: 10-7.

Therefore, it's a crap shoot, whether they will even talk with you. Yes, they must cooperate, so you can complete your investigation, such as providing required statistical data. Don't let them slide. This includes citations. But do not expect them to help you convict them. Even if they speak, their statements may be inadmissible, if the court finds coercion, or involuntariness.

Even if that is not an issue, here is another equally important reason: the *corpus delicti rule* (see Chapter 13). This is commonly referred to by lawyers and judges as the *corpus rule* or simply *corpus*. In other words, admissions alone, from suspects, are never enough to prove your case, even if they are deemed constitutionally okay as evidence. You need more.

The prosecution must present a *prima facie case*, before any admissions of wrongdoing, from the defendant, are admissible. This means you must first present the court enough evidence, separate and apart from any out-of-court admissions by the defendant, to show the defendant probably committed the crime. No such evidence? You, sir or madam, are out of luck.

An example? You are investigating a suspected intoxicated motorist. If so, you will attempt to obtain their complete drinking history, correct? (*Side note: I will cover in depth in one of my next books. Please stand by.*) Drinking history? Standard info you need from a DUI suspect. Call it, the: *who, what, where, when, why,* and *how* they got intoxicated.

Why do you need one? You eliminate any unnecessary wiggle room from a suspect, before a lawyer prepares them for the witness stand. If you obtain a solid history, you will not leave the lawyer much slack.

Assume the motorist admits he consumed ten beers, five shots of tequila, and was driving the vehicle, when it augured into the side of the building you observed, when you arrived on-scene.

If the defense attorney is doing his job, he will correctly object, should the prosecutor attempt to ask you questions about such damaging admissions, unless enough evidence is first presented to establish the crime's corpus.

You must first present *some* evidence the defendant drove, while under the influence, before you can testify about any out-of-court admissions he made. The order, in which you chose to interview parties in the field? Irrelevant, providing you don't impermissibly taints the gathering of evidence, for the courtroom. The corpus rule only pertains to the courtroom.

Even if a traffic court judge might not otherwise require formal adherence, to the rules of evidence, a defense attorney's appearance can quickly increase the level of formality. I can almost promise you a defense attorney's appearance in a courtroom, on behalf of the guy you cited, will prevent you from conducting business in the informal fashion, even if you do so otherwise.

In other words, don't expect to just go to court, take an oath, tell what happened, and thereafter leave. Therefore, go back to basics I preach to cops I teach, over and over again. If you are going to err, do so on the side of caution. Always expect a lawyer to represent the guy you stopped. Over prepared is better.

As for the corpus rule, be ready to prove, each and every element, of each and every crime, you observe, over and above, any admissions of wrongdoing, from the suspect. View any admissions, as merely supplemental statements you have already obtained, from independent witnesses, or in addition to your own observations.

What are *elements of the crime*? Crimes include felonies, misdemeanors, and infractions. All crimes are made up of *elements.* Elements of crimes are their building blocks, somewhat akin to pieces of a jigsaw picture puzzle. Each piece interlocks, with its adjacent neighbor. Prove each and every one, separate and apart, from contiguous cousins.

An example? California Vehicle Code §22350:

"No person shall drive a vehicle upon a highway at a speed greater than is reasonable or prudent having due regard for weather, visibility, the traffic on, and the surface and width of, the highway, and in no event at a speed which endangers the safety of persons or property."

California's basic speed law, broken down into its elements, includes:

1. Driving
2. a vehicle (*as defined in California Vehicle Code §670*)
3. upon a public roadway
4. at a speed greater, than is reasonable or prudent
5. having due regard for actual and potential hazards

Each of the above-numbered items is a separate element of the above-listed crime. Establish each, separate and apart, from any admission made by the suspect. Do this, prior to their introduction, in court.

A nice aspect of traffic law enforcement? Establishing each and every element, solely, with your observations. What if the traffic court judge does not insist on this sort of rigid formality? If he has an appellate court, looking over his proverbial shoulder, he might.

Even if he does not, and a kindly appellate court says that's okay, it does not mean you erred by doing your job correctly. The defense is not expected to prove lack of guilt. Their job? Acquit. Yours? Prove guilt. If you've already testified in traffic court, you should already know how much extra work, if any, the court will require of you. Do not assume I am saying you have to say "element number one", and so on. I am not. Just make sure you cover everything the law requires you to prove.

With most traffic matters, your testimony, based on your own observations, will establish all the elements. If the judge believes you are spending too much time with formality he will tell you so. If the judge insists you do your job right, then you don't worry about your case getting nuked. Either way, it's a win-win proposition.

Is the raw act of proving the elements of the traffic crime you are investigating the only reason to interview potential victims? No. Another reason? This helps you obtain additional evidence. Keep in mind, every traffic case you touch is going to be a bit different from any others. You may interview the victim, and discover he cannot provide you, with a statement, comprehensive enough to prove the case. Does this mean you can't prove your case? No.

You may need to interview additional witnesses, in order to complete your investigation. Maybe, you can rely on your own observations.

Remember, the whole idea of any criminal investigation, including a traffic? Do you have a provable case?

Does the gathered evidence, including interviews, physical evidence, and perceptions of your own senses, tell you the suspect is guilty? If so, prepare for court. If not, then be sure to do the right thing. As my old Vietnam War boss, at the DA's office noted, not every hill is the one we need to die on.

Assume the suspect refuses to talk. The identity of the driver, normally, is *not* considered an element of the crime. *People v. Lopez* (1967) 245 Cal App 2d 185. Ask your local prosecutor, if that is the law in your state.

Can you establish the act of driving, either from the mouth of the suspect, from your own observations, or those of other witnesses? If not, determine if, additional witnesses are capable of providing that information.

Should this happen, can other witnesses put the suspect behind the right steering wheel? Who observed the suspect driving? Does other evidence establish the suspect was driving? For example, in a collision, is the suspect unconscious, and still seat-belted in, behind the steering wheel?

What if the victim cannot identify the perp? Can they provide you with another witness who can provide such information? Does it matter, if the identifying party is a victim or simply a witness? No. If they can fill in the pieces, otherwise missing, you can use them, to complete your investigation. Do not expect to obtain all needed evidence, from a single witness, including yourself. Each case is different. Sometimes one witness does the job. Other times you need several. Remember, this is not a perfect world. Nor, is it necessarily fair.

We spoke earlier about Mirandizing suspects. I am repeating what I shared earlier. It's that important. Before you advise a suspect of his *Miranda* rights, first ascertain: is he a suspect? Is he about to be asked questions producing possible incriminating answers? And, is not free to leave? Are the answers all yes? Mirandize. If not, do not.

"At the outset, if a person in custody is to be subjected to interrogation, he must first be informed in clear and unequivocal terms that he has the right to remain silent." *Miranda v. Arizona* (1966) 384 U.S. 436@468. Does it appear a *Miranda* warning is required in any setting, where someone is detained, including on a traffic stop? Not necessarily.

A subsequent U.S. Supreme Court case, *Berkemer v. McCarty* (1984) 468 U.S. 420 provides the law covering interrogations and temporary roadside detentions. *Berkemer* says if the questions you ask are as likely to produce answers that will free a suspect as take them to jail, you do not need to advise them of their *Miranda* rights, prior to questioning.

"...For Miranda to apply to a traffic stop, however, a defendant must be subject to a 'restraint on his freedom of the degree associated with a formal arrest...' "*California v. Beheler* (1983) 463 U.S. 1121; *U.S. v. Murray* (7th Cir. 1996) 89 F3d 459

What is required of each witness, or victim, in any identification process? First provide them, with an appropriate admonition, before you attempt to obtain any suspect identification statements from them.

If you admonish someone you believe is a witness, and they tell you nothing, all you have invested is your time. On the other side of the coin, if you fail to properly admonish, and they are the witness who gives you the proverbial smoking gun, all you have lost is your entire case. Your call.

Be sure each potential witness understands the admonition. How will you know? Ask. For example: "Sir/madam, do you understand what I've just asked you? Is there anything you'd like me to explain further or clarify?"

Always separate witnesses, from one other, prior to obtaining their statements. Only the one you are interviewing should hear what you say, and vice-versa. You and the prosecutor, must *prove* guilt, beyond a reasonable doubt. A defense attorney's job? *Create* reasonable doubt. Do not give them ammunition. They will gladly shoot holes in your case.

Although you do not necessarily need to make the admonition, as complete as the example I am providing below, it is nonetheless necessary for you to make it clear, to any witness or victim, what their role is. Your department should already have a standard pre-printed admonition you can use. If so, use it exclusively. If your department does not have one or is inadequate, you may share mine with your department. They are more than welcome to use it as the official departmental version. It works. It's tested. And, it's reliable.

A witness must identify real crime suspects, not misidentify innocent people as suspects. Do the admonition, exactly the same way, each time you give it. Remove the ability of a defense attorney, to undo your hard work. Such admonitions ascertain victims and witnesses understand the importance of not mistakenly selecting innocent people as criminal suspects. It helps them to identify actual suspects. Use this admonition, prior to showing any witness, either a photographic six-pack, or an in-person line-up. Read it to witnesses before you ask them to identify a possible suspect.

The sample admonition:

<u>SAMPLE SUSPECT IDENTIFICATION ADMONITION</u>

1. I have asked you to participate in the identification of a possible suspect in a crime.
2. The suspect may or may not be included.
3. Your purpose is to identify the suspect, or to eliminate anyone who is not a suspect.
4. Please keep in mind, hairstyles, length of hair, mustaches, and beards may change from time to time.
   a. (*if photographic*) The lightness, or darkness, of the photographs shown is due to varying development techniques. This is not significant.
5. Be as objective as possible.
6. It is more important to free an innocent person, than to identify a suspect.
7. (*if photographic*) Please indicate the photograph you identify, as the suspect, by circling the photo. Place your initials and today's date by it.

____________________________ ____________________

(Signature of Witness to Crime) (Date & Time)

____________________________ ____________________

(Signature of Officer-Witness) (Date & Time)

Once a witness reads the admonition, and indicates he understands it, next ask them to sign and date it. Also list the time of signature, and time of any viewing. This eliminates any uncertainty, whether the admonition, or viewing, occurred first. Be sure you, not the witness, is the one who lists the time of the admonition and viewing.

Only after this is done, should you allow the witness to attempt to determine, if they can identify anyone, as the actual suspect, in your case. This form should also have a space where the officer in charge of the investigation can sign it, showing they witnessed, the witness sign the admonition.

When you sign you have witnessed the signature, list the time the document was signed. When the witness views the lineup or show-up, then list that time the same way. If you do this the same way each time you conduct one of these, it eliminates possible ammunition for the defense because you can say *"...this is the way I always do it..."*

The admonition must be read, understood, and executed, by both witness and case agent, before any witness is allowed to attempt an identification. Otherwise, you risk dealing with a defense claim you impermissibly tainted the identification of the defendant, assuming the prosecutor even files the case.

The proper way to obtain information from non-victim witnesses, for the purpose of identifying a suspect, is akin to obtaining the same type of information from victims. In other words, whether the witness is merely a witness, or is also the victim, be sure you provide them an admonition like my sample. Obtain the signature indicating they understand it, before you allow them to attempt a suspect identification.

If you fail to do a witness admonition, expect any attempts to identify the suspect in court will fail, *assuming it even gets that far*. Remember, if your case is one the filing prosecutor must first review, and if they are doing their job, your filing request will be rejected. If the prosecutor fails to do their job, and somehow files your case, expect the court to disallow the in-court identification. If the trial judge somehow also lets it slide, there is always an appellate court ready to intervene.

Tainted identification is tainted identification. You cannot fix it! So take your time; do your job properly. You will obtain justice for any victims, and appropriate punishment for the bad guy.

Chapter 4
Reasonable Suspicion vs. Probable Cause

Three different categories define the type of possible contacts between police officer and citizen. Suspect rights you will deal with are those primarily found in the Fourth, Fifth, and Sixth Amendments to the U.S. Constitution. These are not mere procedural issues or technical points. They are hard and fast constitutional rights you must respect.

Ever hear this one? *"...He got off on a technicality..."* This is flat out wrong. These constitutional rights are designed to protect all of us. Yes, I admit many of them protect suspected criminals. But, they also protect each and every one of us who call America home. If you choose to not honor them, expect to find yourself and your agency in federal court as defendants for violating someone's civil rights. While I have found federal court a very nice place to hang out as a lawyer, it is not where you want to be as a defendant.

The landmark case dealing with the extension of Fourth Amendment protections to state court defendants is *Mapp v. Ohio* (1961) 367 U.S. 643. *Mapp*, and its progeny, deal with a wide variety of constitutional issues, in criminal matters.

The three types of contacts, in this chapter, are listed immediately below this paragraph. Each is separate and distinct from the other two, even though a consensual encounter can morph into either of the other two categories, as you will learn. They are:

1. consensual encounters
2. investigative detentions
3. arrests and searches

The least obtrusive contact is a *consensual encounter*. It's neutral. You do not even have to believe you are dealing with a criminal suspect. The second and third types of contacts are with suspects. A *temporary detention* requires you to have a *reasonable suspicion* a crime has been, or is being, committed. Both arrests and searches require you to establish *probable cause* a crime has been, or is being, committed.

If you prepare an incident report, the facts you articulate will be used by any self-respecting defense attorney, trying to spin them to their client's benefit. That's their job. Never expect a defense attorney to give you the benefit of the doubt. If they do, they could face professional disciplinary action for not being zealous enough.

Remember, even if all you do is make notes on the back of your citation, always be factually accurate. Be careful with your use of verbiage. Anything you use, to refresh your recollection, is discoverable by the defendant and his counsel. That means they get to read every embarrassing word. Do not use demeaning language in any notes you write. Be factual. Keep it clean.

Make sure any description you provide concerning any work-related contact is comprehensive enough to allow you to convince the judge the incident happened exactly the way you recall it happening. This is particularly important, if you have to persuade the court, the subject of your contact, was *free to leave*, should the subject claim otherwise. True or not, they probably will.

If you are fresh out of the academy, expect people to lie. That's because they do. Some defendants practically view this as part of their job description. You crossed every T. You dotted every I. Congratulations! But, does that mean the suspect will say it did happened, the way it happened? Some lawyers act as if what their clients tell them is true enough, they can use it in court, even if it sounds preposterous to reasonable people, like us.

From the get-go, their lawyer will try to create reasonable doubt, out of whole cloth, or otherwise. And, they'll rely on their client's version of what happened, irrespective of whether reasonable people believe it smells like garden fertilizer. Nonetheless, this issue may still impact your receipt of statements or physical evidence, seized, if the court determines they were not provided voluntarily.

A temporary detention, or an arrest, may require you to justify the receipt, of evidence you would not have to substantiate, during a consensual encounter. They are not considered a seizure, unlike a detention or an arrest. This makes it easier for the defense to argue coercion played a role, if a suspect provides evidence to you, or a fellow officer. In other words, was it done voluntarily? Yes or no?

Consensual encounters are exactly what the name implies. The subject does not even have to be a suspect in a crime, but could be. A consensual encounter with a typical, middle of the road, citizen is not necessarily what we are envisioning here, although if you and I met in public, that could constitute such an encounter.

For example, let's say you and I have known each other both professionally and socially for many years. If we were to contact one another in public, particularly if you were the one contacting me, rather than vice-versa, technically that could qualify as a consensual encounter, up to the point where I tell you I have other things to do, and need to be elsewhere. At that point, we would wish each other well. We go our separate ways.

Now, let's modify this a bit. You discover facts during this encounter. They cause you to believe criminal activity is afoot. I become a suspect. If you wish to prolong the contact, in the event something develops. You now believe I either have committed, or am committing, a crime. You need to articulate facts. They must establish, at least a reasonable suspicion, I have done so, for you to justify a temporary detention. Otherwise, I am legally free to leave.

Continuing this hypothetical, let's say you learn I am a drug abuser. During our consensual encounter, your training and experience persuades you my pupils are either abnormally dilated, or constricted. Taking this a step further, let's say this tells you I might be under the influence of a central nervous system stimulant, or depressant. That should be sufficient to permit you to escalate the consensual encounter to a reasonable suspicion level, to determine if I am under the influence.

More often than not a consensual encounter is one you have with a suspected criminal, rather than someone you perceive to be law-abiding, correct? Appellate courts generally understand you won't instantly have reasonable suspicion, or probable cause, criminal activity is afoot, every time you encounter someone professionally. Therefore, you are permitted this sort of legal wiggle room, in order to do your job, protecting public safety.

In all probability, the person you contact in such situations, is best described as a *person of interest*. By that, I mean, you have either arrested them before, are someone you know has a criminal record, or is someone who appears to be doing something questionable. They probably are someone who consumes illegal drugs and/or abuses alcohol. We still on the same page?

Your field training officer (*FTO*) taught you about these sorts of scenarios, right? Visualize observing a pedestrian exhibiting, one or more objective symptoms, of being under the influence of an alcoholic beverage, or a drug, in public.

Visualize. Does the subject appear unable to safely take care of their own welfare or the welfare of others? In other words, are they a classic public intoxication case? Assume they stagger, as they walk. Their clothing is disheveled. They are covered in vomit. And, their light colored trousers are wet in the crotch area, consistent with recent urination.

You make contact with this person. Upon getting closer, you smell what appears to be the strong odor of urine, vomit, and an alcoholic beverage. Their eyes are red and watery. You greet them and ask if they are okay. At this point, your contact is still consensual. So far, so good?

When they respond, their speech is slow and slurred. They appear somewhat belligerent. You decide to place them under arrest, for being drunk in public. Next, you inform them they are under arrest. You place them in handcuffs. Alternatively, let's say you do not arrest, but inform them they are not free to leave. Either way, this changes the nature of the contact, from consensual to custodial. Telling your subject they are not free to leave, at a minimum, creates a *temporary detention*.

Placing your subject in handcuffs may or may not constitute an arrest. It depends, in large part, your intention, and what you tell your subject. Tell them, they are under arrest? Or, are they detained? Explain why. Make this part of your standard operating procedure. If you do not tell them, they is being detained, even if they are, their lawyer will argue arrest, rather than detention.

What's the big deal, you ask? Have we not been paying attention? We must be mindful of the role *Berkemer* plays in temporary roadside detentions, allowing questioning. That may or may not call for incriminating answers. With arrests, however, you must Mirandize, before you do so.

Any change in their status may well depend on whether you inform them they are being temporarily detained, or arrested. Be clear, when you make this announcement. If you can lawfully record such verbiage, carry a pocket-size recorder with you. Use it regularly. At the beginning of each shift, audibly record your name, your assigned unit number, the time, and the date.

When you speak with an investigative subject, ask if they understand you. Be sure to get an understandable answer from them. If you do not receive one, repeat your question and ask them to speak louder. Do not rewind. Doing so may allow defense counsel to falsely accuse you of editing responses.

If you have changed the subject's status from consensual contact, to temporary detention, by placing them in handcuffs, and so informing them, remember to explain you are doing so, for reasons of officer safety and/or their safety. You are doing so only until you can complete your investigation.

This is true irrespective of whether you place them in the back seat of a police vehicle, or merely ask them to otherwise remain immobile, until you are done with your investigation. Do not inadvertently give the subject ammo to claim you really arrested them.

Document everything you do. This includes documenting any objective symptoms, as soon as possible, by taking notes. Write an incident report, if that is consistent with departmental policy. Remember to refer to your notes. Develop a methodology you can routinely use, for better accuracy.

According to California Evidence Code §1105, this is called *habit or custom. "Any otherwise admissible evidence of habit or custom is admissible to prove conduct on a specified occasion in conformity with the habit or custom."*

If you are not a Californian, see if your state has a similar provision in your own Evidence Code. I suspect it does. Habit or custom basically means what it says. If you do a certain task the same way each and every time. Even if you are not able to say you specifically remember doing it the same exact way this particular time, it is most likely you did so. Why? This is the way you always do it. Habit or custom.

To bolster this proposition, a California LEO could also rely on Evidence Code §1237, if you are simply not able to recall. Evidence Code §1237 reads:

"(a) Evidence of a statement previously made by a witness is not made inadmissible by the hearsay rule if the statement would have been admissible if made by him while testifying, the statement concerns a matter as to which the witness has insufficient present recollection to enable him to testify fully and accurately, and the statement is contained in a writing which:

(1) Was made at a time when the fact recorded in the writing actually occurred or was fresh in the witness' memory;

(2) Was made (i) by the witness himself or under his direction or (ii) by some other person for the purpose of recording the witness' statement at the time it was made;

(3) Is offered after the witness testifies that the statement he made was a true statement of such fact; and

(4) Is offered after the writing is authenticated as an accurate record of the statement.

(b) The writing may be read into evidence, but the writing itself may not be received in evidence unless offered by an adverse party. Should this happen, the court might let you rely on a document prepared at or near the time of the act, condition or event. This is another good reason to not delay writing reports."

Remember, to establish you wrote your report, when the information was still fresh in your mind. If you did not write it yourself, did the report writer do so, under your direction, for the purpose of recording it? It can be offered, as evidence, once the declarant testifies the statement is a true fact. Offer it, after the writing has been authenticated, as an accurate record of the statement.

If you do not do this, expect a defense attorney to belabor this in the courtroom. Expect opposing counsel to win. If you want to prevail, follow these simple steps. Nonetheless, the modus operandi (*MO*) for many defense attorneys? Throw enough you-know-what against the wall. Some of it may stick.

Consensual encounters are so-called because they require the consent of the subject, you are contacting, in order for you to legally continue them. In other words, during any consensual encounter, the person you contact, must always be free to leave. No exceptions.

Do not visualize your work through your own eyes. Instead, think like defense counsel. And do NOT Mirandize, unless the subject is a suspect, is in custody, and will be asked questions that *may* lead to incriminating answers.

What if the subject does not invoke? Instead, what if they answer your questions, and, what if those answers lead to your seizure of incriminating evidence you plan to use against the subject in court? Do not assume defense attorneys cannot bamboozle the judge into making an erroneous decision. They do. I have seen it first-hand. Maddening, but it happens.

Do not place yourself in the unnecessary position of having to defend against a possible defense charge the evidence you seized is *fruit of the poisonous tree*, per *Wong Sun v. U.S.* (1963) 371 U.S. 471. Fruit of the poisonous tree is a euphemism to describe evidence acquired as the result of illegally seized evidence previously obtained by you, or another peace officer.

If you do this, the defense may try to show you are wrong, or lying, when you describe such an admission, by their client, as having been made consensually. Remember, what you did, has nothing to do with what you may be accused of doing, in court. Despite ad nauseum contrary verbiage to juries, by defense counsel, the truth is secondary to them. They will tell the court, if you read their client their *Miranda* rights, the suspect was not really free to leave. And if he was, why you did you Mirandize them in the first place?

Here's a real life example of what defense attorneys routinely do. Years ago, I was in court opposing yet another motion to suppress evidence. A veteran Palm Springs PD bicycle patrol cop was on duty, after dark. He saw contraband, in plain sight, inside a vehicle, on a public street.

He made this observation, by using his flashlight. In short, according to appellate case law, it was not a search. But the deputy public defender repeatedly called this *plain sight observation,* an *illegal search,* claiming the artificial illumination violated his client's right to privacy, and ergo, an unlawful search.

I cited a case to the judge, analogizing its holding that approved police use of binoculars in the daytime, and reiterated my position this was a *plain sight observation*, merely aided by another type of mechanical device that illuminated since it was nighttime, and informed the court it was perfectly legal to use the flashlight. Why? Just like the officer, with the binoculars, this officer was in a place *where he had a lawful right to be*. I explained this was no different than using binoculars to aid the naked eye. This officer was on a public street. That officer was also in a public place. Binoculars? Flashlight? Doesn't matter.

I correctly criticized the characterization of this plain sight observation, as a search, much less an *illegal* search, and reminded the judge the nature of the contact did not change merely because defense counsel misrepresented it as such. Talk did not change its substance. *Res ipsa loquitur*. The facts spoke for themselves.

As an in-court example, I pointed to counsel table and told His Honor it would not grow tires, and drive away, just because counsel called it a Lamborghini Countach. His Honor grinned, and denied the motion, as he should have done.

Does this sound ludicrous? Welcome to court. It did not stop defense counsel from doing what he did, filing a borderline-at-best suppression motion, as he attempted to fulfill his ethical duties. Therefore, once again, continue to err, on the side of caution. Always assume defense counsel will do their job, even if you have done nothing wrong. Like a good Boy Scout, make sure you prepare.

Be sure what you observe as, a traffic officer, is 100 percent consistent, with what you write, irrespective of whether it's the verbiage on the front and back side of a citation, or the language, contained in an incident report. What if you believe a suspect is intoxicated?

What should you be looking for? Does the subject appear to be under the influence? Does the subject exhibit objective symptoms? If so, what are they? Depending on the chemical body-additive of choice, they may or may not include:

1. red, watery eyes
2. dilated pupils
3. constricted pupils
4. horizontal gaze nystagmus
5. vertical gaze nystagmus
6. hyperactivity
7. lethargy
8. rapid speech
9. slurred speech
10. the odor of an alcoholic beverage about their person
11. track marks on various places from the intravenous injection of drugs
12. reddening of the edges of nostrils
13. drug paraphernalia
14. soiled or disheveled clothing, and so on

Do you have a description of such a suspect? Is it partial or complete? Does this person exhibit any of the characteristics we have just discussed? Do not forget to fully articulate, any and all relevant facts, in any report you write. This includes your notes on the back of a traffic citation.

Does your suspect's physical description, such as ethnicity, age, gender, height, and weight, accurately describe what you have observed? How about clothing? Does location match what is in your report? Was the suspect in a motor vehicle? On a bicycle? On foot? If on foot, is the suspect mobile, or stationary?

Does your report match the facts? Read it again, before you submit it. Always rely on specifics. Never generalize. *Do not be conclusionary*. Your job is to report the facts, just as all your senses report them to you.

As you probably already know, from your own experiences, as a police officer, consensual encounters are an ideal way to make contact, with someone who may have committed a crime, when you lack adequate prior information to either initially detain them, or arrest them. During a consensual encounter, commence talking to the subject. When they responds to your inquiry, they may say something incriminating.

That may establish the reasonable suspicion you need to shift the status of the contact from a consensual encounter to a temporary detention, or perhaps even elevate it to an arrest. Since the subject is not being detained, this means they are free to leave.

Consensual Encounters

Case law lays out the parameters for consensual encounters. *U.S. v. Williams* 945 F. 2d 192@195 (Seventh Circuit 1991) held the degree of criminal conduct required to justify a consensual encounter between a peace officer and a citizen is *zero*. In other words, you do not have to articulate any reason to have a consensual encounter while on duty as a police officer, other than deciding to do so. According to *Williams* (supra), this is because a consensual encounter is not considered a seizure, within the meaning of the Fourth Amendment of the U.S. Constitution.

During a consensual encounter, the subject is free to leave. They have no obligation to remain in your presence, and are able to terminate the contact, by merely telling you they do not wish to deal with you any further. Or, they can simply walk away. If you have evidence which legally permits you to elevate the nature of the contact to a temporary detention, or an arrest, do it.

What if you lack such evidence? This is the time to terminate the contact. Simply wait for another day. Are you an experienced police officer? If you are, you understand why patience is exhibited by folks who fish. The gill-bearing aquatic vertebrate that gets away today is the one you may catch, tomorrow.

The same is true with police investigative work. Criminals tend to not change their lifestyles. They are criminals. That is what they do. That is why they breathe. It's like asking male dogs to not urinate on bushes, or gang-bangers, aka criminals, to not do graffiti. You need no evidence of any criminal wrongdoing to contact anyone, during a consensual encounter. And yes, this includes *contacting criminal suspects.*

Temporary Detentions

Before we get into temporary detentions, remember, never misspeak. Some of the officers I worked with, incorrectly referred to developing *probable cause*, or PC, to make traffic stops. That is utterly wrong. The standard for a temporary detention? *Reasonable suspicion*. This is not my edict. This is federal appellate case law. If you say this, please stop. And if you do not, please do not start. Lawyers string words together into meaningful sentences. So do cops.

Do not do this even when you are discussing it, in the seeming confidentiality found only in, the exclusive company of other officers. Doing so is no more correct than for someone to talk about a *VIN* (*vehicle identification number*) number or a *PIN* (*personal identification number*) number. If you do this, please break the habit immediately. And, make it permanent.

Probable cause deals with the legal ability to make arrests and the legal ability to conduct searches. It has nothing to do with temporary detentions. The correct standard is reasonable suspicion.

We have already discussed questioning suspects, during temporary detentions, permitted in typical roadside encounters, as set forth in *Berkemer*. In order to temporarily detain a suspect, you must first establish reasonable suspicion the suspect either has committed, or is committing a crime.

Temporary detentions, or *investigative* detentions, are considered seizures, within the scope of the Fourth Amendment. Doing so constitutes an intrusion into the life of the person being so detained. What is your reasonable suspicion to interfere with that person's freedom?

A wide number of appellate cases delve into the subject of temporary detentions. You are a police officer. Therefore, in order for you to justify such an incursion into another person's life, you must have *specific, articulable facts* supporting your *reasonable suspicion* the detainee either has committed a crime, or is committing one.

In *Alabama v. White,* (1990) 496 U.S. 325, the U.S. Supreme Court defines what is required for a peace officer to articulate reasonable suspicion: "(r)easonable suspicion is a less demanding standard than probable cause not only in the sense that reasonable suspicion can be established with information that is different in quality or content than that required to establish probable cause, but also in the sense that reasonable suspicion can arise from information that is less reliable than that required to show probable cause." (Emphasis added)

U.S. v. Sokolow (1989) 490 U.S. 1 had this to say about reasonable suspicion: "(t)he Fourth Amendment requires 'some minimal level of objective justification' for making the stop," citing *INS v. Delgado* (1984) 466 U.S. 210. *Sokolow* went on to say "(t)hat level of suspicion is considerably less than proof of wrongdoing by a preponderance of the evidence." (Emphasis added)

One complaint I have voiced for a long time about some appellate courts is what I perceive to be their propensity for making *ivory tower* decisions. By this, I mean their ability to make decisions seems to be limited to the bare appellate record they are asked to review, devoid of any nervous tics, perhaps demonstrated by a defendant, while on the witness stand, in a trial courtroom, including throat clearing, looking at defense counsel for guidance, and the like.

U.S. v. Arvizu (2002) 534 U.S. 266 discusses this issue. Ralph Arvizu was detained by U.S. Border Patrol agents, while driving on an unpaved road, in a rural area of southern Arizona, not far from the Mexican border. A search of his vehicle resulted in the discovery and seizure of more than one hundred pounds of marijuana. Arvizu tried unsuccessfully to suppress the seizure of the marijuana, at the District Court level, but was later successful in convincing the Ninth Circuit Court of Appeals to reverse the lower court's decision.

In *Arvizu*, the U.S. Supreme Court first admonished lower appellate courts reasonable suspicion should be governed by the *totality* of the unique factual circumstances surrounding each case. The court also reminded them to avoid a *"divide and conquer analysis of whatever an officer relies upon in deciding to detain an individual."*

Deferring to trial court judges and local law enforcement officers, *Arvizu* noted "...in light of the District Court's superior access to the evidence and the well-recognized inability of reviewing courts to reconstruct what happened in the courtroom..." The Court echoed my own complaint about that same issue. Nice.

Arvizu delved further into the topic of Monday morning quarterbacking by saying: "(w)hen discussing how reviewing courts should make reasonable suspicion determinations, we have said repeatedly that they must look at the totality of the circumstances of each case to see whether the detaining officer has a particularized and objective basis for suspecting legal wrongdoing. This process allows officers to draw on their own experience and specialized training to make inferences from and deductions about the cumulative information available to them that might well elude an untrained person. (citing *Ornelas v. U.S.* [1996] 517 U.S. 690) Although an officer's reliance on a mere hunch is insufficient, to justify a stop, the likelihood of criminal activity need not rise to the level required for probable cause, and it falls considerably short of satisfying a preponderance of the evidence standard."

In other words, lower courts: *please do not split hairs*. As an editorial aside, this is the same criticism I have levied at appellate jurists who incorrectly use the word *hunch*, to describe actual reliance, by peace officers, on their own unique training and experience, regular people lack.

This, in large part, is what investigative deductive reasoning is all about. If these same appellate justices would take the time to see the world through the windshield of a police car or two, rather than being so knee-jerk quick to criticize the boys and girls who wear badges, I suspect the quality of their decisions on reasonable suspicion, or probable cause issues, would improve significantly.

The high court noted the Ninth Circuit incorrectly chastised the U.S. District Court's denial of Arvizu's motion to suppress by categorizing certain factors that court relied on as being "out of bounds" in deciding if reasonable suspicion to detain existed.

The U.S. Supreme Court, in overturning the Ninth, noted its methodology was not consistent with prior Supreme Court holdings, specifically criticizing the Ninth's "divide and conquer" analysis by holding: "(w)e think that the approach taken by the Court of Appeals here departs sharply from the teachings of these (prior Supreme Court) cases. The court's evaluation and rejection of seven of the listed factors in isolation from each other does not take into account the totality of the circumstances, as our cases have understood the phrase. The court appeared to believe that each observation by Stoddard that was by itself readily susceptible to an innocent explanation was entitled to no weight. (*Terry v. Ohio* [1968] 392 U.S. 1), however, precludes this sort of divide-and-conquer analysis. The officer in *Terry* observed the petitioner and his companions repeatedly walk back and forth, look into a store window, and confer with one another. Although each of the series of acts was perhaps innocent in itself, we held that, taken together, they warranted further investigation."

What better way to commence such an investigation, than by conducting a consensual encounter? See *Sokolow*, supra at p. 9, (pointing out that factors by themselves quite consistent with innocence collectively can amount to reasonable suspicion).

Therefore, when you are attempting to determine if you have amassed adequate reasonable suspicion to detain, my suggestion? Examine all the facts, upon which you wish to rely. Ask yourself if individual factors, may well be consistent with innocence. Will they nonetheless collectively rise to the level of reasonable suspicion? If so, detain.

If you are like every other normal cop, you pride yourself on being a trained observer. This is because your training and experience allows you to make observations untrained folks are simply not equipped to competently make. They include the typical defense attorney, prosecutor, or judge. Ironically, they get to decide if you erred, or not.

What might not rise beyond the level of a hunch, by a regular citizen, may constitute reasonable suspicion for you. What specific articulable facts do you rely on, to buttress your decision making? Do they tell you a crime has been, or is being committed? If so, detain the subject, until you sort out what is happening. Remember, if this is a roadside-type detention *Berkemer* says you are free to question, without need for *Miranda*, if the questions are as likely to free an innocent person, as they are to take a guilty person to jail.

Just be mindful of the admonition of *Beheler* and *Murray*. Do not place a restraint on a detainee's freedom, associated with a formal arrest. Never lose sight of the fact your duties include the investigation of circumstances, not starkly black or white. Remember, this is not TV. This is why you receive training to investigate possible crimes. If it turns out no crime was committed or is being committed? Terminate the investigative detention. Send the person on his way.

Probable Cause to Arrest

An arrest requires a higher burden of proof than a temporary detention. Temporarily detaining someone merely requires you to have reasonable suspicion of criminal activity. An arrest requires *probable cause*. But like a temporary detention, an arrest is a seizure, within the meaning of the Fourth Amendment. In order for you to justify an arrest, you must be able to articulate probable cause. Has the suspect committed, or are they committing, a crime?

Beck v. Ohio (1964) 379 U.S. 89 held that probable cause exists when, at the time of an arrest or a search, "...the facts and circumstances within (*one's*) knowledge and of which (one has) reasonably trustworthy information were sufficient to warrant a prudent man in believing that the (*defendant has*) committed or was committing an offense," quoting *People v. Triggs* (1973) 8 Cal 3d 884.

Probable cause is an objective, rather than a subjective, standard. Therefore, it is irrelevant as to whether you even entertain a belief probable cause exists, if your actions are reasonable under the Fourth Amendment, according to *People v. Gonzales* (1989) 216 Cal. App. 3d 1185. So, if your actions are challenged by the defense, the court is required to measure you "...under a standard of objective reasonableness without regard to (your) underlying intent or motivation..."

According to *People v. Ingle* (1960) 53 Cal 2d 407, probable cause is defined as "...having more evidence for than against...evidence which inclines the mind to believe, but leaves some room for doubt...".

Illinois v. Gates (1983) 462 U.S. 213 held "(p)robable cause requires only a probability or substantial chance of criminal activity, not an actual showing of such activity. By hypothesis, therefore, innocent behavior frequently will provide the basis for a showing of probable cause; to require otherwise would be to sub silentio impose a drastically more rigorous definition of probable cause than the security of our citizens' demands...In making a determination of probable cause the relevant inquiry is not whether particular conduct is 'innocent or guilty,' but the degree of suspicion that attaches to particular types of non-criminal conduct."

Factor in all of the above. Be sure you know the status your own conduct has attached to the subject, with whom you are speaking. Provide whatever admonition is required, if any. If none is required, do not be hell bent on throwing away a free lunch. Is a subject the target of criminal suspicion? Remember to differentiate the nature of the subject's status.

Is the subject in custody, a suspect, and about to be asked questions possibly leading to incriminating answers? Remember to first Mirandize them. Is the contact a consensual encounter, a temporary detention, or an arrest? Irrespective of whatever it is, be sure to treat it appropriately and act accordingly.

Chapter 5
The Importance of Foundation

What is the big deal with foundation? Let me answer you this way. Ever build a house? If so, visualize trying to build one, without adequate foundation. The roof and the walls will have no more structural integrity, than the foundation. In other words, it will fail. But, if there's adequate strength, the walls and roof will have the support they need, in order to do their job protecting the building's inhabitants, from the elements. If the foundation is not right, nothing you do thereafter, to either the walls or the roof, will make up for this major deficiency. In short, it's first things first.

Same is true with a criminal case, including traffic. However, for reasons we will grasp, in a moment, a criminal case takes this even further. Failure to lay adequate foundation does more, than weaken the rest of the process required to complete the job. It will prevent your case from going forward, whatsoever, if your opponent is doing their job. Is the evidence, which requires foundation, the evidence you need to meet your burden of proof? You will lose.

Everyone in a criminal case has a job to do. The judge's job? Rule on evidentiary objections, made by the prosecution and the defense. What if this is an infraction? No attorneys present in the courtroom? It doesn't matter. Same rules.

If your state's evidence code means anything to the judge, they may disallow the introduction of further evidence, if an adequate preliminary foundation has not been laid, by whichever side is attempting to offer the evidence requiring such foundation. I do that as a Judge Pro Tem. In days past, as defense counsel, I convinced judges to do it, with or without a prosecutor present. At the risk of sounding simplistic, the law is the law. Know it or blow it.

Traffic court judges tend to be a wee bit more informal than they probably should be, unless a defense attorney is present to motivate them to be stricter with evidentiary requirements. The quantity of cases dictates function over form.

The prosecutor's job? Dispense justice. This means convicting guilty defendants, acquitting innocent ones, and seeking fair dispositions in every case. Not so with defense counsel. They have an ethical mandate to zealously represent their client, as we discussed, at length, in Chapter 2.

Does it matter if they believe their client is guilty or not guilty? As noted before? No, it does not. Short of suborning perjury, or perpetrating a fraud on the court, they are paid to help their client walk out of court free of the charges they faced, when they walked in. Their job is to keep you from doing your job. That includes preventing you from laying proper foundation.

In legal terms, what do we mean by *foundation*? Let's review statutes from several states to examine some requirements. Immediately below, please find them verbatim. However, be sure you take the time to read your own state's Evidence Code, as needed. Know the exact wording of your state's foundational requirements. Legal research is tedious. There are no shortcuts. But it's worth the effort. I am not trying to make this book an impromptu substitute for law school. But it's important to have a handle on what you need for the courtroom.

California Evidence Code §402

"(a) When the existence of a preliminary fact is disputed, its existence or nonexistence shall be determined as provided in this article.

(b) The court may hear and determine the question of the admissibility of evidence out of the presence or hearing of the jury; but in a criminal action, the court shall hear and determine the question of the admissibility of a confession or admission of the defendant out of the presence and hearing of the jury if any party so requests.

(c) A ruling on the admissibility of evidence implies whatever finding of fact is prerequisite thereto; a separate or formal finding is unnecessary unless required by statute."

Now, let's translate that legalistic mumbo-jumbo, into more rudimentary verbiage we're more comfortable using. What is this really saying? Section 402 says you must first establish a *preliminary* fact, before you are permitted to try proving a *secondary* one.

This includes, but is not limited to, understanding and interpreting topics such as *Engineering and Traffic Surveys* (*ETS*) in states like California, the calibration and testing of radar devices, and the calibration of speedometers, for excessive speed-based citations, in general.

How do other states deal with this? Take a peek at foundational requirements in Texas. Although the wording is a bit different you will discover the requirements are much the same, i.e., first A, then B.

Texas Code of Criminal Procedure, Article 38.22

"A statement of an accused may be used in evidence against him if it appears that the same was freely and voluntarily made without compulsion or persuasion, under the rules hereafter prescribed." (Referring to Article 38.23)

Article 38.22 says the court will permit any statement made by a defendant to be used against that person in court, but only if the statement was made freely and voluntarily, as opposed to being the product of compulsion or persuasion by anyone else. Therefore, the prosecution must first present adequate evidence the statement was made freely and voluntarily in order for it to be deemed admissible. Article 38.23 goes into great detail as to when such statements cannot be used.

Now, let's migrate from the Lone Star state over to the east coast. Does the Empire State have similar foundational requirements? In my state of birth, you will find much the same requirements, as Texas or California.

New York Criminal Procedure Law, Evidence §60.45

"1. Evidence of a written or oral confession, admission, or other statement made by a defendant with respect to his participation or lack of participation in the offense charged, may not be received in evidence against him in a criminal proceeding if such statement was involuntarily made.

2. A confession, admission or other statement is 'involuntarily made' by a defendant when it is obtained from him:

(a) By any person by the use or threatened use of physical force upon the defendant or another person, or by means of any other improper conduct or undue pressure which impaired the defendant's physical or mental condition to the extent of undermining his ability to make a choice whether or not to make a statement; or

(b) By a public servant engaged in law enforcement activity or by a person then acting under his direction or in cooperation with him:

(i) by means of any promise or statement of fact, which promise or statement creates a substantial risk that the defendant might falsely incriminate himself; or

(ii) in violation of such rights as the defendant may derive from the constitution of this state or of the United States."

Section 60.45 prohibits statements made by defendants, from being used against them in court, unless the prosecution first establishes they were made *voluntarily*. Subsection 2 describes what constitutes *involuntariness*, noting use of physical force, the threatened use thereof, any statement made that creates a substantial risk suspects may falsely incriminate themselves. What if you violate state or federal constitutional protections? Doing so renders any such statements involuntary.

Please understand something. The necessity of laying foundation, in a courtroom, before you can prove certain past events occurred, is not limited to traffic court. This is standard operating procedure in the USA. This concept applies to our justice system, in general. This includes our entire criminal justice system; infractions, misdemeanors, felonies, the civil system, and the administrative arena.

As you can see, wording aside, the message is the same. Do not ignore foundation. Laying foundation is an integral part of presenting evidence. Unless you are a lawyer, I do not expect you to have the same grasp of something that's been part of my life, for more than 35 years, if you include law school and law clerking. Visualize starting your motor, before you can drive. First A, then B.

Expect your opponent to out-prepare you. But, don't let them. Foundation pertains to the courtroom, as well as other types of hearings. These include arbitration and mediation. It deals with you presenting evidence. In the criminal courtroom, it's not limited to trials. It also pertains to preliminary hearings, and a shopping list of motion hearings. I had to lay foundation in every major narcotic case I tried, as well as in non-narcotic cases. Why do I include information about narcotics herein? It's not uncommon for traffic officers to arrest suspects for narcotics offenses. Like a Boy Scout, be prepared.

Laying foundation is a two-step process. For dope, the foundation consists of establishing the particular narcotics officer, being examined, is a narcotics expert. This means they testify about all the training and experience they accumulated, prior to the incident that brings them to court. You may be working traffic today, but could well be working dope tomorrow.

Training includes relevant academy classes, tutoring by field training officers, relevant post-academy classes, such as California Peace Officer Standards and Training POST-approved radar and lidar classes, and on-the-job experience. Foundation also pertains to other types of cases, including DUIs, and your ability to offer an expert opinion, based on your own training and experience.

Following testimony about your training and experience? Step two. Depending on where you are, the state regulatory body that approves training, will probably be known by a different name, from the one in other states. And I correctly use the word *we*. That's because laying foundation is a team effort. After we introduce foundational evidence, we next elicit whatever secondary testimony is needed from the same officer. In any narcotics case, the type of case will determine what foundational requirements must be met. The secondary evidence presented, deals with a variety of issues. This will vary, depending on whether the case is one of the following types of narcotic cases:

1. possession for sale
2. transportation
3. sales
4. cultivation
5. clandestine lab operation

What do these foundational issues include? Is the narcotic in question possessed for sale, rather than for mere personal use? Is the suspected dope really dope? The key? Convince the judge the officer is qualified to provide the necessary proof.

After receipt of proper foundational qualifications, a witness can even testify the controlled substance is cocaine, for example, based solely on his training and experience as a police officer at preliminary hearings. This can be done without any crime lab analysis of the substance. In my state, lab results are must be introduced at trial. Why? The standard is proof of guilt, beyond a reasonable doubt, rather than mere probable cause.

Foundational application is limited only to the creativity and imagination of the person seeking to use it. Forget memorization. Just make sure you offer enough relevant foundation, before you attempt to offer whatever secondary evidence you are holding in abeyance. The worst thing any judge can ever tell you is no. Like the good book says, ask and ye shall receive.

You might be surprised at the relative ease required to qualify a police officer, as an expert. I know. I've done it, repeatedly. I have even done it with raw rookies. I'm talking slick-sleeved, snotty-nosed rookies. Guys who still have their training wheels. This is not about me. It is about the training and experience LEOs need to qualify, as experts. Thank them, not me.

The judge needs to know what training and experience you possess, that permits you to offer expert testimony. If you lack proper qualifications, the prosecutor is utterly irrelevant. His job is to simply ask the questions that expose your qualifications. The prosecutor is merely the piano player. In order for the judge to rule you have the qualifications needed to offer an expert opinion, he must be convinced your training and experience supports that belief.

Once the court receives proof of all your relevant training and experience, you must next convince them you can answer whatever questions need to be answered, in order for you to prove the alleged crime occurred, whether or not, a prosecutor is present and working with you, in the courtroom.

For example, if your training and experience is relied on to deal with possession of a specific controlled substance for sale, you must explain, why the evidence you gathered, proves the defendant did in fact possess that specific drug for sale, as opposed to possessing it for mere personal use. Upon what specific facts do you base your opinion?

The same basic methodology pertains to other crimes. First? Prove you are an expert. Next? Use your expertise to explain your opinion as an expert. Depending on the issue, you will not necessarily be able to supply all the foundation yourself. For example: speedometer calibration.

Are you qualified to calibrate speedometers? Did you, in fact, calibrate the speedometer in your police vehicle, used to determine a motorist's speed? If not, you won't be able to testify how fast the motorist was driving. *You must provide adequate foundational proof, as required by your state's Evidence Code.*

If you used radar, are you qualified to properly use it? Did you test it, at the beginning and the end of your shift? Did you do so, prior to using it to determine the motorist's speed? If you did this, you should be able to prove the case, with or without a prosecutor's participation. All he can do is offer what you did, right or wrong. Remember? They are just the piano player. You write the lyrics to describe the motorist's antics.

A defense attorney will challenge everything you do, especially if you are doing it right. Be preemptive. Before you go 10-8, i.e., announcing you are now on duty and in service? What issues would you raise, if you were defense counsel? Remember, they do not have to prove innocence. They only have to create reasonable doubt. One man's ceiling? Another man's floor.

Not every judge makes decisions similar to ones their brethren make. What is admissible to one jurist may be inadmissible to another. Both reasonable and unreasonable minds differ. Rarely do you find judicial minds agreeing on issues. Err on the side of caution.

California is different from other states. Our own Engineering and Traffic Surveys (ETS) differ from the Engineering and Traffic Investigations (ETI) in your own state. Your state's ETI does not mandate traffic court foundational requirements, like my state. California labels compliance failures as *speed trap* violations. That renders any evidence of speed so gathered, inadmissible. Your state's ETI appears to merely establish the ability of designated authorities to increase or decrease posted speed limits, to ensure safe and prudent driving conditions.

Some California judges keep a current ETS in their courtrooms. I don't. If they do this, you do not have to bring one to justify the posted speed limit for certain roadways. In my state, each relevant stretch of highway, defined by statute, requires its own ETS.

If the court has one, make sure it's not out of date. Does it justify the posted limit? Are you sure you are qualified to testify? Is your radar device properly calibrated? Was it tested by you, before you use it? Before you go to court, determine if it's your responsibility to bring a certified copy of the ETS with you, or if the court has one.

Following, you will find an example of how an officer might provide foundational testimony in a narcotics case. As we discussed earlier, the fact you are assigned to traffic does not mean you will not make narcotics arrests.

For many years CHP's sworn personnel were called State Traffic Officers, aka STO. Drug interdiction was a nice addition to their regular duties. Why? Vehicles are ideal mobile storage units for narcotics. CHP's informal motto? *All roads, all codes*. That includes the Health and Safety Code, Penal Code, Vehicle Code, and so on.

In the hypothetical courtroom scenario below, *P* is the prosecutor. *DC* is defense counsel. *CA* is the case agent. The judge is simply identified as Court. This is a typical scenario you will see in virtually any courtroom in America where narcotics cases are prosecuted. It should not matter who the agency is. That's because your state's Evidence Code will dictate what qualifications are required to provide competent foundational testimony.

Does the officer have adequate qualifications, to provide their opinion?

P: "Officer, by whom are you employed?"

CA: "California Highway Patrol." (*Hereinafter CHP*)

P: "In what capacity?"

CA: "I'm a K-9 officer."

P: "Are you currently working in a special assignment?"

CA: "Yes."

P: "And what is that?"

CA: "I'm assigned to our drug interdiction unit."*

P: "What does this unit do?"

CA: "We patrol the roadways of this community, ever alert for illegal drugs being transported on them, in vehicles."

P: "How are narcotics transported, in vehicles?"

CA: "Generally? In *hidden compartments.*"

P: "What is a hidden compartment?"

CA: "A hidden compartment is any area in a motor vehicle where something...in this case, narcotics...can be secreted."

P: "Where are these hidden compartments?"

CA: "Locations are limited, only by the creativity of the cartel doing the smuggling."

P: "Can you give me some examples?"

CA: "Sure."

P: "Please list some."

CA: "Inside doors, door panels, dashboards, gas tanks, spare tires, seats, engine compartments, trunks, between headliners, and vehicle roofs."

P: "What if we're talking about 18 wheelers?"

CA: "This opens up a whole new bunch of places, including dope being hidden in trailers amongst legitimate merchandise being transported."

P: "Ever work any cases where hidden compartments were being built to smuggle narcotics?"

CA: "Yes. We even arrested one guy who was a city councilman. He was using his auto body shop, as a front to build false compartments, in vehicles, so dope, smuggled from Mexico into California, could be hidden in them. My K-9 found three pounds of methamphetamine, in the engine compartment of a motor home, parked at his business the day we did the warrant. (*Smiles*) He's in prison now."

DC: "Objection, (*shrugs*) oh, never mind."

P: "On June 6, 1998, at approximately 10:07 a.m., were you employed and on duty?"

CA: "Yes."

P: "On that date and at that, time did you make a traffic stop, of a certain westbound vehicle, on I-10, just west of Date Palm Drive?"

CA: "Yes sir."

P: "Why?"

CA: "The vehicle was traveling approximately 81 miles per hour."

P: "What's the speed limit there?"

CA: "The maximum speed limit anywhere in California is 70. Actually, the max is 65, unless CalTrans designates otherwise in special geographical areas."

P: "Describe the vehicle."

CA: "It was a 1994 Toyota Camry, dark blue in color, California license plate 'David-Robert-George-Sam-Robert-Union-Sam.'"

P: "In essence, 'drugs are us'?"

CA: "That's what it looked like to me."

P: "Was anyone inside the vehicle?"

CA: "Yes, that gentleman sitting over there at counsel table."

P: "Please describe him further."

CA: "Wearing the orange jail-issue jumpsuit."

P: "Your Honor, he's indicating the defendant."

Court: "The record will so reflect."

P: "Did you learn this person's identity?"

CA: "Yes, John Q. Public."

P: "Anyone else in the vehicle?"

CA: "No."

P: "Did you ask Mr. Public for permission to search the vehicle?"

CA: "Yes."

P: "Did you obtain consent to search?"

CA: "Yes, he indicated by nodding his head up and down, and by saying 'no problem…sure.' He also signed a written consent to search form in my presence."

P: "Did you find anything?"

CA: "Yes."

P: "And what was that?"

CA: "After my K-9 indicated there was something of interest in the trunk area, I searched the trunk, and found a slightly less than nine pounds of cocaine hydrochloride."

DC: "Objection, no foundation. Move to strike."

Court: "Sustained. Motion granted."

(Note: The motion was granted because foundational evidence was not presented that the officer had the requisite training and experience to know what cocaine hydrochloride is, and lacked the expertise to so identify it.)

P: "Officer, as of June 6, 1998, did you have training and experience, enabling you to render an opinion, that a substance you believe to be cocaine, is in fact cocaine?"

CA: "Yes."

P: "Please describe."

CA: (*Describes his narcotics training at CHP academy in Sacramento, as well as in-field training under supervision of a CHP Field Training Officer [FTO] for several weeks following completion of academy. Training at the academy included the identification of different illegal substances such as marijuana, cocaine hydrochloride, cocaine base, different varieties of heroin, and methamphetamine, among other illegal drugs.*

This training also included how to identify paraphernalia used to ingest these drugs, and the field testing of drugs, to determine if the substance appears to be a scheduled narcotic. Training, under the FTO, included a number of narcotic investigations, drug identification, field testing, and suspect examination for usage. The CA next described his own narcotic investigations, following completion of training, under a FTO. This experience also included narcotic identification and field testing.)

P: "So, officer, in your opinion was the substance you found in the trunk of Mr. Public's vehicle cocaine hydrochloride?"

DC: "Objection, lack of foundation."

Court: "Counsel?"

DC: "Your Honor, the officer has merely recited some drug training, and narcotics investigation experience he has received. He still hasn't told us why he believes the substance he found to be cocaine."

Court: "Sustained. People?"

(*Note: Once again, the prosecutor failed to lay adequate foundation. The mere fact the officer recites his training and experience does not tie together why the officer properly believes the substance seized was cocaine.*)

P: "Officer, were you able to determine anything, based on your training and experience, that persuaded you the stuff you found in the trunk of Mr. Public's vehicle was cocaine?"

CA: "Yes."

P: "Describe that."

CA: "I field tested it using a NIK-brand field test kit."

P: "Describe your training and experience, prior to this date, to use the NIK kit."

CA: (*Describes qualifications to use test kit*) "When I introduced the cocaine to the test vial, it turned both blue and clear in color."

P: "In your opinion, did it also appear to resemble powdered cocaine?"

CA: "Yes."

P: "Describe."

CA: "The substance was wrapped in four different plastic bags. It was off white in color, granular, and, well...it smelled like cocaine."

DC: "Objection. Foundation."

Court: "Sustained."

P: "Are you saying you've smelled cocaine before?"

CA: "Yes."

P: "How many times?"

CA: "Dozens. Probably more. Cocaine, either I or other officers, have field-tested as positive, and/or that has produced a positive result at the forensic lab we use."

P: "So, (*beginning to show impatience*) let's try this, again. In your opinion was this stuff cocaine?"

DC: "Objection, lack of foundation."

Court: "No, I'm satisfied adequate foundation has been laid. Overruled."

CA: "Yes."

P: "And on what do you base that opinion?"

CA: "My training and experience I've just outlined. After field testing a portion of the substance found in the vehicle's trunk, using a NIK-brand field test kit, the substance turned both blue and clear in color. According to the manufacturer that is consistent with the detection of cocaine."

As you can see from the preceding example laying foundation is not meant to be a speed contest. The prosecutor took his time, in order to elicit the totality of this officer's training and experience, obtained prior to the date of the relevant investigation.

Granted, the defense was able to successfully object twice, because the prosecutor tried to introduce qualifying evidence, before proper foundation was presented. As you can see, short cuts do not work. Much to their credit, the prosecutor and officer kept moving persistently forward, until the court was ultimately satisfied adequate foundation had been presented.

Despite prosecutorial diligence, defense counsel continued to object, attempting to chip away at the prosecutor's efforts to prove his case, even as the court finally agreed adequate foundation had been presented. The same basic methodology should be followed, whenever foundation must be established, before other evidence is offered. If training and experience is required, present that as foundation. That establishes expertise. It does not matter if the trier of fact is a judge, jury, referee, arbitrator, mediator, or anyone else being asked to make a decision. The relevant question? Has enough evidence been produced, to complete needed foundational requirements?

Expect defense counsel to say something disparaging about your case. That is what they get paid to do, whether they are public or private sector. It does not mean anyone on your side has done anything wrong. If the prosecutor is present in court with you, it likely means your case is solid. Otherwise, they would not be prosecuting it.

It does not matter, if defense criticism is an evidentiary objection, or the use of some other verbiage. Counsel may actually appear sincere as they do this, possibly even strident. Others may simply be good actors. They are simply attempting to get their client acquitted. Instead of focusing on what you hear defense counsel saying, just concentrate on doing your job. Judges have been around the block a few times too. We understand all too well how this game is played.

The same methodical approach is used to lay foundation, for even the most inexperienced officers, in order for you to qualify as an expert, on a variety of topics. While I was in charge of my office's Eastern Division major narcotic unit, I decided to experiment in this area. I was trying to find the outer edges of the courtroom foundational expertise envelope. Why was I doing this?

My mission? Find the outer edge of the envelope, by trying to qualify rookie officers, as experts, on some of my narcotic cases. Some had never even testified before. My goal? Qualify officers, as close to being totally green as possible. If they were able to work, without an FTO, I tried to qualify them as experts. I vaguely recall at least one was still under his FTO's wing.

My reasoning was quite elemental. First, this was strictly no harm, no foul. If the court did not approve any of my attempts, I could try again later, when the particular officer was more qualified. This turned out to be an easy research project. I even surprised myself with the results. Not a single officer failed to qualify, as an expert. Consider suggesting this to your own prosecutors. It's just a matter of educating the judge. An officer's qualifications so provide.

Ironically, I had more difficulty, subsequently, qualifying a former veteran sheriff's deputy, as an expert. He had lateraled over to a city department. He had no prior experience with rock cocaine for sale cases, although his experience making methamphetamine arrests was comparable. The LEO's testimony was fine. For reasons I may never know the judge was just being difficult that day. The Commission on Judicial Performance later removed him from the bench. Allegations? Nose candy aficionado. Do the math.

The first time you qualify as an expert; no matter how inexperienced you are? From that moment forward, you are an expert on that particular subject. What if defense counsel objects to some prosecutor subsequently attempting to elicit your opinion as an expert? If the court is doing its job, you will automatically qualify, as an expert, on that specific issue. That's because you are now an expert. This is akin to losing one's virginity. Once it's gone, it's gone. Conversely, once you're an expert, you remain an expert forever after.

Laying foundation does not always require the introduction of an officer's training and experience. While that is true with an issue such as an officer's identification of suspected narcotics, use of a radar device, or speedometer, it does not apply to something such as an ETS, which requires a different type of foundation. And, that's because you are trying to establish its validity, not your own expertise or someone else's.

If building foundation is required, before you can testify about the speed you have gathered, you must first produce it, before evidence of speed can be introduced. An ETS may be unique to my state. But with radar, I do not know of a single state where you can avoid proving you are qualified to use radar or present proof the device was working properly.

In law enforcement-restrictive California, there are a number of ways, gathering evidence of a motorist's speed, may also be deemed illegal *speed trap evidence*. For instance, our state's traffic officers must be attired in a standard-issue departmental uniform, complete with badge and name plate, as is required by other states.

But, unlike other states, they must also be operating a distinctively marked police vehicle, before they can lawfully issue a speeding citation. And, at trial, they must present evidence of a valid ETS, if evidence of speed was gathered, by use of any type of radar on certain types of roadways. The issue is not guilt or innocence, but whether the officer, and others, remembered to genuflect, and say *mother, may I*, before the T-stop was made.

The ETS must be conducted within a specific period of time, prior to the issuance of the citation. And it must justify the posted limit. This means the survey must not only be conducted, within the required time frame. It must also establish an adequate percentage of motorists are traveling at the posted speed.

This is to avoid setting the posted limit too artificially high or low. For example, if the posted limit is set at 35 mph, but only 10 percent of the motorists surveyed are traveling at that speed, the likelihood is slim the survey will withstand scrutiny for the speed to remain as is. This makes no sense. That's because my state's Legislature allows speeders determine our speed limits.

In California, another foundational example is the introduction of documentary evidence. This normally requires the custodian of records to testify the particular document is what the proponent claims it is. If the document is what is known as an *official* record, then it is self-authenticating. This means no one will have to authenticate it, with testimony.

An official record speaks for itself. An ETS is considered an official record. If a document is not self-authenticating, do not make such decisions unilaterally. Include your prosecutor. If foundational testimony from the custodian of records is required, you must interview the custodian, in conjunction with the prosecutor, to prepare their courtroom testimony.

As an aside, make sure no prosecutor you ever work with interviews witnesses, on any of your cases, unless you or another officer is present, as a percipient witness, to what was said. Ideally, you should conduct the interview, with the prosecutor's guidance.

I never interviewed witnesses myself. Why? It kept me from having to testify, if a witness testified inconsistently with what they said, before they took the witness stand. Doing this presents a conflict of interest. It may force the prosecutors to recuse themselves from the case. That's why the LEO does the interviews.

How did I learn to not do this? It was the mistake another attorney made, in a death penalty case, that was heard by the California Supreme Court. [See *People v. Farmer* (1989) 47 Cal.3d 888] This took place in the early 1980s. The defendant's court-appointed lawyer had to take the witness stand to impeach a witness. Why? He testified inconsistently, with what he previously told the lawyer, during a jailhouse interview. It should have been conducted by an investigator, instead of by the lawyer. It wasn't.

Not only did he not have an investigator do the interview, *as he should have done*, he did the interview, *without* the investigator even being present. Had he done so, he could have avoided the embarrassing trip to the witness stand. His investigator would have testified, to what he heard the witness say, during the interview.

Even worse, the lawyer did not record anything. Absent these mistakes, the court would not have appointed me, to represent the defendant, while his counsel of record twisted in the wind, on the witness stand. Instead, I participated in a historic event. My limited role was to examine that lawyer, while he was on the witness stand. He had to tell the jury what the witness had told him. In the long haul it did not make any difference. The defendant went to Death Row. Nonetheless, it was an avoidable gaffe.

Whether I was asking questions, or was simply present, during any interview, I always had a DA investigator with me, in case a witness' testimony contradicted his previous statement. Be sure you tape record. If your state's laws require this, get the interviewee's permission first. If witnesses go sideways, it means their courtroom testimony will have to be impeached. You do this, in court, by asking them if their previous unsworn statement is inconsistent with their testimony. If they deny that, then you can provide evidence, as to what they previously said. Also, play the tape to impeach them.

Establishing adequate foundation goes beyond properly using an ETS to prove a motorist violated one of your state's speed laws. It also applies to radar and speedometers used to gather evidence of speed. How do we do this?

Let's deal with these issues one by one. First, since radar may be tied into the effective use of an ETS, at least in my state, let's discuss radar first. Whenever one attempts to testify some device was used, in order to prove something else, two foundational aspects must be included. Assume, for this hypothetical, a prosecutor is involved.

First? Prove the device was operating properly. Next, establish the operator was qualified to properly use it. If a full blown evidentiary foundational hearing is required, this should be something the prosecuting attorney's office choreographs. Your role should be limited to following whatever instructions the prosecutor provides. You are the traffic expert. The prosecutor is the courtroom expert. Never confuse the two. Keep the experts in their proper places.

You may be asked to contact the manufacturer of the radar device you used in order to find out who its expert is, if a full blown evidentiary hearing is required to establish the device's reliability. I realize *U.S. v. Dreos* (infra) says radar is presumptively reliable. It does not necessarily mean other jurisdictions will *not* require such a hearing establishing reliability. *Dreos* is not necessarily binding on other circuits.

Make sure the expert has been subpoenaed, timely, for the foundational hearing. To be on the safe side, double-check with the prosecutor. The expert should also be prepared to provide testimony, about the sort of training you need, in order to use the device correctly. View *Dreos* to radar as you might *Lowe* to speedometers, except the former is federal court, and the latter is Superior Court Appellate Division.

If your jurisdiction follows Fourth Circuit Court of Appeals rulings (MD, NC, SC, VA & WV), *U.S. v. Dreos* 946 Fed 2nd 888 holds radar is generally accepted, as reliable, if foundational evidence is first presented:

1. it was properly tested and checked
2. it was manned by a competent operator
3. proper procedures were followed
4. proper records were maintained

In non-*Dreos* jurisdictions, foundation must first be laid, by an expert, to establish the device's reliability. Once such a full blown hearing is conducted, in your jurisdiction, future area hearings should only require LEO testimony the LEO is individually qualified and used the device properly. At any future hearing, the court can take judicial notice of its own records, including testimony from the hearing that established the device's reliability.

The same basic kind of preparation is needed, to lay foundation, to prove speed, if you used your vehicle's speedometer, or some other authorized device to make that determination.

Let's use your speedometer as an example. You can testify your speedometer indicated the speed your vehicle was traveling, as you bumper paced the suspected offender, assuming it's calibrated properly. That will be meaningless, without prior foundational evidence, the speedometer was, in fact, properly calibrated.

A lot depends on your own state's lawmakers. Are they helping you protect highway safety? Do any statutes make police department speedometer calibration records self-authenticating official records? *Lowe* (supra) comes close to doing that. Alternatively, your department can train each traffic officer to be a custodian of records for business records, allowing you to authenticate them. Either way provides foundation for you to testify you used your speedometer to determine an offender's speed, without additional witnesses.

Are you working with a prosecutor? A trial run in their office is always helpful, so no unexpected surprises take place, derailing things, in court. Mistakes are going to be made. Part of learning? Trial and error. The place to make those errors? Before you enter the courtroom. With all due respect, to any prosecutor, never assume they are an expert, in the subject matter at hand, and will instantly correct any mistakes you make. There are too many laws. Always take the time to do your job properly. Never assume someone else will fill in any missing gaps, if you did not do your own job.

Therefore, be sure you are satisfied adequate preparation has gone into the equation. We spoke earlier about the speeding citations I defended, and how I was able to succeed, by preventing foundation from being laid, to prove the speedometer was properly calibrated. With cases like *Lowe*, that probably would not work today. The solution is quite simple. I realize most speeding stops today rely on the use of radar. That makes bumper-pacing an unlikely way to prove a motorist was speeding. But we cannot assume you will never have to establish speed by bumper-pacing. I still see its use in traffic court, on a fairly regular basis. Candidly, the reliance on bumper-pacing surprises me. Therefore, be sure you are tuned in to its proper use.

Your state's Evidence Code contains exceptions to the hearsay rule. Business records are one of those exceptions, admissible, only if proper foundation is first presented. The custodian of records must testify to properly authenticate any challenged document, as a business record. Once they do so, the document is admissible, as an exception to the hearsay rule.

Who is the custodian of records? The custodian is anyone qualified to authenticate a business record, as being what it purports to be, providing they meet the requirements spelled out in the statute. How many custodians can you have? I am not aware of anything, limiting the number of people who can qualify, as a custodian of records. Nor am I aware of police officers being prohibited from so qualifying.

Let's reflect back on our earlier discussion about the cases I won as a defense attorney. I did that because officers did not lay adequate foundation to support their observations a motorist was speeding. I didn't necessarily win because my clients were innocent. Officers naively assumed no one would challenge what their speedometer told them a motorist's speed was. In other words, they did not prove their patrol vehicles' speedometer was properly calibrated. My job was not to show them how to do that. In fact, I was ethically mandated to do just the opposite, and prevent them from offering such evidence to the court.

Therefore, isn't the simplest solution, to this unnecessary problem, better utilization of the very folks who issue speeding citations? Traffic divisions should train their officers so each can qualify, as a custodian of records, for the documents that establish the speedometer of your assigned unit is properly calibrated, if a custodian of records is required to testify.

The custodian of records must meet statutory requirements, and testify to their qualifications. As an example, California Evidence Code §1271 spells out the foundational requirements you must meet, to qualify as the custodian of a business record. Your own state should have fairly similar foundational requirements.

Required training needed to do this should not be that involved. Each officer authorized to issue traffic citations simply needs to be able to introduce the document reflecting speedometer calibration was done properly. The officer must show the document is what it purports to be. And lastly, the document and the method of its preparation must establish it as trustworthy.

If the document qualifies as an official record, treat it as such. Any officer can offer it to the court, as a self-authenticating document. If it is a certified copy, then you should have no trouble presenting it to the traffic court jurist, as admissible evidence. In most traffic courts, the judge will examine it, and return it to you, so you can use it next time you have to testify concerning unlawful speed.

Chapter 6

Foundational Requirements: California vs. Other States

As noted earlier, I wrote my first book in 1987. Like most first time authors, I was satisfied *CATCH 55: Courtroom Survival for Traffic Officers* was a good book; a solid book, even. And I still am. That's because it contains a lot of useful information.

When I wrote it, however, I chose to not rely on any third party input. I did so, much more from ignorance, than arrogance. So, while it contained depth, in retrospect, it lacked needed breadth. Lesson learned there, and applied herein.

I decided to take a different approach this time, and rely on LEOs from throughout America. From my early days as a DA, I have gotten to know many officers. Many are the boys and girls I was privileged to serve with, until I retired from public service.

Some are former students. Others I've met elsewhere. Some of these LEOs are still active duty. Others are now honorably retired, like me. Status aside, various officers in several states have shared their knowledge to help me write this book. The end result is an extensiveness and balance *CATCH 55* quite simply lacked.

This book combines many of the legal procedures I've practiced, during several decades in the legal profession, with a representative sampling of LEO opinions throughout America. My intent is not to merely infuse you, with so-called black letter law. Frankly, there are too many laws, to comfortably fit all of them into one book. My goal is to show you how to obtain needed information, in your own cases and statutes.

This book's task is to show you how to find what you need, so you can go into court, and confidently take care of business. As a long time lawyer, in California, I have done enough research to understand the parameters of traffic court. If you apply what we have all learned, you can relate that to your own state, by doing your own analyses.

TEXAS

Lt. Mark Reynolds is the man in charge of academy training for the Comal County Sheriff's Office in New Braunfels. On the issue of testing radar units to make sure they are working properly in his state of Texas, Mark provided a very helpful tip.

I had the pleasure of meeting Mark when I taught my own sixteen hour *Courtroom Survival for Peace Officers*™ class for them a few years ago. He takes great exception with what he calls the misapplication of the word *calibrate*, rather than *test*, to describe how LEOs confirm a radar device is operational. Per Reynolds, testing ascertains, if a radar device is functioning correctly, before a traffic officer goes 10-8. Calibration, on the other hand, is done solely by the manufacturer.

Here's what he said.

"When any officers from Comal County attend the Radar Certification course, we make it perfectly clear to them they do not 'calibrate' the radar. That is done only by the manufacturer. The tuning forks are not calibrating the radar. They test the device to make sure it is working properly. If it isn't, it is immediately removed from the vehicle and taken out of service for repair by the manufacturer. Students are instructed, if they testify in court, they may testify as to how the radar unit is operated, i.e., their proficiency to do so. But they do not calibrate. That is the manufacturer's exclusive turf.

In fact, we even removed an incorrect portion from our department's traffic citations. Previously, our citations contained a box that read: **Radar Calibrated**. Officers would check 'yes' or 'no.' Doing this, put them in the frame of mind they were 'calibrating' radar units by checking them with tuning forks. They weren't. They were testing them.

We contacted our county Justices of the Peace to see if they had any objection to that particular language being removed because it was not correct. None of them objected. In fact some even observed that our officers were having difficulties in court with defense attorneys because of the term 'calibrating.' We instruct each officer to test the unit before and after duty to make sure the unit is functioning properly."

At **Texas Statutes-Title 7: VEHICLES AND TRAFFIC**, you will find the traffic regulatory statutes in Lt. Reynolds' state. It does not matter where you are. The same ground rules apply. Just be sure you know your own state's applicable laws.

Chapter 545, Subchapter H, and its included sections, cover speed restrictions, spelling out the legal capacity of the Texas Transportation

Commission, and local authorities, to set speed limits, via Engineering and Traffic Investigations. These do not entail the same foundational requirements, to measure speed, as California does, with our periodic surveys to justify existing posted limits, to avoid speed traps. Nonetheless, Texas still mandates properly functioning radar devices and suitably trained operators.

In fact, §545.363, relying on Engineering and Traffic Investigations, even goes in the opposite direction. If you look at it you'll see it authorizes setting *minimum* speed limits, on certain roadways, under specified circumstances.

Texas Statutes 545.363 MINIMUM SPEED REGULATIONS

"(a) An operator may not drive so slowly as to impede the normal and reasonable movement of traffic, except when reduced speed is necessary for safe operation or in compliance with law.

(b) When the Texas Transportation Commission, the Texas Turnpike Authority, the commissioners court of a county, or the governing body of a municipality, within the jurisdiction of each, as applicable, as specified in Sections 545.353 to 545.357, determines from the results of an engineering and traffic investigation that slow speeds on a part of a highway consistently impede the normal and reasonable movement of traffic, the commission, authority, county commissioners court, or governing body may determine and declare a minimum speed limit on the highway.

(c) If appropriate signs are erected giving notice of a minimum speed limit adopted under this section an operator may not drive a vehicle more slowly than that limit except as necessary for safe operation or in compliance with law."

It does not matter which state you serve in. Your job is to enforce the laws your lawmakers create. They ultimately determine what you must do, in order to present competent evidence in traffic court. Legislators draft the laws. Meanwhile, their judicial brethren interpret what such language means for those on the law enforcement team, who must maintain highway safety. As the tip of the spear, you must function competently in court, for any of those laws to really mean anything to the public you serve.

MARYLAND

As I ambled virtually around the USA, looking for answers, I also spoke with two retired Annapolis PD officers, my longtime buddy Sgt. John Groh, sadly now deceased, and his former lieutenant, Russell Hall, to get their perspectives on what you should expect in a typical Maryland traffic court. At the time, Russ was a paralegal in attorney Mark Howes' law firm;

himself a retired Anne Arundel PD sergeant. These three Maryland men knew each other, since their days working the streets. John was kind enough to introduce me to them.

Lt. Hall was kind enough to actually send me copies of relevant Maryland statutes, and supporting appellate cases, dealing with the use of radar, to determine the speed of motorists. They also explain what a police car is, for traffic enforcement purposes.

Vehicle Law 10-301 covers the use of radio-microwaves, to prove the speed of vehicles. If you review this section, in an annotated edition, you will see a cited case, *U.S. v. Dreos*, 156 F. Supp. 200 (D. Md. 1957). *Dreos* says radar is now presumed to be reliable, providing the officer is qualified to use it, and they follow proper procedures.

Maryland Vehicle Laws 10-301 RADIO MICROWAVES

The speed of a motor vehicle may be proved, by evidence of a test made upon it, with a device designed to measure and indicate the speed of a moving object, by means of radio-micro waves.

Vehicle Law 10-301 does not address the issues of foundation and hearsay, in terms of establishing devices, such as speedometers, have been properly calibrated, and radar units have been properly tested, checked, or whatever other correct descriptive word is currently in vogue, in that particular jurisdiction. I am not making light of the selection of descriptive verbiage.

Having said this, there are simply too many communities in America for me, or any other traffic disciple, to be able to stay on top of what is considered all of the currently acceptable local language. That's why you must do your own homework, on such issues. Remember, lawyers get paid to string words together into meaningful sentences. Irrespective of whether they are prosecution or defense, that's what they do.

You have previously endured my rant about why you never say VIN *number* or PIN *number*. Therefore, take the time to confer with knowledgeable local legal folks. Ask them what descriptive language is correct, in your own area, concerning checking radar devices. Be sure you are not professionally misspeaking. Talk to your department's training officer, and your local prosecutors. Appellate case law will provide the answers. It does no good to know how to do it if you cannot correctly explain what you did.

Once you are satisfied you are using the right verbiage, you need to confirm each device you use is functioning properly, before you rely on any of them, to determine an offending motorist's speed, if you want the judge to accept your testimony. If proper foundation is not provided, no matter where you are, you have wasted your time.

Essentially, all 10-301 says is radar devices are respectable enough today for the public to rely on them. It's still up to you to establish, to the satisfaction of the judge, the device you used accurately allowed you to reasonably state what the motorist's speed was, when you observed the motorist traveling faster than deemed legally acceptable.

If you are not able to do that even if the device is considered scientifically acceptable, it is about as worthwhile to you, as nothing. Russ Hall turned out to be a veritable treasure trove of information, also alerting me to Vehicle Law 16-112, dealing with the requirement to produce a driver's license, upon demand of uniformed peace officers, and 21-106 dealing with emergency vehicles.

Maryland Vehicle Laws 16-112 DRIVERS' LICENSES

"(a) 'Display' defined. In this section, 'display' means the manual surrender of the licensee's license into the hands of the demanding officer for inspection.

(b) Carrying license with driver. Each individual driving a motor vehicle on any highway in this State shall have his license with him.

(c) Display to uniformed police officers. Each individual driving a motor vehicle on any highway in this State shall display the license to any uniformed police officer who demands it.

(d) Signature in presence of officer. Each individual driving a motor vehicle on any highway in this State shall, if requested by the officer, sign his usual signature in the presence of the officer so that the officer may determine whether he is the licensee.

(e) Giving false name. A person may not give the name of another person or give a false or fictitious name to any uniformed police officer who is attempting to determine the identity of a driver of a motor vehicle."

Maryland Vehicle Law 16-112 requires motorists to permit a uniformed officer to inspect their driver's license, while an officer not in uniform is only entitled to request a motorist's registration documents. Both Sgt. Groh and Lt. Hall point that out. Maryland appellate cases Taylor v. State 9 Md. App. 402 (1970), Cornish v. State 215 Md. 264 (1957) and Goode v. State 41 Md. App. 623 (1979) confirm this. Maryland Vehicle Law §21-106 subsection (c)(1) states an emergency vehicle operated as a police vehicle need not be equipped with or display the visual signals.

Maryland Vehicle Laws 21-106 EMERGENCY VEHICLES

"(a) Circumstances for which privileges granted. Subject to the conditions stated in this section, the driver of an emergency vehicle registered in any state may exercise the privileges set forth in this section while:

(1) Responding to an emergency call;

(2) Pursuing a violator or suspected violator of the law; or

(3) Responding to, but not while returning from, a fire alarm.

(b) Enumeration of privileges. Under the circumstances stated in subsection (a) of this section, the driver of an emergency vehicle may:

(1) Park or stand without regard to the other provisions of this title;

(2) Pass a red or stop signal, a stop sign, or a yield sign, but only after slowing down as necessary for safety;

(3) Exceed any maximum speed limit, but only so long as the driver does not endanger life or property; and

(4) Disregard any traffic control device or regulation governing direction of movement or turning in a specified direction.

(c) Use of audible and visual signs required.

(1) Subject to paragraph (2) of this subsection, the privileges set forth in this section apply only while the emergency vehicle is using audible and visual signals that meet the requirements of §22-218 of this article, except that an emergency vehicle operated as a police vehicle need not be equipped with or display the visual signals.

(2) The privileges set forth in subsection (b) (1) of this section apply only while the emergency vehicle is using visual signals that meet the requirements of §22-218 of this article.

(3) (i) The driver of an emergency vehicle may not use flashing lights or a bell, siren, or exhaust whistle while returning from an emergency call or fire alarm, except that fire apparatus carrying standing firemen may use flashing lights that are visible only to the rear.

(ii) The driver of an emergency vehicle, while parking or backing the emergency vehicle, may use flashing lights within 100 feet of the entrance ramp to a:

1. Fire station; or

2. Rescue station.

(d) Driver not relieved from duty of care. This section does not relieve the driver of an emergency vehicle from the duty to drive with due regard for the safety of *all persons."*

This issue was raised and the principal was upheld in *Taylor v. Mayor of Baltimore* 314 Md. 125 (1988). By contrast, California would not permit this. My state requires speeding citations to be issued, only by uniformed LEOs driving garden variety patrol units, with all the bells and whistles.

ARKANSAS

I next obtained information from Officer Mark Grant of Monticello PD, now with University of Arkansas at Monticello. When I asked him about speed traps in Arkansas, considering the role speed traps play, in the enforcement of California speed limits, here's what he said:

"The only thing I can find on speed traps is that towns cannot use speeding tickets as a primary 'money maker' for the community, so to speak. I have not been able to find any legislation in Arkansas state law that really gives any other type of restrictions due to speed traps."

My standard operating procedure is to do my own supplemental research, in order to confirm any outside information I receive is correct. I did this with each officer I consulted. This does not mean I distrust any of these dedicated LEOs. It means I am as cautious writing books, as I was practicing law.

I got into the habit of doing my own research in law school. Dealing with defense counsel, as a DA, I had to do this to be sure they were correctly representing case citations to the court. Anyone who knows me should not find this continuing attention to detail surprising.

Frankly, it's a habit that has served me so well for so long I find no compelling reason to abandon it. This continues in my role as a Judge Pro Tem. Therefore, after speaking with Grant, I did what I do. I reviewed the Arkansas Code, focusing on laws pertaining to the operation of motor vehicles, and the authority of Arkansas law enforcement officers to regulate this, as well as some collateral issues.

My first area of review was Title 12, including a careful review of 12-8-401, et seq, which is Arkansas's version of a speed trap law. Section 402 defines

it.

Arkansas Code 12-8-402 SPEED TRAP LAW

"As used in this subchapter:

(1) 'Abusing police power' means the exercise of police power to enforce criminal and traffic laws for the principal purpose of raising revenue for the municipality and not for the purpose of public safety and welfare;

(2) 'Affected highway' means any highway which is part of the state highway system; and

(3) 'Affected municipality' means any city of the second class or incorporated town through which passes an affected highway."

This confirmed the accuracy of Grant's own efficacious research, as set forth in the Arkansas Speed Trap Law. Arkansas Code 12-8-402 limits the discussion of speed traps to prohibiting both criminal and traffic enforcement schemes that are for "...the principal purpose of raising revenue..." It was just as Officer Grant told me.

Let's discuss Title 12 further, before we delve into Title 27. By researching Arkansas law, I next discovered its state police officers are required to wear distinctive uniforms, like California Highway Patrol officers must do. That provision is also found in Title 12.

Arkansas Code 12-8-213 deals with equipment and uniforms, spelling out what uniform patrol officers of the Arkansas State Police must wear at all times while on duty. Their uniform, badge, and other accoutrements are designated by the director of the Arkansas State Police. This section also says state police personnel shall have the equipment they need to do their jobs.

Arkansas Code 12-8-213 EQUIPMENT AND UNIFORMS

"(a) Such motorcycles, automobiles, and other vehicles, equipment, and supplies as may be necessary for the proper and efficient operation of the Department of Arkansas State Police and as may be necessary for the proper enforcement of this chapter shall be furnished to the officers and patrol personnel by the department.

(b) The officers and patrol personnel shall wear and display upon their person a metal badge or other insignia as the director of the department shall require, bearing the words 'Arkansas State Police.'

(c) All such patrol personnel and officers shall wear such uniforms at such times and places as shall be designated and required by the director."

That led me to research the portion of Arkansas law, dealing with certification of officers, qualified to use radar, as more fully set forth in Title 12. The Arkansas Commission on Law Enforcement Standards and Training is Arkansas' version of POST, in my own state. Title 12 spells out minimum radar certification requirements. Such officers must successfully complete training, enunciated by Arkansas Code 12-9-403. It is important to note this section does not preclude local authorities, from requiring such operators and instructors to meet even higher standards than their own.

However, despite extensive research, I was unable to find any Arkansas mandates comparable to my state's Engineering and Traffic

Survey requirements. Practicing law this many years has taught me to never assume I am conclusively correct about anything.

Arkansas Code 12-9-403 APPOINTMENT AND TRAINING

"(a) No person shall be appointed as a police traffic radar operator or police traffic radar instructor until the minimum standards for training requirements have been completed.

(b) The training requirements for police traffic radar operators or police traffic radar instructors shall be established by the Arkansas Commission on Law Enforcement Standards and Training.

(c) The commission may issue a certificate evidencing satisfactory completion of the requirements of this subchapter when evidence is submitted by the law enforcement agency director, chief, or county sheriff that the police traffic radar operator has met the training requirements.

(d) Nothing in this section shall be construed to preclude any law enforcement agency from establishing qualifications and standards for appointing and training of police traffic radar operators and police traffic radar instructors that exceed those set by this subchapter or by the commission.

(e) Any police traffic radar operator or police traffic radar instructor failing to meet the training requirements as set forth in this subchapter shall lose his or her authority to operate a police traffic radar for enforcement purposes.

(f) A law enforcement officer shall complete the commission-required training for officer certification before being eligible for certification as a police traffic radar operator.

(g) Only a full-time law enforcement officer, part-time I law enforcement officer, and part-time II law enforcement officer, as defined by commission regulation, will be eligible for certification as a police traffic radar operator."

I have been performing legal research since I began law school in 1975, and remain fully confident Officer Grant's shared information about speed traps is correct, because it is what I found set forth in Title 12, from my own research.

I also reviewed Title 27, which deals with speed limits. Title 27, Chapter 51, Subchapter 2, §201, dealing with what Arkansas lawmakers call Engineering and Traffic Investigations, sets forth the authority of the State Highway Commission to establish speed limits, on what are called controlled access highways. However, it does not set forth any foundational requirements for traffic court.

Arkansas Code 27-51-201 LIMITATIONS GENERALLY

"(a)(1) No person shall drive a vehicle on a highway at a speed greater than is reasonable and prudent under the conditions and having regard to the actual and potential hazards then existing.

(2) In every event, speed shall be so controlled as may be necessary to avoid colliding with any person, vehicle, or other conveyance on or entering the highway in compliance with legal requirements and the duty of all persons to use due care.

(b)(1) The maximum speed limits set forth in subsection (c) of this section shall not apply to controlled-access highways.

(2)(A) Upon an engineering and traffic investigation, the State Highway Commission shall determine the maximum permissible speeds on controlled-access highways which shall be effective when appropriate signs giving notice are erected along the highway.

(B) The commission shall fix the maximum permissible speed of trucks with one and one-half (1 1/2) ton capacity or more at ten (10) miles per hour below the maximum permissible speed for automobiles.

(c) On all facilities other than controlled-access highways, except when a special hazard exists that requires lower speed for compliance with subsection (a) of this section, the limits specified in this section or established as authorized shall be maximum lawful speeds, and no person shall drive a vehicle on a highway at a speed in excess of the following limits:

(1) Thirty (30) miles per hour in any urban district;

(2) Fifty (50) miles per hour for trucks of one and one-half (1 1/2) ton capacity or more in other locations; and

(3) Sixty (60) miles per hour for other vehicles in other locations;

(4) No vehicle which is over width, over length, or over height or the gross load of which is in excess of sixty-four thousand pounds (64,000 lbs.), excluding the front axle, even if operated under a special permit, shall be operated in excess of thirty (30) miles per hour.

(d) Consistent with the requirements of subsection (a) of this section, the driver of every vehicle shall drive at an appropriate reduced speed when approaching and crossing an intersection or railway grade crossing, when approaching and going around a curve, when approaching the crest of a hill, when traveling upon any narrow or winding roadway, and when special hazard exists with respect to pedestrians or other traffic or by reason of weather or highway conditions.

(e) In every charge of violation of this section, the complaint and the summons or notice to appear shall specify the speed at which the defendant is alleged to have driven and the prima facie speed applicable within the district or location.

(f) No person shall operate any motor-driven cycle at any time mentioned in 27-36-204(a) at a speed greater than thirty-five (35) miles per hour unless such motor-driven cycle is equipped with a headlamp or headlamps which are adequate to reveal a person or vehicle at a distance of three hundred feet (300') ahead.

(g) The provisions of this section shall not be construed to relieve the plaintiff in any civil action from the burden of proving negligence upon the part of the defendant as the proximate cause of the accident."

ARIZONA

Arizona lawmakers appear to be in sync with Arkansas and Texas, on the issue of Engineering and Traffic Investigations. Maricopa County Sheriff's Sgt. Jeff Sprong took time out, from his own busy schedule, to educate me on some of the finer points of Arizona law. And in case any of you are wondering, yes, this is the same Maricopa County where legendary Sheriff Joe Arpaio has been housing his prisoners in tents, at his Estrella Jail, in Phoenix, since 1993. *America's Two Toughest Sheriffs'* covers Joe's competition, with retired Sheriff Andy Lee. Now available, in both print and Kindle, just type **Brhel** into the search bar at Amazon.com. Chapters 23-40 explore Arpaio's unexpected public battle, with the administration of Barack Hussein Obama II. Sadly, my research uncovered unprecedented misbehavior, by federal officials, whom Americans should simply be able to trust, but apparently cannot and should not. *Sheriffs'* 811 end note Bibliography relies on a host of very credible sources.

Grand Canyon State traffic enforcement aficionados need to familiarize themselves with Title 28 of Arizona Revised Statutes, Transportation, Chapter 3, Traffic and Vehicle Regulations. The primary statute dealing with speed limit enforcement is 28-701.A. Subsection A prohibits any speeds, greater than *reasonable and prudent.* I invite you to read the entire statute.

Arizona Revised Statutes 28-701 REASONABLE AND PRUDENT SPEED

"A. A person shall not drive a vehicle on a highway at a speed greater than is reasonable and prudent under the circumstances, conditions and actual and potential hazards then existing. A person shall control the speed of a vehicle as necessary to avoid colliding with any object, person, vehicle or other conveyance on, entering or adjacent to the highway in compliance with legal requirements and the duty of all persons to exercise reasonable care for the protection of others.

B. Except as provided in subsections C and D of this section or except if a special hazard requires a lesser speed, any speed in excess of the following speeds is prima facie evidence that the speed is too great and therefore unreasonable:

1. Fifteen miles per hour approaching a school crossing.

2. Twenty-five miles per hour in a business or residential district.

3. Sixty-five miles per hour in other locations.

C. The speed limits prescribed in this section may be altered as authorized in sections 28-702 and 28-703.

D. The maximum speed provided in this section is reduced to the speed that is reasonable and prudent under the conditions and with regard to the actual and potential hazards then existing, including the following conditions:

1. Approaching and crossing an intersection or railroad crossing.

2. Approaching and going around a curve.

3. Approaching a hillcrest.

4. Traveling on a narrow or winding roadway.

5. A special hazard exists with respect to pedestrians or other traffic or by reason of weather or highway conditions.

E. A person shall not drive a motor vehicle at a speed that is less than the speed that is reasonable and prudent under existing conditions unless the speed that is reasonable and prudent exceeds the maximum safe operating speed of the lawfully operated implement of husbandry."

I asked Sgt. Sprong if his state has obstacles like California does, specifically speed traps, for non-compliance with Engineering and Traffic Surveys, the need for marked vehicles, or uniforms, in order to issue speeding citations. He assured me that was not necessary. In fact, he shared "...I am not aware of any types of laws that prohibit (that). In all of my traffic court dates I have always been able to bring up the speed in court..."

Predictably, to ensure accuracy, I did my own research, but couldn't find any prohibitive statutes dealing with this issue, either. In fact, as close as I could get to Engineering and Traffic Surveys is language from 28-703 that deals with Engineering and Traffic Investigations, which authorizes local authorities to alter speed limits.

MICHIGAN

Another state where I received guidance was Michigan. My consultant was an old friend, Deputy Sharon Beltz, with the Oakland County SO. The questions I posed were the same ones I asked of every other LEO, with whom I communicated. Basically, I wanted to know if speeding citations could be issued by non-uniformed officers, and if they had to present evidence they had complied with any Engineering and Traffic Surveys, if they used radar. If radar was used, what sort of ground rules applied?

Deputy Beltz informed me a marked unit or uniform was not required, in order to write speeding citations. However, she did say her state requires its officers, who operate radar, to be qualified to operate the devices they use, in order for their testimony, about gathering evidence of illegal speed, to be admissible. And, of course, the devices must be operated properly, just as is required in other states. Both requirements are fair and reasonable. Beltz referred me to the Michigan Vehicle Code, aka Act 300 of 1949, §257.627 and 257.633, which regulate speed in her state.

Michigan Vehicle Code 257.627 SPEED LIMITATIONS

"(1) A person operating a vehicle on a highway shall operate that vehicle at a careful and prudent speed not greater than nor less than is reasonable and proper, having due regard to the traffic, surface, and width of the highway and of any other condition then existing. A person shall not operate a vehicle upon a highway at a speed greater than that which will permit a stop within the assured, clear distance ahead.

(2) Except in those instances where a lower speed is specified in this chapter or the speed is unsafe pursuant to subsection (1), it is prima facie lawful for the operator of a vehicle to operate that vehicle at a speed not exceeding the following, except when this speed would be unsafe:

(a) 25 miles per hour on all highways in a business district as that term is defined in section 5.

(b) 25 miles per hour in public parks unless a different speed is fixed and duly posted.

(c) 25 miles per hour on all highways or parts of highways within the boundaries of land platted under the land division act, 1967 PA 288, MCL 560.101 to 560.293, or the condominium act, 1978 PA 59, MCL 559.101 to 559.276, unless a different speed is fixed and posted.

(d) 25 miles per hour on a highway segment with 60 or more vehicular access points within 1/2 mile.

(e) 35 miles per hour on a highway segment with not less than 45 vehicular access points but no more than 59 vehicular access points within 1/2 mile.

(f) 45 miles per hour on a highway segment with not less than 30 vehicular access points but no more than 44 vehicular access points within 1/2 mile.

(3) It is prima facie unlawful for a person to exceed the speed limits prescribed in subsection (2), except as provided in section 629.

(4) A person operating a vehicle in a mobile home park as defined in section 2 of the mobile home commission act, 1987 PA 96, MCL 125.2302, shall operate that vehicle at a careful and prudent speed, not greater than a speed that is reasonable and proper, having due regard for the traffic, surface, width of the roadway, and all other conditions existing, and not greater than a speed that permits a stop within the assured clear distance ahead. It is prima facie unlawful for the operator of a vehicle to operate that vehicle at a speed exceeding 15 miles an hour in a mobile home park as defined in section 2 of the mobile home commission act, 1987 PA 96, MCL 125.2302.

(5) A person operating a passenger vehicle drawing another vehicle or trailer shall not exceed the posted speed limit.

(6) Except as otherwise provided in this subsection, a person operating a truck with a gross weight of 10,000 pounds or more, a truck-tractor, a truck-tractor with a semi-trailer or trailer, or a combination of these vehicles shall not exceed a speed of 55 miles per hour on highways, streets, or freeways and shall not exceed a speed of 35 miles per hour during the period when reduced loadings are being enforced in accordance with this chapter. However, a person operating a school bus, a truck, a truck-tractor, or a truck-tractor with a semi-trailer or trailer described in this subsection shall not exceed a speed of 60 miles per hour on a freeway if the maximum speed limit on that freeway is 70 miles per hour.

(7) Except as otherwise provided in subsection (6), a person operating a school bus shall not exceed the speed of 55 miles per hour.

(8) The maximum rates of speeds allowed under this section are subject to the maximum rate established under section 629b.

(9) A person operating a vehicle on a highway, when entering and passing through a work zone described in section 79d(a) where a normal lane or part of the lane of traffic has been closed due to highway construction, maintenance, or surveying activities, shall not exceed a speed of 45 miles per hour unless a different speed limit is determined for that work zone by the state transportation department, a county road commission, or a local authority, based on accepted engineering practice. The state transportation department, a county road commission, or a local authority shall post speed limit signs in each work zone described in section 79d(a) that indicate the speed limit in that work zone and shall identify that

work zone with any other traffic control devices necessary to conform to the Michigan manual of uniform traffic control devices. A person shall not exceed a speed limit established under this section or a speed limit established under section 628 or 629.

(10) Subject to subsections (1) and (2)(c), speed limits established pursuant to this section are not valid unless properly posted. In the absence of a properly posted sign, the speed limit in effect shall be the general speed limit pursuant to section 628(1).

(11) Nothing in this section prevents the establishment of an absolute speed limit pursuant to section 628. Subject to subsection (1), an absolute speed limit established pursuant to section 628 supersedes a prima facie speed limit established pursuant to this section.

(12) Nothing in this section shall be construed as justification to deny a traffic and engineering investigation.

(13) As used in this section, 'vehicular access point' means a driveway or intersecting roadway.

(14) A person who violates this section is responsible for a civil infraction."

Deputy Beltz guided me to Michigan Vehicle Code 257.633, listed immediately below. It spells out how excessive speed violations are dealt with, by the LEO who issues the citation:

Michigan Vehicle Code 257.633 VIOLATIONS OF SPEED REGULATION

"(1) In every charge of a violation of a speed regulation in this chapter the complaint or citation and the summons or notice to appear, shall specify the speed at which the defendant is alleged to have driven and the speed applicable within the district or at the location.

(2) The provision of this chapter declaring speed limitations shall not be construed to relieve the plaintiff in a civil action from the burden of proving negligence on the part of the defendant as the proximate cause of an accident."

As with the input from the other LEOs, I did my own research and found nothing to dispute what Beltz had told me. I even located a complete section dealing with what Michigan calls Engineering and Traffic Investigations, as do several other states, located in Michigan Vehicle Code 257.628.

Michigan Vehicle Code 257.628 MAXIMUM OR MINIMUM SPEED LIMITS

"(1) If the state transportation department and the department of state police jointly determine upon the basis of an engineering and traffic investigation that the speed of vehicular traffic on a state trunk line highway is greater or less than is reasonable or safe under the conditions found to exist at an intersection or other place or upon a part of the highway, the departments acting jointly may determine and declare a reasonable and safe maximum or minimum speed limit on that state trunk line highway or intersection that shall be effective at the times determined when appropriate signs giving notice of the speed limit are erected at the intersection or other place or part of the highway. The maximum speed limit on all highways or parts of highways upon which a maximum speed limit is not otherwise fixed under this act is 55 miles per hour, which shall be known and may be referred to as the 'general speed limit'.

(2) If the county road commission, the township board, and the department of state police unanimously determine upon the basis of an engineering and traffic investigation that the speed of vehicular traffic on a county highway is greater or less than is reasonable or safe under the conditions found to exist upon any part of the highway, then acting unanimously they may establish a reasonable and safe maximum or minimum speed limit on that county highway that is effective at the times determined when appropriate signs giving notice of the speed limit are erected on the highway. A township board that does not wish to continue as part of the process provided by this subsection shall notify in writing the county road commission. As used in this subsection, 'county road commission' means the board of county road commissioners elected or appointed under section 6 of chapter IV of 1909 PA 283, MCL 224.6, or, in the case of a charter county with a population of 2,000,000 or more with an elected county executive that does not have a board of county road commissioners, the county executive.

(3) If a superintendent of a school district determines that the speed of vehicular traffic on a state trunk line or county highway, which is within 1,000 feet of a school in the school district of which that person is the superintendent, is greater or less than is reasonable or safe, the officials identified in subsection (1) or (2), as appropriate, shall include the superintendent of the school district affected in acting jointly in determining and declaring a reasonable and safe maximum or minimum speed limit on that state trunk line or county highway.

(4) In the case of a county highway of not less than 1 mile with residential lots with road frontage of 300 feet or less along either side of the highway for the length of that part of the highway that is under review for a

proposed change in the speed limit, the township board may petition the county road commission or in charter counties where there is no road commission, but there is a county board of commissioners, the township board may petition the county board of commissioners for a proposed change in the speed limit. The county road commission or in charter counties where there is no road commission, but there is a county board of commissioners, the township board may petition the county board of commissioners to approve the proposed change in the speed limit without the necessity of an engineering and traffic investigation.

(5) If upon investigation the state transportation department or county road commission and the department of state police find it in the interest of public safety, they may order the township board, or city or village officials to erect and maintain, take down, or regulate the speed control signs, signals, or devices as directed, and in default of an order the state transportation department or county road commission may cause the designated signs, signals, and devices to be erected and maintained, taken down, regulated, or controlled, in the manner previously directed, and pay for the erecting and maintenance, removal, regulation, or control of the sign, signal, or device out of the highway fund designated.

(6) A public record of all speed control signs, signals, or devices authorized under this section shall be filed in the office of the county clerk of the county in which the highway is located, and a certified copy shall be prima facie evidence in all courts of the issuance of the authorization. The public record with the county clerk shall not be required as prima facie evidence of authorization in the case of signs erected or placed temporarily for the control of speed or direction of traffic at points where construction, repairs, or maintenance of highways is in progress, or along a temporary alternate route established to avoid the construction, repair, or maintenance of a highway, if the signs are of uniform design approved by the state transportation department and the department of state police and clearly indicate a special control, when proved in court that the temporary traffic control sign was placed by the state transportation department or on the authority of the state transportation department and the department of state police or by the county road commission or on the authority of the county road commission, at a specified location.

(7) A person who fails to observe an authorized speed or traffic control sign, signal, or device is responsible for a civil infraction.

(8) Except as otherwise provided in this section, the maximum speed limit on all freeways shall be 70 miles per hour except that if the state transportation department and the department of state police jointly determine upon the basis of an engineering and traffic investigation that the speed of vehicular traffic on a freeway is greater or less than is reasonable

or safe under the conditions found to exist upon a part of the freeway, the departments acting jointly may determine and declare a reasonable and safe maximum or minimum speed limit on that freeway that is not more than 70 miles per hour but not less than 55 miles per hour and that shall be effective when appropriate signs giving notice of the speed limit are erected. The minimum speed limit on all freeways is 55 miles per hour except if reduced speed is necessary for safe operation or in compliance with law or in compliance with a special permit issued by an appropriate authority.

(9) The maximum rates of speed allowed under this section are subject to the maximum rates established under section 629b, section 627(5) to (7) for certain vehicles and vehicle combinations, and section 629(4).

(10) Except for the general speed limit described in subsection (1), speed limits established pursuant to this section shall be known as absolute speed limits."

As with the other states, none of the language appears to require proof of dated Engineering and Traffic Surveys that justify the posted speed limit in order for her state's LEOs to lawfully use radar to measure speed.

NEW JERSEY

In the Garden State, I was blessed to be able to rely on my old buddy, Cpl. Gary Hughes, Passaic County SO. Gary is a great guy who almost sounded apologetic for what he believed was a paucity of information about his state's legal requirements for use of radar. Frankly, I wanted to kiss the guy. He actually took the time to dig up a bunch of New Jersey appellate cases.

If I may say so, without sounding overly critical of New Jersey's state legislators, it is easily the most difficult state, in which I have done legal research. For one thing, it is nearly impossible to navigate the Table of Contents, in order to find the relevant statutes. And, even when you find it, the work is certainly no picnic. Word to the wise, NJ lawmakers, please rethink this. A good descriptive word of your work is *tedious*. Anyhow, what you read here is a combination of me locating statutes, and Cpl. Hughes locating cases. However, on the subject of making life easier for their own state's officers, my hat is off to New Jersey's lawmakers. Why do I say that? Let me share what Gary had to say:

"Well in N.J. they do not use the term *speed traps*. We call it *radar enforcement*. Really, the only way to beat a radar ticket in NJ is if the officer is not certified, the radar unit is not certified, and the tuning forks aren't certified, or (if) the car is not calibrated, if doing pace radar. All documents must be presented at trial. If you're also asking, if the officer has to be in a marked vehicle, no, they don't. We can run radar day or night. We also do not have to be visible...We also can run radar from an overpass and radio the info to another officer down the road or highway to conduct the motor vehicle stop. I've also enclosed some case law from NJ...and a link from NJDCJ for certification for officers."

Wow, what can a humble DA say, other than THANK YOU, GARY? Here are the case citations Hughes provided: *State v Dantonio* 18 N.J.570 (1955), *State v Bookbinder* 82 N.J. Super 179 183 (App. Div. 1964), *State v Readding* 169 N.J. Super 238 (Law Div. 1978), and, *State v Wojtkowiak* 170 N.J. Super. 44 (Law Div. 1979).

In *Dantonio*, the court determined use of radar is legally acceptable, providing it is working properly, and the operator is adequately competent, by concluding:

"We are satisfied that readings on radar speedmeters which have been set up and operated in the manner established by the evidence in the instant matter constitute legally admissible evidence which may readily support a finding of guilt by the trier of the facts."

In Bookbinder, the court noted: "...if the defendant is found guilty, the trial court should determine the quantum of excess was so many miles per hour in exercising its discretion as to the penalty to be imposed within the statutory limitation. The precise speed a motorist was traveling thus is material only on the question as to the penalty to be imposed, not on the question of guilt or innocence."

In *Readding*, the court stated the general rule that "...in order for the radar speedometer reading to be admissible into evidence, it should be established that: (l) the device is scientifically reliable; (2) the particular speedometer used in the case being tried is accurate; (3) the operator is qualified; and (4) the device was operated properly in the case being tried...."

In Wojtkowiak, the court ruled "...the K-55 Radar is an accurate and reliable tool for the measurement of speed, its accuracy and reliability in any case are no better than the skill of the person operating the radar...a calibration check is accomplished with the use of two tuning forks and their accuracy must be the subject of the documentary proof...Use of the K-55 does not eliminate the need for such proof..."

The obvious message from *Wojtkowiak* was for any departments using such devices, to first adequately train any officers who would operate them. Interestingly, the court found no impediment to the use of the words *calibration check*, referring to the use of tuning forks to test the device.

This suggests to me the words *check* and *test* are viewed by this court, as being synonymous. And this also appears inconsistent with Comal County SO's Lt. Reynolds' insistence *test* be used by his department's peace officers, rather than *calibration*. If you recall, Mark said the latter verbiage is the exclusive province of the manufacturer. So, ascertain how your state views such issues.

The link Cpl. Hughes provided, regarding certification of radar operators is www.state.nj.us/lps/dcj/njpdresources/radar.htm. For your edification, he is certified to operate radar in his state. In order to avoid relaying incorrect information, I have taken the liberty of copying and pasting, verbatim, what NJ requires, of both its operators and instructors, as set forth in New Jersey

Administrative Code 13:1-4.4.

New Jersey Administrative Code 13:1-4.4 RADAR CERTIFICATION

"Requirements for Certification

Operator (3 year certification)

Minimum of four (4) hours classroom instruction on the Division of Criminal Justice RADAR manual.

Minimum of four (4) hours supervised hands-on practical training in RADAR operation.

Minimum of eighty (80) hours hands-on non-enforcement operation of the RADAR equipment.

Upon completion of the above requirements, application must be made to the Division of Criminal Justice for certification.

Instructor (3 year certification)

Satisfactory completion of RADAR operator requirements.

Two years' experience as a RADAR operator.

Completion of a course for RADAR instructors approved by the Police Training Commission.

In order to instruct RADAR in the Basic Course for Police Officers and the RADAR Instructor's Course the instructor must meet the Methods of Instruction requirements specified in N.J.A.C. 13:1-4.4. THIS IS FOR ACADEMY LEVEL TRAINING ONLY. Upon completion of these requirements application must be made to the Division of Criminal Justice for certification.

Recertification as a Radar Operator

Two (2) years of continuous RADAR operation following initial certification.

Four (4) hours of in-service training during the last year of the operator's current certification period by a certified instructor. The training must include two hours of classroom instruction with updates on court decisions or related training issues and two hours of practical exercise using a vehicle mounted RADAR unit or equivalent training device. Upon completion of these requirements application must be made to the Division of Criminal Justice for recertification.

Recertification as a Radar Instructor

Presentation of at least one (1) RADAR course at a certified police academy or police department during the instructor's current certification period.

Attendance at a Division of Criminal Justice approved RADAR instructor refresher course or equivalent course.

Upon completion of these requirements application must be made to the Division of Criminal Justice for recertification. **THIS IS SATISFIED UPON COMPLETION OF THE RADAR INSTRUCTOR REFRESHER COURSE.**"

Although I admittedly found New Jersey's code system more than a bit trying, as far as having to research it, if Hughes could trudge through it, I decided I could too. So with that thought in mind, curious to learn, if I could find any more similarities between my state and others, I pursued the question of any requirement for state police uniforms.

Here is what I located in New Jersey Permanent Statutes. Separate uniforms are spelled out, for both winter and summer usage. Talk about attention to detail. So it appears the same basic uniform requirements for my state's CHP officers apply in Cpl. Hughes' own state.

New Jersey Permanent Statutes 53:3-5. UNIFORMS FOR STATE POLICE

"The members of the department of state police shall wear the following standard uniform, subject to state police regulations:

a. Winter uniform: French blue blouse, dark blue breeches with yellow stripe, cap with dark blue band and French blue bell, black boots, black pistol belt, long dark blue trousers with yellow stripe for officers, French blue overcoat; all according to state police specifications.

b. Summer uniform: French blue shirt, dark blue breeches with yellow stripe, cap with dark blue band and French blue bell, black boots, black pistol belt, long dark blue trousers with yellow stripe for officers, French blue overcoat; all according to state police specifications."

MISSOURI

Last, but certainly not least, is my old buddy, retired Crystal Lakes PD Chief Dennis Postel. As a point of reference, Dennis is the first Hispanic chief at that particular department. He and I generally e-mail each other daily. Like me, Dennis seems to have difficulty saying no to new professional challenges, as evidenced by his own dislike of things sedentary, unless he is also enjoying a nice cigar, just as I try to do, when time permits. He currently holds the rank of reservist captain elsewhere. I asked Chief Postel the same questions I asked officers from other states. Here's what he said:

"I attended an instructor's class to teach others to work radar. The only requirements are training which may be on the job. The radar unit and forks must be certified once a year. The officer must testify that he checked the radar unit with the tuning forks. Some do it at the beginning of setting up and then when they conclude. I always checked before and after each traffic stop, as I felt it was more credible. When I taught radar I issued a card indicating the officer attended my class and I signed off on the card. I generally took the original certificate to court in case questions arose. I did some research and there is not law or requirement that officers must be in full uniform to issue a traffic summons/citation."

Like any self-respecting LEO or prosecutor, Dennis was not content to rely on his own information. He got on the horn, with one of his own local Das, to see what she had to say about her opinions. The DA quickly confirmed he was right, even going so far as to cite Missouri Revised Statute 70.820. In California, we refer to this as mutual assistance. This is a legal vehicle that authorizes different agencies to come to the aid of another agency under certain specified conditions.

Missouri Revised Statute 70.820 AUTHORITY OF PEACE OFFICERS, etc.

"1. Any law enforcement officer as defined by section 556.061, full-time peace officer as defined by section 590.100, of a county or a full-time peace officer of any political subdivision who is certified pursuant to chapter 590, or a chief executive officer as defined by section 590.100, of a county or any political subdivision, certified pursuant to chapter 590 shall have the authority to respond to an emergency situation outside the boundaries of the political subdivision from which such peace officer's authority is derived. This section does not apply to any peace officer certified pursuant to subsection 6 of section 590.105.

2. Before a peace officer shall have the authority to respond to an emergency situation outside the boundaries of the political subdivision from

which the officer's authority is derived pursuant to subsection 1 of this section, the authority shall be first authorized by ordinance, order, or other ruling by the governing body of the political subdivision from which the officer derives such officer's authority and by the governing body of the political subdivision in which the emergency situation is alleged to be occurring and by the board of police established by section 84.020 or by the board of police commissioners established by section 84.350 if the officer derives his authority from either board or if the emergency situation is alleged to be occurring within the jurisdiction of either board.

3. As used in this section, 'emergency situation' means any situation in which the law enforcement officer has a reasonable belief that a crime is about to be committed, is being committed, or has been committed involving injury or threat of injury to any person, property, or governmental interest and such officer's response is reasonably necessary to prevent or end such emergency situation or mitigate the likelihood of injury involved in such emergency situation. The determination of the existence of any emergency situation shall be in the discretion of the officer making the response or in the discretion of an officer or governmental officer of the political subdivision in which the emergency situation is alleged to be occurring.

4. As used in this section, 'response' shall mean to take any and all action which the officer may lawfully take as if exercising his powers within his own jurisdiction.

5. In addition to the emergency response powers prescribed in subsection 1 of this section, any peace officer of a county of the first classification with a charter form of government, or any peace officer of any political subdivision within any county of the first classification with a charter form of government, or any peace officer of any city not within a county, who has completed the basic peace training program pursuant to chapter 590 may arrest persons who violate any provision of state law within the boundaries of any county of the first classification or of any city not within a county.

6. In addition to the powers prescribed in subsections 1 and 5 of this section, section 544.216, and any other arrest powers, a law enforcement officer or federal law enforcement officer as defined in subsection 8 of this section, may arrest on view, and without a warrant, at any place within this state, any person the officer sees asserting physical force or using forcible compulsion for the purpose of causing or creating a substantial risk of death or serious physical injury to any person or any person the officer sees committing a dangerous felony as defined in section 556.061. Any such action shall be deemed to be within the scope of the officer's employment.

7. To provide assistance to law enforcement officers, a federal law enforcement officer shall have the same authority as a law enforcement officer where:

(1) The federal law enforcement officer is rendering assistance at the request of any law enforcement officer of this state; or

(2) The federal law enforcement officer is effecting an arrest or providing assistance as part of a bona fide task force or joint investigation in which law enforcement officers of this state are participating.

8. A federal law enforcement officer is a person employed by the United States government who is empowered to effect an arrest with or without a warrant for violation of the United States Code and who is authorized to carry a firearm in the performance of the person's official duties as a federal law enforcement officer and includes a law enforcement officer as defined in section 556.061."

As with California, New Jersey and other jurisdictions, it appears Missouri Highway Patrol officers are required to be attired in a specified uniform while on duty, as set forth in MRS 43.130.

Missouri Revised Statutes 43.130 UNIFORMS

"1. The superintendent shall prescribe a distinctive style of uniform and badge for members of the patrol to be made of the material and of the color he specifies, and it shall be unlawful for any person to wear the prescribed uniform or badge, or any distinctive part thereof, except on order of the superintendent. The uniform shall be purchased at the times the superintendent requires, and the superintendent shall fix a uniform allowance for such purpose for each member of the patrol.

2. The members of the patrol shall, at the expense of the state, be furnished with the vehicles, equipment, arms, ammunition, supplies and insignia of office as the superintendent deems necessary, all of which shall remain the property of the state and be strictly accounted for by each member of the patrol. All such vehicles and equipment shall be distinctively marked, and all vehicles used by members of the patrol shall be distinctively lighted at night.

3. Members of the patrol shall wear their uniform and insignia of office at all times when on duty, unless otherwise designated by the superintendent."

As I was digesting all this, I also did my own research, just to make sure no one missed anything. I went so far, as to review MRS 300.205, in order to learn if at least one state, other than my own, had laws similar to mine dealing with the use of radar. All I found was language, basically saying the state could regulate speed limits in municipalities, but not vice-versa. I found no Engineering and Traffic Surveys.

Missouri Revised Statutes 300.205 STATE SPEED LAWS

"The state traffic laws regulating the speed of vehicles shall be applicable upon all streets within the city, except that the city may by ordinance declare and determine upon the basis of engineering and traffic investigation that certain speed regulations shall be applicable upon specified streets or in certain areas, in which event it shall be unlawful for any person to drive a vehicle at a speed in excess of any speed so declared when signs are in place giving notice thereof, but no city ordinance shall regulate the speed of vehicles upon controlled access highways of the state."

So all in all, every state requires its radar operators to be fully trained to use radar while on duty to determine speed of motorists. They require radar devices to function properly. But only California appears to mandate proof of Engineering and Traffic Surveys before an officer can produce proof of a motorist's speed captured by a radar device without risking being accused of doing so by way of impermissible speed traps.

Chapter 7
Use of Radar

(*Sgt. Dan Devinny*)

Note: As mentioned previously, I wrote this chapter, thanks to the expertise of Dan Devinny. As noted in From the Author, "Dan-Dan the Traffic Man" is a Riverside County, California Sheriff's sergeant. Danny brings an absolute wealth of traffic enforcement experience to the table. Dan has been a peace officer since 1986 and has also taught traffic classes at his department's academy where I've taught. I worked with him, while I was still a DA, and attest first-hand to the impeccable quality of his work.

The purpose of this chapter? The role radar and lidar may each play, in your life, as a traffic officer. First, radar stands for *radio detection and ranging*. It's an acronym made of the first two letters in radio and the first letter in the next three words in this phrase. Lidar is an acronym for *light detection and ranging*. It's an improved version of radar, and is used, by relying on the same concepts and procedures, as radar.

There are three basic types of radar you may use, in the course and scope of your duties, as a traffic officer: *stationary, moving*, and *handheld* radar. We'll discuss how each of these is used, in a bit.

Please remember, as the operator, you *test* a radar device. Only the manufacturer *calibrates* it. I have received negative reports, concerning the operation of radar, from LEOs. They complain about courtroom scenarios where defense counsel has successfully challenged their use of the word calibrate, in lieu of test. You can avoid this potential courtroom issue by not using this verbiage interchangeably, unless you are sure it's acceptable in your jurisdiction.

Stationary radar is mounted in police vehicles, and may have either one or two antennae. A stationary unit is normally mounted on your unit's dashboard. You operate it, when your unit is also stationary. Hence, the name. Visualize a traffic unit parked, while the officer operating it is using radar, to monitor speed enforcement.

Stationary devices are so named because they are operated from a stationary position. Such devices are installed in traffic units. They remain there for their working lives, unless they need to be removed for maintenance.

Moving radar, on the other hand, as the name implies, can be operated while your unit is also moving. The idea is to track a moving target, when your patrol vehicle is mobile. As the name suggests, moving radar is in use while you are traveling. Essentially, you will operate your patrol vehicle, in much the same fashion you would, if you were bumper-pacing a suspected speeder.

Handheld devices, on the other hand, like speed guns, used to measure the speed of balls thrown by baseball pitchers, can bc quickly pointed in any direction. Handheld units are mostly battery powered. For the most part, they are used by motor officers. As a practical matter, as with any other device powered by a battery, make sure the battery is adequately charged before you go 10-8.

Any of these types of devices—stationary, moving, or handheld—will require calibration and testing, before you can offer admissible testimony, in court, about any speed you have determined, with their use. In practical terms, this means defense counsel can attack your acquisition of a motorist's speed, by challenging the qualifications required to properly check these devices. Counsel can, and will, also contest your ability to properly operate such a device.

The primary components of stationary radar are an antenna, a counting unit, and a power source. Handheld units, on the other hand, integrate the antenna, the counting unit, and the power source, into one unit. This simplifies the set-up. Handheld devices are both cord-connected and cordless.

Cordless handheld radar devices integrate the power source into a rechargeable battery pack. Obviously the convenience of this speaks for itself. And once again, at the risk of being accused of redundancy, remember to always keep the battery pack adequately charged.

Before we delve deeper into the use of radar, it's important to first understand the importance of why radar is useful. Enforcing speed limits protects public safety, and saves lives. There is a direct correlation between excessive speed, and other factors, which result in traffic collisions with major injuries and fatalities.

Because of this unfortunate relationship, there are safety benefits to be gained from effective speed regulation and enforcement. What specific causes of traffic collisions should we be aware? These include, but are not necessarily limited to:

1. unsafe speed for conditions
2. driving under the influence of alcohol and/or drugs
3. driving on the wrong side of the road
4. improper turning movements
5. right of way violations
6. failure to obey traffic control devices such as stop signs and traffic lights

Radar Features (*control panel*)
1. Range Control (*sensitivity of radar, wider beam or narrower beam*)
2. Audio Doppler tone generator (*confirms acquisition of vehicle, vehicle speed, etc.*)
3. Internal circuitry test (*confirms radar equipment is operational*)
4. Lock/Hold option (*displays and holds speed of violator on the unit's display*)
5. Fast Mode (*on or off: freeway speed or city traffic*)
6. Auto-lock/Alarms (*can set specific speed at which radar will lock on a target vehicle; will notify operator by sounding alarm/Doppler tone*)

Set-up and testing of Radar Unit
1. Mount antenna and counting unit securely
2. Confirm antenna is clear of any and all obstructions
3. Route power cord away from counting unit
4. Mount antenna away from counting unit to prevent feedback

Testing the Radar
1. Examine the overall condition of the radar unit, the display window, the case, and the power cord, if it has one:
    a. Caution: Confirm unit has not been dropped
        i. Insure there is adequate power supplied to the radar unit
        ii. Insure the area in front of the radar is free from obstructions, with no external interferences, e.g., close-by radio frequency interference (RFI) or electromagnetic interference (*EMI*)
        iii. Verify all segments of the display, such as light emitting diodes (*LED*) or liquid crystal displays (*LCD*) are working properly. Verify the radar is sending out a signal at the designated frequency.

Most radar units have a TEST button. When depressed, the radar unit is programmed to cycle through the internal circuitry test (*ICT*). The radar unit will first check the lamp/segments of the display, and then test the internal signal calibration. If the radar is sending out the proper radar signal, most radar units will generate a pre-determined speed in the display window. These speeds are usually 32 mph or 40 mph depending on which radar you have (*check your operator's manual to determine the ICT display speed of your radar unit*).

The radar unit will have "PASSED" the ICT if:

1. All segments/lamps on the display are working properly
2. The ICT display indicated is correct with no deviation

External Circuitry Test (*Tuning Fork Test*)

The tuning fork was invented in 1711, by Englishman John Shore. It is a small, two-pronged metal device used by musicians to provide a fixed pitch by which to tone instruments. Tuning forks are sometimes also used in physics and acoustical experiments.

The Tuning Fork Test

The tuning fork, when lightly tapped, produces a fixed harmonic tune. This harmonic tune influences the transmitted radar signal, resulting in a predictable and uniform speed reading, by the radar device.

1. Tuning forks are produced for individual bands of radar and must be used with the correct band
2. A tuning fork may have a tolerance of plus or minus 1 mph
3. Tuning forks should be calibrated and kept with the radar device it is used to check

CAVEAT: Tuning forks must not be interchanged with other radar units

Performing a Tuning Fork Test

1. Gently tap the fork ends against a solid surface causing the tuning fork to generate a harmonic tone.
2. Holding the tuning fork upright, align the forks one-half inch to two inches away from the radar antenna, and activate the radar device.

The tuning fork should cause the radar device to immediately read a speed on the display. If the radar device display speed is within plus or minus 1 mph of the tuning fork speed, it has passed the test. You have properly tested the fork.

Tracking History-Stationary

1. Visual Observations
2. Audio Observations
3. Radar Observations

Visual Observations

1. Identify target vehicle (*i.e., which vehicle is speeding, pulling away from others*)
2. Estimate target vehicle's speed (*ability learned with experience; assists in confirmation of radar speed*)
3. Check range (*determine if target is within radar's range*)
4. Check environment (*confirm or dispel other vehicles or collateral interference*)

Audio Doppler Tone consistent with your estimated speed in:
1. Pitch (*higher pitch equals higher speed*)
2. Clarity (*loud uninterrupted tone*)

Audio Observations
1. Pitch (*higher pitch equals higher speed*)
2. Clarity (*loud uninterrupted tone*)

Radar Observations
1. Confirm your radar's indicated speed:
   a. Stable Reading (*not fluctuating up and down)*
   b. Lock/No-lock option (*if unlocked stable reading, lock display to save*)

Moving Radar

Basic Principle

Moving radar, like stationary radar, uses the "Doppler Principle" to acquire target signals, and determine target speeds. However, because the "Doppler Principle" uses relative motion, the speed of your police unit now becomes relative motion, in the speed equation. Moving Radar separates the return signals into two categories:

1. High Doppler Signals
2. Low Doppler Signals

High Doppler Signal
1. The High Doppler signal is the relative speed between your police vehicle and the speed of another moving object in your radar's zone of influence

Low Doppler Signal
1. The Low Doppler signal is the relative speed between your police vehicle and stationary objects

Moving Radar Fundamentals

1 The moving radar is manufactured and programmed to calculate the target vehicle speed by subtracting the low Doppler signal from the high Doppler signal

2. Target speed equals closing speed minus patrol speed

Moving Radar Set-Up and Testing

1. Moving radar is set-up and tested in the same way as stationary radar, with one exception—The Tuning Fork Test

Moving Radar–Tuning Fork Test

1. As the name implies, moving radar operates while the police unit is moving

a. Therefore, to properly test the radar reception and computation you must use two tuning forks as opposed to just one

2. Always make sure the tuning forks you are using are properly calibrated and designed for the specific radar you are testing

a. If they are not, any calibration performed will be invalid

Special Problems with operating Moving Mode Radar

Trigonometric functions, also known as circular functions, are functions of an angle. You use them to relate a triangle's angles to the lengths of its sides. The most familiar trigonometric functions are *sine*, *cosine* and *tangent.*

The *sine* of an angle is the ratio of the length of the opposite side to the length of the hypotenuse, or the longest side of a right-angled triangle, i.e., the side opposite the right angle. The sine function takes an angle and tells you the length of the y-component of that triangle, also known as the *rise*.

The *cosine* of an angle is the ratio of the length of the adjacent side to the length of the hypotenuse. The cosine function takes an angle and tells you the length of that triangle, also known as the *run*.

The *tangent* of an angle is the ratio of the length of the opposite side to the length of the adjacent side. The tangent function takes an angle and tells you what the result is when you divide the y-component by the x-component. This is also known as the *slope*.

1. Low Doppler/High Doppler Cosine

2. Doppler radar, named after Austrian physicist Christian Doppler, functions by beaming a microwave signal toward a selected target, listening for its reflection, then analyzing how the original signal has been altered by the target. Avoid possible confusion that can occur as your radar device's signal is reflected by both stationary and moving objects.

3. Shadowing Effect *(see following pages for explanation)*

4. Batching Effect *(see following pages for explanation)*

5. Control/Switching errors *(see following pages for explanation)*

Multi-Tasking Operations

1. Unlike stationary mode radar operations, as a moving mode radar operator, you must divide your attention, on the tracking history and target speed acquisition while you are also safely operating your vehicle.

   a. **NOTE:** Divided attention is an issue that pertains to suspects who operate a motor vehicle, while under the influence of alcohol or a controlled substance. An example? A motorist trying to maintain a straight line of travel, while observing their speedometer, thereby creating the expression *divided attention impairment*. Even if a motorist, such as a law enforcement officer, is not under the influence of an intoxicant, such multi-tasking nonetheless requires appropriate levels of concentration. Therefore, expect defense counsel to raise this as a DUI issue, whether factual or not, in order to attempt to create reasonable doubt as to their client's guilt.

Radar Site Selection

1. When choosing a location to work radar enforcement you should consider the following:
2. Ability to set-up without impeding traffic
3. Ability to safely enter traffic stream to commence a pursuit
4. Availability of safe locations to stop violators
5. Demonstrated need, such as collisions or complaints
6. Reasonably clear and unobstructed view of traffic
7. Not excessively hilly or curvy
8. Reasonably well-spaced traffic (no "stop and go" traffic)

Radar Effects

Radar Effects Groups

1. Natural Effects (*e.g., terrain, other obstructions*)
2. Manmade Effects (*e.g., buildings, signs*)
3. Operator Effects (*i.e., distance, angle of radar, control settings*)

Natural Effects

1. Natural effects may hamper the sensitivity of the radar by reducing its effective range, but it NEVER affects the radar unit's accuracy, including:

   a. Rain
   b. Snow

c. Fog
d. Moisture in the atmosphere
e. High/low temperatures

Manmade Effects

1. Interference (RFI, EMI)
2. Proper Use of Equipment
3. Microwave Transmissions
4. High tension wires
5. Harmonic Interference
6. External Mechanical Interference

Operator Effects Stationary or Moving modes

1. Reflected Signal
2. Double Bounce
3. Improper Control Setting
4. Feedback or Panning
5. Harmonic Interference
6. External Mechanical Interference
7. Side Lobe Effect
8. Scanning or Sweeping effect
9. Window obstructions
10. Operator effects

Moving mode only

1. Shadowing
2. Low/High Doppler Cosine (*angle at which the target vehicle is measured, the greater the angle the lower the speed projected; thus benefiting violator*)
3. Own speed capture
4. Pulsating Amplitude Effect

Shadowing Effect

1. This occurs when your antenna is misaligned, and/or you are following a vehicle so closely, it causes your low Doppler signal to become the closing rate of speed, between you and the vehicle you are trailing. This again will cause the counting unit of the radar to not subtract out enough patrol speed, and again inflate the target vehicle speed.

Low Doppler/High Doppler Cosine

1. As in stationary mode, cosine angles affect the relative motion between you and the target vehicle. Because you are moving, a cosine effect on your low Doppler, or patrol speed, can result in a lower than actual

indicated patrol speed. When the radar subtracts the patrol speed, from the closing speed, to calculate the target speed, it does not subtract out enough patrol speed, thus inflating the target vehicle's speed, and displaying a *higher* than actual speed, for the target vehicle.

Batching Effect

1. This occurs, when you are rapidly accelerating, or decelerating your police unit, caused by slight time lags, in the moving radar's sensing/computing cycle. Like the cosine and shadowing effects, this can lead to either higher or lower target vehicle speed results, depending on the circumstances.

Tracking History Moving Mode Radar

1. Visual Observations
2. Audio Observations
3. Radar Observations
4. Speedometer Verification

Radar Detectors and Radar Jammers

Are radar detectors legal to use? That depends. Radar detectors are legal for all vehicles, except commercial vehicles, in the State of California, for example. **Code of Federal Regulations,** Chapter III–Federal Motor Carrier Safety Administration, Department of Transportation. Part 392–Driving of Commercial Motor Vehicles. Subpart G–Prohibited Practices. Sec. 392.71 Radar detectors; use and/or possession:

(a) "No driver shall use a radar detector in a commercial vehicle, or operate a commercial motor vehicle that is equipped with or contains any radar detector.

(b) No motor carrier shall require or permit a driver to violate paragraph (a) of this section."

Radar Jammers vs. Detectors

A radar jammer differs from a radar detector, in that it is actively transmitting radio wave signals from the device. In other words, a radar detector's function is to *detect* law enforcement radar units. A jammer, on the other hand, is used to *interfere with* your radar unit's ability to determine a traffic violator's speed. Because it is transmitting a radio wave signal, it would require Federal Communication Commission (FCC) licensing. Radar jammers are *illegal* to use in the state of California, for example, in all vehicles.

National Case Law

1. *State of Delaware vs. Moffitt* (1953)
2. *State of New Jersey vs. D'Antonio* (1955)
3. *State of Conn. vs. Tomanelli* (1966)
4. *State of Kentucky vs. Honeycutt* (1966)
5. *State of Wisconsin vs. Hanson* (1978)

State of Delaware vs. Moffitt

In 1953, the defendant was issued a citation by state troopers, using an S band radar device. The issue, before the court, was the validity of the Doppler principle. The prosecution was required to present foundational testimony, in order to establish the reliability of radar.

State of New Jersey vs. Dominic D'Antonio

In 1955, the defendant was issued a citation by New Jersey state troopers using an S band radar device, which was challenged by the defense as to:

1. the validity of the Doppler principle
2. the proper setup and testing of the radar device
3. qualifications of the officers to operate the radar device

Judicial notice was taken on the reliability of radar, eliminating the requirement of expert testimony on this issue.

State of Connecticut vs. Tomanelli

In 1966, the defendant was issued a citation by Connecticut police officers. The citation was challenged, by the defense, on the following issues:

1. the validity of the Doppler principle.
2. outside influences possibly affecting the accuracy of readings
3. qualifications of the officers to operate the radar device
4. use of tuning forks to test the accuracy of the radar device

Judicial notice was taken, of the issue of the reliability of radar, eliminating the requirement of expert testimony. The court also found the use of tuning forks was an accepted method of testing the accuracy of a radar device, and assumed accurate, if not challenged by the defense.

State of Kentucky vs. Honeycutt

In 1966, the defendant was issued a citation by police officers for traveling 60 mph in a 35 mph speed zone. The court took judicial notice of the Doppler principle. Issues included:

1. Accuracy of the device and how it functioned *(out front and closest)*
2. Proper setup and testing of radar
3. Training of operators
4. Identification of target vehicle *(tracking history)*

The court held the prosecution must establish the accuracy of the radar device, on the date and time of the reading, including proper setup and testing. The operator need not be an expert in the internal workings of the device, somewhat akin to acknowledging a motorist does not have to know how to tear down his vehicle's motor, in order to drive it. The court found a few hours of training, in the use a radar device, was sufficient.

State of Wisconsin vs. Hanson

On January 4, 1975, the defendant was ticketed for speeding on U.S. Highway 18-151. He was allegedly traveling at a speed of 68 mph in a 55 mph zone. Hanson's speed was measured using a Kustom electronic Model MR-7 Moving radar unit. The court took judicial notice of the Doppler principle. Issues included:

1. Accuracy of the radar device and how it functioned (*one window operator switched back and forth*)
2. Proper setup and testing of radar (*two tuning forks*)
3. Experience and training of operator
4. The need to operate a radar device in an area free of distortion

The court found the following:

1. Verification of patrol speed on radar display to patrol unit speedometer
2. An officer using the device must have adequate training and experience
3. The officer must testify to the setup and testing of the radar unit
4. Equipment was operated with minimal possibility of distortion
5. An external test was performed by a calibrated second vehicle or the use of a tuning fork

Dade County Florida-May 7, 1979–Judge Nesbitt's ruling

Eighty cases were consolidated, and heard, in court, pursuant to a motion to suppress evidence. Thirty experts in the field of radar, engineering, physics, mathematics, and law enforcement testified. There were thirty-three exhibits, and over two thousand pages of documentati.

This case gained national notoriety (*60 Minutes*, etc.), and caught the eye of the National Highway Traffic Safety Administration (*NHTSA*). The judgment favored the defense, and set the use of radar back many years, in the state of Florida.

Issues included:

1. Training of Radar Operators
2. Radar Errors *(effects)*
3. Reliability of the radar device

This ruling prompted NHTSA to establish a 24-hour radar operator program, and a testing program for radar devices. This case pointed out the real significance of tracking history, as evidence a radar device only supports the officer's observations. In Florida, radar operators must attend a 40-hour course, every two years, to maintain certification, and a radar instructor must attend a radar operator course, and a 40-hour instructor course, every two years, to maintain their certification.

The court held, "Dr. Nichols has prescribed an intensive course of training in both classroom and in the field with written examination for proof of qualification, conducted by an independent, highly skilled radar operator and not by a manufacturer's agent or his students. This would only be a lessening of the problems.

All of this morphs into one main issue, to wit; the reliability of radar speed-measuring devices as used today. 'Based upon all of the testimony, exhibits, and argument of counsel, I find that the reliability of the radar speed measuring devices as used in their present modes and particularly in these cases, has not been established beyond and to the exclusion of every reasonable doubt nor has it met the test of reasonable scientific certainty'."

Legal Aspects of Radar

California Vehicle Code §40800 (*Uniform Used by Officers*)
"Every traffic officer on duty for the exclusive or main purpose of enforcing the provisions of division 10 or 11 of this code shall wear a full distinctive uniform, and if the officer while so on duty uses a motor vehicle, it must be painted a distinctive color specified by the commissioner."
"This section does not apply to an officer assigned exclusively to the duty of investigating and securing evidence in reference to any theft of a vehicle or failure of a person to stop in the event of an accident of violation 23109 or in reference to any felony charge, or to any officer engaged in serving

any warrant when the officer is not engaged in patrolling the highways for the purpose of enforcing the traffic laws."

California Vehicle Code §40801 (*Speed Trap Prohibition*)
"No peace officer or other person shall use a speed trap in arresting, or participating or assisting in the arrest of, any person for any alleged violation of this code nor shall any speed trap be used in securing evidence as to the speed of any vehicle for the purpose of an arrest or prosecution under this code."

California Vehicle Code §40802 (*Speed Traps*)

(a) "A 'speed trap' is either of the following:

(1) A particular section of a highway measured as to distance and width boundaries marked, designated, or otherwise determined in order that the speed of a vehicle may be calculated by securing the time it takes the vehicle to travel the known distance."

(2) "A particular section of a highway with a prima facie speed limit that is provided by this code or by local ordinance under subparagraph (A) of paragraph (2) of subdivision (a) of section 22352, or established under section 22354, 22357, 22358, or 22358.3, if that prima facie speed limit is not justified by an engineering and traffic survey conducted within five years prior to the date of the alleged violation. And enforcement of the speed limit involves the use of radar or any other electronic device that measures the speed of moving objects. This paragraph does not apply to a local street, road, or school zone."

(b) (1) "For purposes of this section, a local street or road is defined by the latest functional usage and federal-aid system maps submitted to the federal Highway Administration, except that when these maps have not been submitted, or when the street or road is not shown on the maps, a (local street or road) means a street or road that primarily provides access to abutting residential property and meets the following three conditions:

A) Roadway width of not more than 40 feet.

B) Not more than one-half of a mile of uninterrupted length.

C) Not more than one traffic lane in each direction.

(2) For purposes of this section, 'school zone' means that area approaching or passing a school building or the grounds thereof that is contiguous to a highway and on which is posted a standard 'SCHOOL' warning sign, while children are going to or leaving the school either during school hours or during the noon recess period.

'School zone' also includes the area approaching or passing any school grounds that are not separated from the highway by a fence, gate, or other physical barrier while the grounds are in use by children if that highway is posted with a standard 'SCHOOL' warning sign.

(c)(1) When all the following criteria are met, paragraph (2) of this subdivision shall be applicable and subdivision (a) shall not be applicable:

(A) When radar is used, the arresting officer has successfully completed a radar operator course of not less than 24 hours on the use of police traffic radar, and the course was approved and certified by the Commission on Peace Officer Standards and Training.

(B) When laser or any other electronic device is used to measure the speed of moving objects, the arresting officer has successfully completed the training required in subparagraph (A) and an additional training course of not less than two hours approved and certified by the Commission on Peace Officer Standards and Training.

(C) (i) The prosecution proved that the arresting officer complied with subparagraphs (A) and (B) and that an engineering and traffic survey has been conducted in accordance with subparagraph (B) of paragraph (2). The prosecution proved that, prior to the officer issuing the notice to appear, the arresting officer established that the radar, laser, or other electronic device conformed to the requirements of subparagraph (D).

(ii) The prosecution proved the speed of the accused was unsafe for the conditions present at the time of alleged violation unless the citation was for a violation of Section 22349, 22356, or 22406.

(D) The radar, laser, or other electronic device used to measure the speed of the accused meets or exceeds the minimal operational standards of the National Traffic Highway Safety Administration, and has been calibrated within the three years prior to the date of the alleged violation by an independent certified laser or radar repair and testing or calibration facility.

(2) A 'speed trap' is either of the following:

(A) A particular section of a highway measured as to distance and with boundaries marked, designated, or otherwise determined in order that the speed of a vehicle may be calculated by securing the time it takes the vehicle to travel the known distance.

(B) (i) A particular section of a highway or state highway with a prima facie speed limit that is provided by this code or by local ordinance under subparagraph (A) of paragraph (2) of subdivision (a) of Section 22352, or established under Section 22354, 22357, 22358, or 22358.3, if that prima facie speed limit is not justified by an engineering and traffic survey conducted within one of the following time periods, prior to the date of the alleged violation, and enforcement of the speed limit involves the use of radar or any other electronic device that measures the speed of moving objects:

(I) Except as specified in sub-clause (II), seven years.

(II) If an engineering and traffic survey was conducted more than seven years prior to the date of the alleged violation, and a registered engineer evaluates the section of the highway and determines that no significant changes in roadway or traffic conditions have occurred, including, but not limited to, changes in adjoining property or land use, roadway width, or traffic volume, 10 years.

(ii) This subparagraph does not apply to a local street, road, or school zone."

California Vehicle Code §40803 (*Speed Trap Evidence*)

a) "No evidence as to the speed of a vehicle upon a highway shall be admitted in any court upon the trial of any person in any prosecution under this code upon a charge involving the speed of a vehicle when the evidence is based upon or obtained from or by the maintenance or use of a speed trap.
(b) In any prosecution under this code of a charge involving of a vehicle, where enforcement involves the use of radar or other electronic devices which measure the speed of moving objects, the prosecution shall establish, as part of its prima facie case, that the evidence or testimony presented is not based upon a speed trap as defined in paragraph (2) or subdivision (a) of section 40802.

When a traffic and engineering survey is required pursuant to paragraph (2) of subdivision (a) of section 40802, evidence that a traffic and engineering survey has been conducted within five years of the date of the alleged violation or evidence that the offense was committed on a local street or roadway as defined in paragraph (2) of subdivision (a) of section 40802 shall constitute a prima facie case that the evidence or testimony is not based upon a speed trap as defined in paragraph (2) of subdivision (a) of section 40802."

California Vehicle Code §40804 (*Testimony Based on Speed Trap*)

(a) "In any prosecution under this code upon a charge involving the speed of a vehicle, any officer or other person shall be incompetent as a witness if the testimony is based upon or obtained from or by the maintenance or use of a speed trap.

(b) Every officer arresting, or participating, or assisting in the arrest of, a person so charges while on duty for the exclusive or main purpose of enforcing the provisions of divisions 10 and 11 is incompetent as a witness if at the time of such arrest he was not wearing a distinctive uniform, or was using a motor vehicle not painted the distinctive color specified by the commissioner."

California Vehicle Code §40805 (*Admission of Speed Trap Evidence*)
"Every court shall be without jurisdiction to render a judgment of conviction against any person for a violation of this code involving the speed of a vehicle if the court admits any evidence or testimony secured in violation of, or which is inadmissible under this article."

With the exception of California's legislative micromanaging, requiring strict adherence to Engineering and Traffic Surveys, and the attendant speed trap prohibitions, it appears the requirements for approved use of radar are relatively uniform throughout America.

Operators must successfully complete an accepted certification course, followed by a periodic refresher course mandated by your state, and test the radar device used, both before and after each shift it is used. Proper policy and procedure must be followed by any LEO using such a device.

Radar devices must be properly calibrated by the manufacturer, prior to being placed in service, and returned to the manufacturer for servicing, should they stop functioning properly. Case law appears to have resolved the issue of whether radar technology has advanced to a point where the use of radar is deemed adequately reliable to measure the speed of offending motorists. In short, it has.

Chapter 8
Traffic Collision Investigation & Reconstruction

(*Sr. Officer Michael J. Van Gorder*)

NOTE: When he wrote this chapter, Mike Van Gorder was a traffic officer for Cathedral City PD, riding a police motorcycle. Mike has been a peace officer, continuously, since 1995 and is someone I served with when I was still a DA. Although years apart, we also graduated from the same high school. Van Gorder is someone I respect tremendously. Without Mike, this chapter simply would not exist. He wrote it, doing so while on vacation.

This chapter, as the name implies, deals with traffic collision investigation and reconstruction, the process of collecting, analyzing, and recording information, at the scene of a traffic collision. The collision may be one of many identifiable types, ranging from non-injury ones, to complaints of pain and minor injury, all the way to major injuries, and even fatalities.

Victims of a crash vary, ranging from a single driver, to several drivers, and/or occupants, even occasional pedestrians, or occupants of structures. *(I trust you have heard of the occasional vehicle that crashes into a store or a restaurant, due to a mechanical malfunction, or because the driver loses control.)* Involved vehicles may include a solo sedan versus a fixed object, a solo vehicle, multiple vehicles, or multiple fixed objects. This includes literally every type of collision imaginable.

Throughout the course of this chapter, we refer to any vehicle contact as a *collision* or a *crash* rather than an *accident*. (*I say we because Mike is my mentor. I am his humble student.)* Most people incorrectly refer to such incidents as accidents. We do not subscribe to such a description for a basic reason. An accident is something unavoidable.

Referring to a collision as an accident is somewhat akin to saying *VIN-number* or *PIN-number*. Using the latter expressions is wrong because they are redundant. Saying this is like saying Vehicle Identification Number-*Number* or Personal Identification Number-*Number*. If you wish to abbreviate them, simply call them VINs and PINs. Similarly, calling a collision an accident is wrong because it is incorrect, even though it involves no redundancy.

Although most people do not intend to be involved in a crash, rarely are they a true accident. For example, if one party goes through a red light, and collides with another vehicle, it happens because one party violated a section of the state's Vehicle Code, i.e., failing to stop at a limit line, before entering an intersection, thus causing the collision.

This is not the same, as a person driving on a mountain road, and having a tree drop immediately in front of his vehicle, due to a lighting strike. That would be an *unavoidable* accident. Collisions caused by inadvertence or inattention are not accidents.

In the first scenario, the motorist has control, but fails to properly exercise it, and does not stop, as required by law for a traffic light that has cycled, from green to yellow to red. In the second one, the driver has no control over the falling tree. Hence we have the difference between a traffic collision and a traffic accident. Think of this as an act of man vs. an act of God. The latter we truly have no control over.

Investigative Process

Collision investigations are handled differently depending on the agency, in whose jurisdiction they occur. For those departments, lacking a dedicated traffic collision investigation team, the beat officer is the one responsible for handling the call. On the other hand, for those departments with such a team, the process begins, when an assigned traffic investigator responds to a call, and arrives on scene.

This may occur, when the investigator is on duty, during day shift, or off duty, in the middle of the night. Upon receiving the call, the involved officer assesses the facts, and obtains needed pertinent information, prior to responding.

If the call concerns a major injury, or a fatality, the officer may need to first respond to the station, to obtain equipment, such as a *fatal box*, i.e., a computer-automated mapping device, and any other equipment needed to do a proper and thorough investigation.

Investigators from smaller departments use fatal boxes that include numerous tape measures, road crayons, roll-a-tapes, digital cameras, and hand tools, such as hammers, etching devices, and tee squares. Bigger departments will generally have computer-automated mapping devices, commonly known as *total stations*. *(We will refer to measuring and mapping later in this chapter.)*

If the crash occurs at nighttime, you will most likely have standup floodlights to help illuminate the area, or be able to use the lighting equipment, from assisting patrol vehicles, and fire engine equipment. If the scene is already secure, officers will be strategically located, on either end of the roadway, and will have diverted traffic, in an effort to close down, the impacted area. If not, you will need to take appropriate steps, to make sure the scene is secure.

A most important factor, in any traffic collision scene, is the safety of involved law enforcement personnel, citizens, and surrounding property. Many times, while in the process of investigating a collision, drivers will attempt to cross into the area of a crash, either inadvertently or intentionally. This behavior is not only dangerous for the personnel working the collision, but is also likely to destroy any evidence, such as tire friction marks (*skids*), blood, hair, and any other physical evidence, needed to conduct a proper investigation. A contaminated crime scene yields contaminated evidence.

It is important, as a collision investigator, to obtain all possible information, while on scene, or at the hospital. At the time of the collision, the roadway must be shut down, and safe, for you to collect every bit of obtainable evidence.

Depending on the area, you can keep the road closed, for as long as necessary. In other words, you are done, when you are done. However, once the road is again open, minute evidence will most certainly be lost. This is why you must know what evidence is material, what is not, and why you need to develop guidelines.

Many times there is evidence present, at the scene, that may not be a part of the collision; in other words, simple roadway debris. Just because something looks like trash, at first blush, does not mean it is. A piece of broken glass, an old tennis shoe, or a bumper rubber, in the roadway, may prove critically important to your case's end result.

A good investigator will rely on his judgment, experience, and resulting expertise. You know it is always better to obtain too much evidence, rather than too little. You also know, once the road re-opens, your chance of locating further evidence collection is virtually lost. Therefore, if you are not sure, gather the evidence, tag it, and sort it out later. Better to gather too much, than too little.

Equally important, is evidence collected from the victim, or suspect, at the hospital. Clothing from a victim should be collected and booked properly. Small bits of paint transfer, or a smear of mud on a victim's leg, or torso, can be overlooked, if you are not adequately conducting your investigation. Be cautious how you obtain evidence, including statements, or physical evidence, from any suspect.

If in doubt, take the time to confer with the on-call prosecutor. See if you need to first Mirandize a suspect, or if you need a search warrant to seize any evidence from a potential suspect. In other words, at this point, is it still a consensual encounter, a temporary detention or an arrest? Know when *Berkemer* applies, rather than *Miranda*.

Statements and dying declarations are of the utmost importance to an investigation. You must be sure you obtain them, lawfully, so you can introduce them in court. Whenever possible, be sure to digitally record any such statements. Planning to pass constitutional muster, on appeal, should always be part of your agenda.

Collision investigation should be a team effort. Any information gathered at a collision scene, may be done by one person, or by many. A good collision investigation team will work together, as one, to obtain all the facts, and then recreate what actually happened moments before, during and after, impact. The information can relate to a chain of events that will have an everlasting effect on those involved.

Training

Traffic collision investigators are often called to court to testify as to the causal facts, underlying the occurrence of a collision. A good investigator must be able to back up his testimony, with proof, and mathematical calculations.

You must have confidence in your ability to examine the facts, and relate them through written documentation, so you can interpret, and explain them, to members of a jury, at any time.

A competent traffic collision investigator must realize most jurors are not versed in the area of traffic collision investigation and reconstruction. Therefore, you must be able to perform your calculations for them, and handle questions, from both prosecution and defense. Always talk *to* the jury, not *down at* them.

As a well-rounded traffic collision investigator, you will take instruction in numerous classes, and will have to pass rigorous tests, along the way. The classes will not only include basic traffic collision investigation, but also intermediate and advanced investigation, skid analysis, vehicle versus pedestrian collisions, computer diagramming, and staged collisions, to name just a few.

Collision investigation is a fascinating area of physics, and requires dedication from those who have chosen to enter this sphere of police work. It can be extremely rewarding and can provide a family with closure to an unfortunate, and, on many occasions, a tragic time in their lives.

If you have chosen to go the distance, and obtain additional training, beyond the investigative process, traffic collision reconstruction is a step beyond. It adds an extra degree to your résumé, as a traffic investigator. Reconstruction is defined as *the effort to determine, from whatever information is available, how the collision happened.*

Reconstruction was formerly referred to, as determining *behavioral* or *mediate* causes of a collision. It is the process of actually going back in time, and rebuilding, moment-by-moment, and step-by-step, the events and circumstances that led to a collision.[1] The reconstruction of a traffic collision results in conclusions, usually in the form of statements. The final document includes *opinions*, *deductions*, and *inferences* on the part of the reconstructionist. It can be questioned, by prosecutor or defense counsel, in court.

A reconstructionist can be an on-duty police officer, trained in the field of reconstruction, or a private company retained by the family, or a law firm representing a party involved in a collision. The reconstructionist will commence work, subsequent to the collision, and will take the facts presented by the investigating officer, analyze them, and determine the validity of various factors, including a myriad of variables contributing to the collision.

The variables are different, but apply to virtually any collision. Some play a major role in the outcome of the investigation. The variables should be determined, and documented, by the original investigating officer. However, based on the experience the officer possesses, some pertinent facts may be omitted.

Therefore, it is up to the reconstructionist to locate and apply these variables, in order to obtain the most realistic results. Some of these variables include:

1. speed
2. positions of vehicles and pedestrians during impact
3. how injuries were received
4. which occupant was driving
5. how road, driver and vehicle conditions contributed to the collision
6. description of driver tactics and strategy

---

[1] Baker, J. Stannard: *Traffic Investigation Manual for Police* (Section 54) 1960, The Northwestern University Traffic Institute, Evanston IL 60204

7. How a particular driver or pedestrian might have avoided the collision

Skills must be developed to perform special tasks, involved in reconstruction. Classes taken in the training for reconstruction provide this technical training, and necessitate the knowledge of higher math. Reconstructionists are highly trained individuals who possess certain characteristics, including the ability to:

1. Compute energy losses and momentum exchanged in involved, colliding vehicles
2. Make momentum diagrams and bodies in collisions
3. Compare possible and actual driving tactics and strategy
4. Estimate driver or pedestrian perception delays
5. Design experiments in driver or pedestrian behavior
6. Design experiments to determine performance of a vehicle[2]

As noted, reconstruction skills require a working knowledge of higher mathematical skills, such as algebra and trigonometry. The investigating officer, or reconstructionist, must have a grasp of physics, an understanding of dynamics, as applied to vehicles, and must understand perception, and reaction time delays. All these events, working in concert with one another, provide the end user with the most realistic and pragmatic results possible.

Speed Analysis

Many times traffic collisions involve parties that are the sole individuals, on scene. The crash can be vehicle versus vehicle, vehicle versus pedestrian, or vehicle versus fixed object. The driver may have been driving too fast for conditions, and simply drove off the roadway. Or, while under the influence of alcohol, or drugs, the motorist may have crashed into another vehicle, or a fixed object.

In situations such as these, fatalities are frequent. Obtaining a statement may be virtually impossible; as when a driver at fault does not die. For example, the driver may be injured to the point where he cannot provide a statement. Even in circumstances where he can communicate, he may or may not provide a truthful, or an accurate statement. This is when the traffic collision investigator, or reconstructionist, becomes the voice of the deceased.

Skid analysis is one of the ways you can do this. Skid analysis is an area of investigation, 100 percent physics and mathematics. Skid marks can

---

[2] Baker, J. Stannard: *The Traffic Accident Investigation Manual* (Section 1) 1986, The Northwestern University Traffic Institute, Evanston IL 60204

also be referred to as *tire friction* marks, and are the result of a vehicle's forward momentum being faster, than the wheel's ability to turn.

As the vehicle moves forward, and the brakes are applied, the wheels are turning slower, than the forward momentum. Rubber from the *contact patch*, i.e., area of contact between the tire and roadway, remains on the road, in what is commonly referred to as, a skid mark.

Skids come in different types. They should be identified, by the investigating officer, to determine their role in a collision. They can range from locked rubber on solid pavement, to a shallow furrow on loose gravel, or a dirt roadway edge. There are acceleration and deceleration skid marks. Each is easily identifiable.

Tire friction marks can be identified as skid marks, yaw marks, acceleration scuffs, flat tire marks, centrifugal skids, and imprints. Skid marks can be straight, curved, or angled. And, they can be solid, or striated.

Each has a different meaning and reason for its presence. Striations in skids can prove the presence of a particular brand of tire, at a collision scene. *Note: This type of skid mark is essential, and can play a key role in the prosecution, of a driver of a vehicle involved, in a hit and run collision.* Sadly, in southern California this is an all too common event, as a traffic officer, or trial prosecutor can attest.

By looking at, and analyzing, a particular skid mark, a vehicle's point of impact can be determined, in a collision. As a vehicle travels forward, and the driver heavily applies the brakes, causing the tires to lock, the vehicle will continue forward, for a distance, depending on the roadway surface and makeup.

As it slides, and is suddenly impacted by another vehicle, from an opposite, or an angular, direction, the movement of the vehicle continues. But, a different direction of travel occurs.

The skidding and locked tires are forced in an offset direction. The rubber on the roadway forms a distinct angle, indicating the exact point of impact. This is an essential fact in a collision investigation.

Centrifugal skids can prove important, in establishing a vehicle was turning, at an intersection, or going around a curve, on a mountain road. Centrifugal skids are those tire friction marks left, having the appearance of a distinct curve.

By measuring the chord, i.e., the straight line connecting the ends of an arc, or two points on curve, the mid-ordinate, i.e., the center of the arc to the chord, and applying a specified formula, the speed can be determined accurately.

The same principle can be applied by measuring straight line skid marks. A quick way to do this, is by applying the *30df* equation. This equation is explained, by multiplying a constant of (*30*) times the distance of the skid mark (*d*), times the coefficient of friction (*f*), of a surface of a roadway. After obtaining the sum, the final step is to take that number, and find the square root. The number represents the minimal speed of the vehicle, at the time of impact.

For example, a vehicle collides, into a stopped vehicle, after the brakes are applied, leaving 150 feet of locked rubber skid. The surface of an asphalt roadway is .7, and the constant formula is 30. Therefore, (30)(150)(.7) equals 3150, and the square root of 3150 equals 56.124; an approximate minimum speed of 56 mph at impact.

The *Conservation of Linear Momentum* is another process, by which speed is determined. You do this, by computing entry and departure angles of vehicles at impact, the vehicle weights, and known post-impact speeds. It can be quite complicated, to the average patrol officer, but is very interesting, and is extremely accurate.

The *six point crush analysis* is also a process for determining speed. This type of speed determination is performed, by taking the damaged vehicle, and an identical undamaged one, and placing each inside a box drawn on the ground. Several measurements are taken, at the same points around both vehicles, and an equation, consisting of 33 variables, is applied. Speed is then determined through a process of algebraic problems, being broken down.

Through these, and other mathematical formulas, you can determine the speed of a vehicle, even if there is no one to say what happened, prior to the collision. Scene measurement and evidence placement is another major concern, in traffic collision investigation and reconstruction. As the investigator, when a collision occurs, you must determine the point of impact.

Sometimes it is difficult to locate the exact point of impact. Weather conditions, emergency personnel on scene, good Samaritans, and other factors cause significant evidence to be moved, lost, stepped on, or even destroyed. That is why initial containment, at a scene, is so critically important. Evidence can be strewn about the collision scene, and these factors need to be measured, for diagram and sketching purposes.

Things to be aware of, and to consider, at a collision scene that must be measured are listed as follows:

1. Post-collision positions of vehicles
2. Point, or area, of impact
3. Body placement of dead, or injured, persons, if thrown from a vehicle

4. Gouge marks left by bumpers, or other metal objects, at the moment of contact
5. Scratches or scrapes, left in the roadway, by metal vehicle parts
6. Tire marks, significant to the collision
7. Scars (*ruts or furrows*) on the roadside, or the shoulder area
8. Various types of debris, such as vehicle parts, and fluid, hats, or other personal items from pedestrians; blood, tissue, or any other items pertinent to the collision[3]

Methods of Measurement

There are four basic methods for measuring a collision scene. Each works well, but some are more accurate than others. In the event of a major injury, or fatality, accurate measurements are surely mandatory, as the case will most likely be adjudicated, in a civil and/or a criminal courtroom.

In any case, prosecuting and defense attorneys, judges, insurance adjustors, and a virtual plethora of other people will read your report, and will interpret it toward their own best interests. For that reason, it is important to use a measuring system that fits the seriousness of the collision. The four methods:

1. Cartesian coordinate method
2. Station line method
3. Triangulation method
4. Computer-aided mapping, or total station, method

The most common form of measurement is the *Cartesian coordinate* method. This method is commonly used, in non-injury collisions, or other minor collisions where pinpoint accuracy is not required.

The Cartesian coordinate method is quick and easy, only requiring a roll-a-tape. When a collision occurs, on a roadway the impact will occur either in the middle of an intersection, or a distance away from one.

The curb line, or roadway edge, is the first point from which to measure to the variable, i.e., vehicle, skid mark, etc. If no intersection is nearby, a fixed point of interest such as a *mile marker* can be used, as a secondary measuring point, from which to begin.

For example, a non-injury collision occurs, in the middle of an intersection, at Main Street and First Avenue, in the #1 southbound lane. Main Street runs east and west. First Avenue runs north and south. Using the Cartesian coordinate method, take your measurements, starting from the

---

[3] Baker, J. Stannard: *The Traffic Accident Investigation Manual* (Section §28) 1960, The Northwestern University Traffic Institute, Evanston IL 60204

closest curb line, or roadway edge, and measure toward the variable, to which it is measured.

Variables may include:

1. Vehicle point of rest
2. Skid marks
3. Gouges left in the roadway
4. Any other item, considered important to your investigation

An example of a point of impact measured by the Cartesian coordinate method would be 124'6" north of the north curb line prolongation, also noted as n/nclp, of Main Street, and 24'4" west of the west curb line prolongation (w/wclp) of First Avenue. The prolongation represents an extension of that area, beyond the curb line.

The next method of measurement is the *station line* method. This method incorporates a single commencement point. In other words, use something that will never change, and will never move, such as an Edison box or an underground electrical vault. After choosing the commencement point, the point is measured, via the Cartesian coordinate method.

From that point, a 100 foot tape measure is placed on the street, in a straight line, traveling from the commencement point, going toward the collision scene. Measurements are taken along the station line, and a second tape measure is used, to measure the distance, from the station line to the variable.

Depending on the area of the collision scene, a station line can run hundreds of feet, or longer. For that reason, the commencement point, and first one hundred feet of a station line, is represented as 00+1(to 99). The second hundred feet, along a station line, is represented as 01+1(to 99), and so on.

A second measurement is taken that records the distance, either north or south, east or west, of the station line, depending on the station line's direction of travel. An example of a point of impact, measured by the station line method, would be 00+83'10" east, 36'5" south.

The third method of measurement is the *triangulation* method. The triangulation method is used, when there is not a good reference point available, such as a clear roadway edge, or a curb line. When the area to be measured is more than 30 feet off the roadway, or is located within a difficult area, triangulation works best.

The idea of triangulation is really very simple. The distance of the variable to be located, is measured directly from each of the two reference points. Two landmarks, such as an Edison vault (reference point 1, or rp1), and a fire hydrant, (reference point 2 or rp2) will serve as the reference points.

Assume the variable to be measured is a car door, torn off at the point of impact. The distance from the Edison vault, and the fire hydrant, will locate the car door. A triangle is formed, by the car door, and the aforedescribed reference points. This is why this method is called triangulation.

The fourth method of measurement is called *computer aided diagramming and mapping*. Many cities today use a system called a *total station*, defined as "an optical instrument used in modern surveying." This is a combination of an electronic theodolite (transit), an electronic distance measuring device (EDM), and software running on an external computer.[4]

When using a total station, the collision investigator, or reconstructionist, determines distances, from the instrument, to measurement points, such as pieces of evidence, points of rest, areas of impact, and so on.

Through the use of trigonometry, angles and distances gathered by the transit, are used to calculate the coordinate points of evidence, and then are stored in the transit. The data is downloaded from the transit to a computer, and application software will create an exact scaled map of the collision scene.

Some modern total stations integrate the use of a single operator, and allow you to control the machine, from a distance, by remote control. This eliminates the need for a second officer to hold the reflector prism, over the point to be measured. You hold the reflector yourself, and control the machine, from the observed point.

On the positive side, total stations are extremely accurate, and provide a precise drawing, that can be used later in a courtroom setting. In addition, they can be used on crime scenes, as well as traffic collision scenes.

Many larger agencies have begun to use total stations for traffic investigations, as have some smaller departments. On the negative side, they can be very costly at the onset, but do pay for themselves, by the amount of time saved, in measuring the scene, and drawing factual diagrams. Many states provide grants, available to police departments that wish to purchase these accurate and time-saving devices.

Photography

Traffic collision investigation reports are official documents that will inevitably be used, in some civil or criminal courtroom, perhaps both, at a

---

[4] http://en.wikpedia.org/wiki/Total_station

later date. In order to provide the best possible report, it is crucial to have the best documentation, including recorded information in the form of audio, video, or still photographs.

Photography is defined by Webster's Dictionary as *"...the art or process of producing images by the action of radiant energy and especially light on the sensitive surface."*[5] It is the method of capturing visual images to film, or other electronic devices.

Photographs are vital. They provide a lasting representation of the scene, as it existed, at the time of the collision and post-collision. They assist the investigator's recollection of what he saw, on his arrival. They assist you, in explaining to others what you observed at the time, including the conditions present that may or may not have contributed to the collision.

They can help prove, or disprove, statements made by a party involved, and prevent civil litigation, after the scene has been contaminated by emergency response personnel, among others. Photos at a crash scene should be taken as soon as the scene is secured, and is safe for all involved.

Normally, the traffic investigator, or motor officer, is in charge of the scene, and will direct other officers to perform certain tasks. After the injured are tended to, gathering information, taking measurements, and obtaining photographs are among the most important jobs, at the scene of any traffic collision.

The officer in charge will normally be the one to take the photos, or may instruct another trusted officer to do so. Photography is important, as the scene will change, from moment to moment, and will not be the same, when you return at a later time.

The best time to obtain photographs is while the roadway is closed. This allows you to take all the photos you want, in the order of how you wish to do so. You can obtain close-up photos of skid marks, blood, hair, or other bodily fluids in the roadway, areas of impact, and any other close, intricate photos of items you deem necessary.

It is always wise to include a fixed landmark to show the placement of evidence, and directional points (*north/south/east/west*). Never be in a hurry, when photographing the area. Take your time, and do your best possible job. Remember, once you release the scene, and leave, you will not have the opportunity to photograph the scene the way it was depicted, when you arrived.

When considering what to photograph, the following is a decent rule of thumb:

---

[5] http://www.m-w.com/dictionary/photography

1. All vehicles involved, at their points of rest
2. Sustained damage to vehicles, and any other property involved
3. Speedometer(s), if possible (*to record speeds at point of impact*)
4. Lighting equipment controllers, such as headlights, turn indicators, four-way flashers, and so on
5. Seat belt placement, and/or web stretching (*indicating use or non-use*)
6. Significant evidence, such as skid marks, shoes, hats, gouge marks, and areas of impact
7. Immediate scene, from all directions of travel, and at a distance determined, by the investigator
8. Roadway markings, caution signs, overhead lighting (*if nighttime*), speed limit signs, regulatory signs, traffic signals, and so on
9. Body positions, in and out of vehicles
10. Body points of impact on the vehicle, or roadway, as represented by blood, hair, brain, or organ tissue
11. Close up photos of injuries sustained

It is important to take photographs, from all angles. Point of view can skew the perspective of a photo. Therefore, be sure you take numerous photos, from as many angles as possible. This is especially easy and inexpensive, with a digital camera. The height, stance, and location can change the viewer's perspective of the scene.[6]

From a vehicular standpoint, a minimum of eight photos, of each vehicle, should be taken. One photo should be taken, from each of the middle of the four sides, and one at each corner. Aerial photography is another tool available to most traffic investigators, should you decide you wish to do so, and if it's available.

This is always a good idea, and can be done with the assistance of the local fire department. Most fire agencies have ladder trucks, with the ability to elevate their ladders, for distances, up to 100 feet, or more. In the case of a very large scene, use a helicopter, or an airplane, to obtain these photos, if one is available.

Aerial photography can accurately depict the design of the roadway, lane markers, and approaches, to and from an intersection. It can show overhead traffic signals, skid marks, and areas of impact, all from a bird's eye view. This can be helpful to a city attorney who has to defend, against a roadway design lawsuit.

---

[6] Faulkner, David *Collision Investigation for the Patrol Officer* (Chapter 4) 1999, LawTech Publishing Company, San Clemente CA 92673

Digital photography is an asset to today's investigator, and reconstructionist. The number of photos taken is limited, only by the size of the camera's memory card, i.e., storage capacity. The pictures taken can be stored in the memory card, or transferred to a personal computer, and stored there.

The results can be shown in an instant, as opposed to the old style 35mm cameras, with film that must be developed, and stored, but without the possibility of loss or damage. Of course, it is always wise to back up a computer's hard drive, in the event of a computer crash. Remember Murphy's Law. If anything can go wrong, it will.

These suggestions should be used, as only a guideline of what and how to photograph a collision scene. Each individual agency has certain criteria established for its own needs and requirements. Photography is one of the more important aspects of collision investigation. It can show a jury what a driver saw, right before impact, and can help in determining liability.

For that reason, it is important to take copious pictures. It's always better to take too many, than not enough. That's the beauty of digital cameras. You are mainly limited, by the size of the memory card. Remember the rule of thumb throughout this book. If you are going to err, always err on the side of caution.

Make sure you do not delete any pictures you take during any investigation. Granted, this is extremely easy to do, with a digital camera, and is something routinely done, when taking pictures with your own personal digital camera. Consider obtaining a separate memory card for each investigation. Then, when the pictures are no longer needed, they can be deleted, and the card can be reused for future cases.

In a potential criminal investigation, do not give the defense any unnecessary ammunition. If you make it a standard practice to not delete any pictures you take, in any departmental investigation, then no one can wrongly accuse you of destroying evidence, and creating an issue, pursuant to *Brady v. Maryland* (1963) 373 U.S. 83.

That's the landmark U.S. Supreme Court case which mandates the prosecution must voluntarily turn over, *any and all*, exculpatory evidence to the defense. This is required, even absent, a defense request for same.

Exculpatory evidence is evidence that *tends to* exonerate the defendant. Even if a deleted picture is not the least bit exculpatory, it will not necessarily stop defense counsel from calling it exculpatory (*the instant they discover it's been deleted.*) And if they are doing their job, expect them to do just that. The operative phrase is *reasonable doubt*.

In other words, the defendant can, and probably will, use such a deletion, to create reasonable doubt. So once again, erring on the side of caution, let's assume you take a digital picture. It's either too dark, too blurry, or otherwise is worthless as evidence to either side, because it failed to clearly capture an image.

To save memory space, just as you would with your own personal digital camera, out of force of habit you delete it. Even though you have done nothing wrong, expect the defense to latch onto this simple, innocent act, and accuse you of destroying exculpatory evidence, especially in a criminal prosecution.

Without the picture you cannot defend yourself, against such a baseless claim. You may even face sanctions, including dismissal of your entire case. Depending on how creative defense counsel is, they might even find it plausible to allege you violated their client's civil rights.

If so, your next stop could be in federal court, as a defendant, in a civil rights case. It's not what you did, or did not, do. It's what an enterprising attorney's imagination can persuade someone to do. It's all about perception. Juries can be unpredictably naïve. A couple of murder cases with aberrant verdicts immediately come to mind; one in CA, another in FL.

So be sure to book all photos properly, per departmental policy, and do so in a timely manner. When assembling a final set of photographs for a PowerPoint presentation in court, a planned set of photos is more informative, than a random set. Take the time to plan this properly. A picture truly can be worth a thousand words.

A well done PowerPoint presentation, standing alone, can be powerful. Add appropriate photos to that mix? You can command the jury's attention. Plan and present a professional series of photos, and be prepared to explain each one. A well-presented visual presentation of the chain of events, pre-collision, and post-collision, will aid in the prosecutorial process, and will ultimately prove advantageous for your case.

Other Points to Consider

There are many other factors involved in a comprehensive traffic collision investigation, and reconstruction. Lighting is a major concern, in any investigation, whether it's too much, or not enough. Early morning crashes occur, when the sun is directly in a driver's eyes, and may have temporarily blinded them, when they entered an intersection, or a roadway.

When this happens it is best to note the specific time of day, and actual placement of the sun. Twilight crashes pose the same type of issue, as the sun is setting on the horizon. Once again, a driver is blinded, by a natural phenomenon.

When darkness covers the area, street lighting is a factor you must consider. Were streetlights present? If so, how many were there? Were they working properly? What color clothing was a pedestrian wearing? Does it appear the pedestrian could have been seen easily, by the driver, prior to impact?

Vehicle lighting is an issue that must be addressed, in any traffic collision investigation. The question of driver and vehicle visibility is always one that should be present, in any investigator's mind.

Collisions can occur, because one driver may have failed to turn on his vehicle's headlights. Or perhaps the headlights did not illuminate because they were burned out, or otherwise defective. Being able to ascertain lighting status, at the time of a crash, is a science all its own. Be sure you factor this into your investigation.

Factors, identified as *cold shock* and *hot shock,* focus on identifying whether the bulb was illuminated or not illuminated, immediately before impact. This is done by analyzing the coiled filament of a light bulb.

The filament is a very brittle piece of metal. Upon sudden impact, it may or may not break. In a *cold shock* condition, the filament can quite possibly look unaffected, or may be broken, anywhere along the coil itself. This indicates the bulb was *off* at the moment of impact.

Assume the coiled filament is stretched out, and still attached to the main arch of the bulb, the indication is the bulb was *on* during impact. This condition is called *hot shock,* and can prove the presence of an illuminated bulb.

Cold shock and hot shock are significant factors in a vehicle inspection, subsequent to any crash, you investigate. It is the condition that can confirm illuminated, or non-illuminated, brake lights, headlights, turn signals, etc. It is a critical piece of evidence, especially at night, if one of the involved drivers states he never saw the other motorist. Cold shock means off. Hot shock means on.

Vehicle/Pedestrian Crashes

In a vehicle/pedestrian crash, shoes, and hat placement are most important. Be sure to document, and photograph them, carefully. Separate or together, they are valuable pieces of evidence. Here is why they are significant. These items can provide essential information, relating to the point of impact. Many times, in such encounters, the investigating officer will find the victim-pedestrian missing one or both shoes.

This is because the pedestrian is literally knocked out of their shoes, at the moment of impact, due to the sheer force of the vehicle which strikes them. If you look carefully enough, you can locate a small rubber scuff mark, indicating the point of impact. If the pedestrian was wearing a hat, the same is true. At impact, the pedestrian is struck with such force, they are virtually knocked out, from underneath their hat. Gravity pulls on the hat. It falls to the ground. Physics.

Signal phasing and operation is another important factor, if the collision occurs at a regulated intersection. It is advisable to check the green, yellow, and red light phasing, and timing, to insure proper operation of the signal itself. Check the *walk/don't walk* intervals, if they are present. Timed intervals of the directional lights are most important. All of this will most certainly be an issue, in either a civil or a criminal trial.

Collision investigation, and reconstruction, is an amazing science, and is the voice of the unheard. It is the job of the traffic collision investigator, and reconstructionist, to do a thorough job. Consider all the questions an ordinary police officer may overlook. A small scuff mark, a broken lens, or a tiny bit of rubber, may prove to be the missing piece of a jigsaw puzzle that will solve a hit and run fatality, bringing an unsuspecting, and otherwise free driver, to justice.

Just as important, it may also help bring a conclusion to a family tragedy.

Chapter 9
Proper Preparation

The purpose of this chapter is to show you how to properly prepare your case, from beginning to end. You must comprehensively prepare for the courtroom, by organizing each of your cases, from your initial observation of a suspected traffic violation, up through and including the very last thing you do, before you leave the courtroom.

Proper preparation means paying attention to details. To the unaccustomed, this may seem like you are being asked to take micromanaging to a new level. This is not what I'm suggesting. In fact, this does not require any more detail coordination, than your day-to-day duties.

You are a trained observer. You even pride yourself on this, correct? I do not know a single LEO who does not view themselves as one. Therefore, the first thing you need to do, even before you activate your emergency lights, is to articulate the section of your state's traffic laws, the motorist you are observing, just violated. If the motorist just violated the law, your observation provides reasonable suspicion to make a traffic stop; all the legal justification you need to intrude into that motorist's life.

This is important for a number of reasons. First, do not go to automatic pilot, and assume every traffic stop will deal exclusively with a traffic-related issue. You may decide to only issue the driver a warning, to be more careful, with their driving in the future. Or, it may result in a misdemeanor or felony arrest, and prosecution of one or more of the vehicle's occupants.

That felony could be a serious one, such as a Three Strikes case, where defense counsel will pull every stop available, in their representation of the defendant. Your workaday world is full of surprises. You are used to its unpredictability. The driver of the vehicle, you just stopped, may not have a valid license. Maybe it's suspended.

Perhaps the driver, or one of their passengers, has an outstanding arrest warrant. Maybe they have just done an armed robbery. If not, one of the occupants could nonetheless be in possession of contraband. This could include illicit narcotics, illegal weapons, or stolen property.

Irrespective of the reason for the stop, someone in the vehicle may decide to not cooperate, and end up being arrested for interfering with you, or battering you, for simply trying to do your job. Maybe someone has a weapon they plan to use, on you. In fact, the nature of this contact could be downright dynamic. The consequences could rise far beyond a routine traffic stop. And, you'll need to be certain you've elevated your documentation, to take that into account.

Should this be the case, it opens the door to a number of other issues, not part of the usual vehicle stop. Misdemeanors or felonies can result in jail, or prison. Convictions for either may have collateral consequences. It may include registration, as a drug offender, or sex offender. A life sentence is even possible, if your subject has prior convictions, qualifying them as a Three Striker, should your state's lawmakers have the vision to have implemented such a law, as did California voters once did.

With such added consequences, expect to deal with a defense attorney, at some point following the traffic stop. If that person is doing their job, expect the initial contact to occur, long before the first court appearance. If the contact morphs into a Three Strikes case, sentencing consequences will be at least as onerous as a murder conviction.

In fact, be surprised if you do not receive at least a phone call from the suspect's attorney, or the attorney's investigator asking to speak with you. While we are on that subject, what should you do, if you receive such an inquiry? I will not tell you to *not* speak with any defense representatives. If you chose not to do that, however, I will not criticize that decision. No law requires you to speak or not speak, with them.

If you decide to speak with the defense, be cautious. Defense counsel's job is not to make your job easier. In fact, it is just the opposite. Their job is to keep you from doing yours. That is their ethical duty. It's called *zealous representation*. Their sole job is to free their client from the charges they face. This is true, whether or not they believe their client is guilty. Irrelevant. This may, or may not, lead to a bonafide search for the truth by them.

As we have discussed previously, to avoid possible professional discipline, their job is to make you look like a fool or a liar, if necessary, in order to provide adequate representation for the accused. The only thing a defense attorney *cannot* do is intentionally mislead the court, or ask witnesses to lie under oath to material issues. No perpetration of a fraud on the court or subornation of perjury. Everything else is fair game.

This same zeal is supposed be there, whether you deal directly with the lawyer, or their representative. So should you speak to a criminal defense attorney or their chosen representative, including their investigator? Are we talking about a civil matter? That is different. They can take your deposition and you are not at liberty to disobey such a subpoena. Doing so could result in a contempt citation, a warrant being issued for your arrest, or both.

In terms of whether you should talk to a criminal defendant's counsel, at the risk of giving you a typical lawyer-sounding answer, the answer to that question depends on certain facts. I do not think you should ever do so *without* the prosecutor's participation. In fact, before you decide to speak to the other side, take the time to speak with the prosecutor. Ask whether you should. Let's face it. Some defense attorneys are more trustworthy than others. Most are. But, a select few are simply not trustworthy. I know. I've dealt with both types.

Your own prosecutor will probably tell you the same thing I am telling you. It was not beneath my dignity as a DA to ask police officers so contacted, if they were satisfied with the incident report they had written. Whenever I was assured they were, I would follow that up, by asking what they expected to gain, by talking to the defense, before trial. I reminded them they could do all their talking from the witness stand, if they so chose.

Team work is important. This is what I expect your prosecutor will say. I expect them to tell you it's solely your decision, as to whether you speak to anyone outside of the courtroom. However, I also expect them to suggest you simply rely on your report, until you can elaborate further from the witness stand under oath. Should you choose to speak, there is always a risk you could be falsely accused of making a prior inconsistent statement. A DA colleague was so accused, following a fatal OIS. He is now a convicted felon. Do the math.

Although it is your decision, speaking to the defense is not without risk because someone may try to twist what you say. Should you choose to speak, tell them you will do so, only if you can record any such conversation. If you record it, be sure you first inform everyone, and obtain permission to do so, in order to avoid being accused of violating privacy rights, or worse.

Should you decide to not speak with the defense, here is what I would tell them if I were you. Simply tell them what you have to say is already documented in your report, and will be repeated by you on the witness stand. If you choose to *not* communicate with the defense, expect them to make a big deal out of it when you are on the witness stand, in order to paint the picture that you are being less than candid. But, that is still better, than an alleged prior inconsistent statement.

However, if the reason you made that decision is because they refused to allow you to use your tape recorder, then you can point that out in your courtroom testimony. Make sure the prosecutor is aware of this. In fact, be sure to tell them about it, as soon as possible. That way, the prosecution can elicit testimony from you concerning that fact, so the judge or jury is not misled, as to why you were not interviewed. It was due to their intransigence, not yours.

The escalation of the hypothetical traffic stop, from a simple citation to a misdemeanor or a felony arrest, will broaden your playing field accordingly, and will also add potential consequences that would not otherwise exist. This can include the addition of an array of pre-trial motions, such as motions to suppress evidence, or motions to exclude confessions. It may include a jury trial. And if the defendant is convicted, it may include one or more appeals.

Additionally, depending on the circumstances, the defendant may even choose to sue you. But, you say, how can I be sued if I've done nothing wrong? That's easy. Defendants sue police officers, whether the officer did anything wrong, or not. Getting sued can add anxiety and stress, you have not previously had to carry, on your own shoulders. This can go on for a number of years, before it finally concludes.

The fact you have done nothing to warrant being named a defendant, in a state or federal civil rights lawsuit, does not mean it will not happen. Be sure to carefully document everything you believe is relevant. That is important for a number of reasons.

First, be prepared for any criminal prosecution that follows your traffic stop. Secondly, if you are sued, to be prepared for that eventuality. The same person who wrongfully sues you, may even file a personnel complaint against you. Use your report to later refresh your recollection. While you cannot include every single bit of minutiae that occurs, during your contact with the subject of any investigation, you must include as many significant, relevant details as possible.

What if you do not issue a citation? If not, is this an appropriate situation to complete a Field Identification card? I cannot answer that for you. Follow your department's policies and procedures, and your own protocol. If in doubt, out of earshot of the folks in the stopped vehicle, consult your supervisor. What if your department does not have a policy on this issue, or you cannot contact a supervisor? If in doubt, fill it out. After all, you are simply doing what you are getting paid to do. You are gathering information. The motorist validated the reason for the T-stop. It's called reasonable suspicion. Federal courts approve.

In the event you issue the motorist a citation, as we've already discussed, you will make notes on its back side, of any relevant information. Remember, those notes are discoverable in court, particularly if you use them to refresh your recollection. Therefore, be sure they do not include something, later embarrassing for you. Do not be conclusionary, by doing something halfway, such as describing the motorist as a jerk, or worse. Be descriptive. Be objective. Be professional.

Now, let's take things to the next step in the equation. Aside from making written notes you can later read, do you need to do anything else? Do you need to interview any witnesses, including any victims? Are you going to interrogate any suspects? If so, unless it's a temporary roadside *Berkemer* detention, do not forget to first Mirandize subjects, if you suspect them of criminal activity, they are not free to leave, and are about to be asked questions that may lead to incriminating answers.

If you Mirandize, does your department have a written admonition form the suspect must sign, before you commence questioning? If so, use it, following your own department's approved procedures. Make sure you always read it verbatim, even if you have committed it to memory. Habit or custom.

Are you going to search the vehicle, or do more than a cursory Terry-type pat down of any suspect? Do you plan to do this, by obtaining the subject's consent? If so, does your department have a written *consent to search* form? If so, once again, be sure to obtain all necessary signatures first. And, make sure you sign the form, to indicate you witnessed the signature. Have you remembered to list the time it was signed?

Are there any other aspects of the investigation you plan to conduct, such as taking photographs, making measurements, or any other normal investigative functions? Do you need to inform your supervisor? Should you contact the forensic people at your department, or ask your supervisor to do it? Or, if your department is not big enough to employ such vitally necessary staff, does it have a mutual aid-type reciprocal agreement, with a bigger local agency, so you can use their specialists? If so, do you need them?

Are there other personnel you need to contact, in order to competently complete your work at the scene? Do you need to contact a K-9 officer, with a trained drug-sniffing dog? Should you request the assistance of narcotics investigators? Is a Physician's Desk Reference needed, if you located any pills? Even if pills are in a standard pharmacy-issued container, be sure to confirm they are prescribed, by a licensed medical doctor. The fact a suspect tells you they are legitimate, does not mean they are.

What about explosives experts? Hazardous device personnel do more than disassemble bombs. I've actually used an ordinance expert, in a methamphetamine lab jury trial, because one of the seized items of contraband turned out to be a rocket launcher. Since I am not foolish enough to claim to have all the statutes of every state digested, ascertain if your state's hazardous device laws include more than just things go bang.

Every state's laws are going to differ slightly, from those of neighboring states, even if the general concepts are similar. Take the time to know your own state's relevant laws. Use the local law library, or go online, to references such as FindLaw.com. Never be shy about talking to your local prosecutor. They are on your team.

It might be a nice idea to prepare a checklist, before you even go 10-8, for the first time. Make sure it contains a list of all the possible things you need to do. Remember, you can never have too much money in the bank. Such a list can never be too comprehensive. I would type it on something compact, such as a 3x5 card. Laminate it, so it is durable. Doing this will permit you to keep it in a shirt pocket, or in your posse box, without concern it will degrade, and become unreadable. I'm a big fan of lamination.

Once you are done at the scene, what are the other things you need to do? Do you need to forward any of your work to your supervisor, for approval? Do you need to send anything to the court? Or, does it need to go to the local prosecuting attorney's office, for filing review? Is any forensic analysis needed? Is there a special place you keep your work-related paperwork, at the station, such as your reports, and any subpoenas? Do not let this get away from you, as you will be shocked to find out just how fast paperwork can pile up. Confirmation of doing this complies with departmental policy? Be sure you do not miss any deadlines.

Let's talk about *hero sheets*, i.e., your résumé. From the time you begin your academy, you should begin compiling a professional résumé. It should contain all your relevant training, and experience, including academy training, FTO training, your work experience, and any follow-up training you receive, as you receive it, including intra-agency and extra-agency classes.

You need to update your sheet every time you learn or do something new, significant enough to so record. This includes professional classes, and on the job training. If you have not already done so, start your résumé today. Keep it updated, faithfully.

As soon as you know you are going to attend a class, participate in any assignment you have not experienced previously, such as search warrant service, or attend any variety of court appearances, take the time to add it to your sheet. Never rely on your memory for such issues. If you have a personal computer, this should be an easy task.

My friend who was in charge of area CHP drug interdiction while I was in charge of major narcotic prosecution updated his résumé every time he did something new. And because he was also a K-9 officer, his pooch also had a résumé that got updated regularly. As you might imagine, both had rather extensive hero sheets.

If the local prosecuting attorney's office plays a role in your case, what relationship should you have with them? You are both on the same team, and must work like one, if public safety is to be protected. If you have not already done so, make arrangements to meet with the assigned prosecutor, at your earliest opportunity.

On that subject, if you refer any cases to the prosecutor, for filing reviews, are they routine ones? Or, do any of them require special handling? If a case appears to have any extraordinary features, do not just send it to the prosecutor, and hope for the best. Contact the filing deputy, and make arrangements to hand carry it to them. You need to sit down, and explain any unique aspects, so there is no misunderstanding. Never assume.

Murphy's Law declares "...if anything can go wrong, it will..." With the exception of understanding Murphy's Law, make no other assumptions. Never assume the prosecutor has seen previous cases like this one. And do not assume the prosecutor necessarily knows the law that applies either. Big mistake.

Before seeing the prosecutor, research whatever case or statutory law pertains to your case's unique facts. Expect to educate prosecutors. Never expect them to know the law, just because they are lawyers. We don't! There are way too many laws, for even the most diligent to know all of them. And, you will probably need to justify why a filing decision is appropriate.

At the risk of appearing to criticize my prosecutorial brethren, they are not fungible. Some understand their job means helping you get your product to the market place, i.e., the courtroom. Others do not have this philosophy and never will. Irrespective of where their heads are, they will handle far more cases daily than there are available prosecutors. Therefore, even subconsciously, some may look for reasons to reject filing requests. If they can reject it that is easier than finding a reason to later dismiss it if the case develops proof problems

This is particularly true if the matter is a *paper case*. By paper case, I mean you prove it, by introducing lots of documents. Some folks call them *white collar crimes*. Do not assume you will not handle any, just because your turf is traffic. For example, if the T-stop you just made, was on a stolen vehicle, you will need to establish ownership, with both documents, and testimony of the registered owner. Their testimony, alone, will not be enough to prove ownership.

These are paper cases. It has been my experience many untrained cops and prosecutors are apprehensive about handling paper cases, simply due to the huge quantity of paperwork involved. I admit it. They concerned me, until I learned how. There is no reason to harbor such fear. While we are on this subject, let me just point out how you prove these types of cases, document by document, essentially the same way you prove a traffic collision…dent by dent.

Unless the documents are self-authenticating, as in *official records*, you must first elicit testimony, from the custodian of records, to establish what each document is. Next, offer each, as an exhibit, once the clerk has marked it for identification. If you have such a case, you will actually have a prosecutor handling all this. This is a far simpler process, than you might otherwise believe. Just be methodical. View proving such a case, akin to the old story about eating a grizzly bear. You do it one little bite at a time.

Irrespective of the type of case, when you meet with any filing deputy, plan to walk them through any special handling-type case, witness by witness, and document by document. Follow the same approach with a paper case. Leave nothing to guesswork, or to chance.

If a prosecutor has been assigned to any of your cases, once you get a subpoena, contact them. Request a face-to-face, pre-trial, preparation meeting. Are you the case agent, i.e., the primary report writer? View the case as one you personally need to shepherd. Make sure all witnesses are accounted for and all evidence is ready for court. You're the sheep dog, shepherding everyone else.

Contact all witnesses and remind them of the time, place, and date, they are to testify. Examine each and every piece of evidence. Do this, with the prosecutor at your side, so you both will know what each evidentiary item really is. Make sure you are not overstepping your bounds. All this will make a huge difference, when preparing for court.

Is another officer the case agent? If so, contact them and see if there is anything he needs you to do, other than to simply show up for court. Did you log any physical or documentary evidence? If so, ask if you need to bring any of that with you to court.

When you do this, have your report ready, so you can refer to each item number, from the evidence list, so you don't risk leaving something to chance. Are there other witnesses, such as additional officers? Civilians? Do they also need to attend this meeting? Be sure every officer who wrote a report, no matter how insignificant it appears to be, brings it with them, to any preparatory meetings, as well as to court.

If the case remains a simple traffic infraction case that results in you merely writing a citation, and doing nothing more, bring your copy of the citation to court, so you can use it. Use the notes you wrote, on its back side, to refresh your recollection. The passage of time dulls our memories. Without memory aids, you may not even recall enough of the underlying facts to otherwise identify the motorist. That's reality. I've dismissed traffic citations at the request of officers who didn't recall important details. Avoid that! Take careful notes.

Add the overall number of cases you deal with? The need for a meaningful memory aid becomes all the more evident. I have seen this happen first-hand. And as we both know, traffic covers a very wide swath of violations, ranging literally from jaywalking to murder.

What if a simple traffic case escalates to either misdemeanor or felony status? What's an example of this? A traffic stop for speeding ends up with you taking the driver, or a passenger, to jail, for possession of a controlled substance. Or, maybe you arrest the driver for felony driving under the influence.

If a T-stop becomes a felony, you may be in a jurisdiction where you have to testify at a preliminary hearing, or before a grand jury. If you are in such a state, are you allowed to testify to what would otherwise constitute inadmissible hearsay of fellow officers, such as Proposition 115-approved hearsay, in California? Treat your time, as a witness, no differently, than you would, were you in front of a jury. This is serious stuff, but the basics are quite simple, providing you do not unnecessarily overcomplicate things.

Take your report with you, to the witness stand. If you did not write paper, get a copy of another officer's report. You can use it to refresh your recollection. Do not answer any question, until the *entire* question has been asked. Never answer any question, *unless and until*, you are sure you understand it. If you do not comprehend a question, immediately request clarification. Say: *"I don't understand,"* or words to that effect. What if the question is repeated, or even rephrased, and you still do not understand? That's easy. Just keep requesting clarification, until you do. No exceptions.

Do not guess. Making an estimate is acceptable. Guessing is not. Ever! What's the difference? You can *estimate* the length of your own dining room table. You cannot estimate the length of mine, unless you have been in my home. Why? For one thing, you may not even know if I have a house, much less a dining room, or a dining room table. I could be living under a bush somewhere.

Never assume. Without such information you are in no position to make any estimates. This reduces you to merely guessing. Never argue with defense counsel. It is not dignified. If you do, the judge will probably chew you a new one. Even I might do so. Courtroom order is important to the dispensation of justice, for the defendant and the prosecution.

Speak slowly, clearly, and loud enough to be understood. Do not shout. But, do not mumble. Be responsive to the question. Speak, only when you are answering questions. And, never volunteer information. Make eyeball contact with the jury. Develop rapport with them. If you do not, they may think you are trying to hide something.

What if you do not know something? Admit it. If you are questioned about making a mistake, and you did in fact err, say so. Juries love candor. So do judges. Do not be a robot. The integrity of your career depends on your ongoing honesty. Do not come across as arrogant. That's a real jury turnoff.

Early in my prosecutorial career I lost a jury trial because a big-headed case agent alienated the jury. As I gained prosecutorial traction, that did not happen anymore. The reason? I learned to *not* try cases, for haughty case agents. Other people appreciate genuine humility. Be yourself. You are selling your product to the buyers, at the marketplace. That's the courtroom. The shoppers are the jury. Develop your people skills. You have them. They just need polishing.

If you are the case agent, does your case have multiple witnesses? If so, the prosecutor will count on your capable assistance, if they operate like me. This means you will be in the courtroom, the morning of the scheduled trial, even before the judge calls the case. Although you will not play a specific role, in this part of the trial, you may get to watch the prosecutor argue what are called *In Limine motions*. In Limine motions may be argued by either counsel, or by both. These ask the court to do, or not do, something, in connection with the pending trial. This may include asking the court to rule on issues such as:

1. the admissibility of evidence
2. the order of the appearance of witnesses
3. the exclusion of witnesses
4. admonishing witnesses to not discuss their testimony with others
5. anything else attorneys deem a matter for the court's pre-trial attention

Motions to exclude and admonish witnesses involve two separate issues. The first part, when granted by the court, excludes all witnesses from the courtroom, other than the one on the witness stand. Such a motion requires you, as the case agent, to immediately tell all other prosecution witnesses they are excluded, and are not to discuss any aspect of their testimony with anyone else, other than the court or the lawyers. A prep meeting tutorial by the prosecutor is a must!

Violation of this order can mean several things will happen. First and foremost? A very angry judge. They are ticked off because someone violated one of their own orders. This may result in a mistrial, a contempt citation, exclusion of evidence your side would have otherwise presented, or all of the above. Expect your boss will be notified, too.

If a mistrial motion, by the defense, is granted it means you must start at the beginning, and do the trial all over again. But if the mistake is made by the prosecution? It could mean a dismissal, if jeopardy has attached. Depending on your jurisdiction, this may happen once the jury is empanelled, or when the first witness is sworn. A contempt citation is not to be taken lightly. It may mean a fine, or a jail sentence for the offender. Exclusion of evidence may mean an acquittal of the defendant. Any of these happenings may mean professional discipline for the offender. Don't let this be you! So, if you are going to screw anything up, make sure it is not one of these orders.

The reason I always relied on my case agent to help me pick juries? If anyone has a finger on the community's pulse, generally better than anyone else does, it's a street cop. First, prospective jurors do not necessarily tell the truth. Therefore, without your input, a prosecutor might inadvertently keep someone on a jury, you know should be excused, from jury service. It could be someone you have arrested, or is related to someone else you, or a fellow officer, has arrested.

It could even be a member of a family your department has dealt with negatively, over and over again. Sadly, every community has such residents. Remember, most prosecutors do not see the world through the windshields of police cars. Therefore, this sort of input is both invaluable and incalculable.

Aside from jury selection, I also depended on my case agents to maintain the evidence list, at counsel table. This includes listing each item, by name and number, on the court's evidence list, describing the item, and noting whether it has merely been *marked for identification*, or had actually been *received into evidence*, by the court. This is not some paltry procedural point. Here's why it is so important. Until an item has been ordered into evidence, by the court, it is not evidence. It is merely pending that status. Therefore, a case agent attending to this can prevent the prosecutor from forgetting to make this request. It happens.

This is critically important at closing argument. A prosecutor is not allowed to refer to an item during closing argument, not received into evidence, by the court. Doing so could mean a mistrial. A request by the prosecutor, that an item be received as evidence, means nothing, unless the court grants the order.

Such an error can result in a mistrial, and a fanny-chewing by the judge. The prosecutor could even be disciplined by the state bar. I've learned something from firsthand experience. Most appellate judges do not have very good senses of humor. Reading about yourself, in an appellate decision, is never fun, if the appellate court is castigating you. Let's leave it at that.

A case agent is once again very useful, whenever evidence is presented. No matter how prepared a prosecutor is, there will always be things, unintentionally omitted. This includes questions that need to be asked. I always kept a lined legal pad, at counsel table, between any case agent and me. That was for the case agent to write on if they thought I forgot to ask any relevant questions, of any witness.

Both of us could use this pad to jot down any notes we deemed necessary. It's also quieter than talking to each other during trial. It avoids interrupting the proceedings, and prevents defense counsel from overhearing trial tactics, or forcing the prosecutor to lose track of what he is doing. Two heads are better than one. It's all about teamwork.

During closing argument, the case agent does more than simply complete the evidence list. I routinely relied on my case agent to physically hand me the actual exhibit I needed next, as I did my show and tell presentation, for the jury. This includes documents, physical evidence and any items needed to present to the jury.

Once the case is presented to the jury, and they retire to deliberate, any evidence not received, but tagged, as an exhibit, by the courtroom clerk, is gathered up by you, and returned to your department's evidence locker, where it is maintained until your agency can legally dispose of it.

Assuming the jury returns a guilty verdict, you may still play a role at sentencing, first by being interviewed by the probation officer who writes the pre-sentence report. The prosecutor may also ask you to participate at sentencing, including being sworn as a witness, and providing testimony.

In summary, if the case is going to withstand constitutional scrutiny on appeal, you must be adequately prepared from the very moment you, and the case, meet one another, continuing forward, until it concludes in the trial court.

Chapter 10
Sell That Citation

What do I mean when I say *sell the citation*? I mean you must convince a motorist the citation you issued is supported by the facts and the law. Never issue a citation, if you do not know the law, underlying it, well enough to do so. If this is not the case, you will lack the confidence you need, in what you just did, to sell the citation.

A motorist must believe they will waste their time going to court to contest it. Use your people skills. Use honey, not vinegar. Educate. Don't intimidate. But, you cannot educate, if you are operating from a position of ignorance. The average driver knows why you stopped them. So do you. He may be ready to pay the fine.

Do not give motorists an excuse to demand a trial they probably do not even want. People sense fear. If you do not project confidence, in what you just did, or have a lousy attitude, you make their choice to opt for trial, far easier than it needs to be. Clearly articulate what you did, and why. Do it calmly, objectively, and professionally.

Trial should be their last choice, not their first. If you do your job properly, it probably will be. Even if a motorist did something really stupid, do not pour accelerant, onto the flames, by giving them a lecture they doesn't need. By the time you contact them, they are not likely to be in a good mood.

An assortment of alternatives to trial exists, if any motorist you issue a citation to, decides they do not wish to go to trial. The ultimate call belongs to the motorist. Avoid talking down to them. If they ask for possible alternatives, take the time to adequately explain them. If they ask you to explain the citation, take the time to do this. You can play a meaningful role, in any decision making. Treat motorists with at least as much dignity and respect, as you believe you are entitled to personally experience.

Part of your job is developing your people skills, to the point where you can sell your product at the marketplace, whether it's in the courtroom or during a roadside encounter with a motorist. Begin the sales process early. If you do, you may avoid traffic court, more often than not, by persuading motorists that will not be a productive expenditure of their time or energy. More road time, equals more citations, equals more public safety.

Avoid giving motorists a reason to want to embarrass you in a courtroom. A big benefit that comes from trying to sell a citation? Everybody wins. Part of this is convincing any motorist you actually did them a favor, by issuing the citation.

What is the purpose of traffic law enforcement? Hopefully, your answer is roadway safety. It is. Traffic enforcement is meant to prevent unnecessary bad driving. Do you honestly believe battling folks in traffic court is going to provide the educational tools they need? If that's not true, then what really is gained from traffic court, other than overtime pay you might not otherwise earn?

Consider your life, before you became a police officer. Did any of your pre-law enforcement experiences include going to traffic court, as a defendant? If so, I suspect you did not enjoy the experience, any more than anyone else does. Did you go to court because you wanted to teach some badge-heavy cop a lesson? If your answer is *yes*, remember to not repeat this mistake yourself. Does it matter, if the trip to court is a motorist's doing, in the first place, even if they honestly believe they did not violate the law? The object of the exercise is to do what best protects highway safety. That is not going to happen, in the courtroom. The preferred situs? Where the rubber meets the road. Does your typical roadside encounter include a free lecture? If so, why? Veteran CHP officers I served with have an expression: *bite me or cite me*. In other words, give the motorist a lecture, or write a citation. Don't do both. Is any lecture likely to improve driving skills? If not, what should you do instead?

Is your answer: *I should sell any citation I issue to offending motorists?* If it is, we are on the same page. Explain the basis of the citation. Do they have any questions? Ask: *do you have any questions, sir/ma'am?* Allow them to drive away from the stop, without feeling like they lost their dignity.

Before we get into any specifics, let's stop a moment. You need to take stock of yourself, immediately prior to your initial contact, with any hypothetical motorist. I realize we all have lives, outside of what we do for a paycheck. This may involve distractions we deal with. This may even cause us to leave our residences, in less than cheerful moods, as we head to work. This is particularly true, if we are in less than peaceful personal relationships. Been there. Not good.

If that's the case, and you arrive at the cop shop, in a lousy mood, find a way to lose it, before you meet your public you protect and serve. Irrespective of whether they are acting responsibly or not, the motoring public is not paying you, to share your bad attitude, with them. Do not give them a view of law enforcement they do not need to see. You are better than that.

Do not give a motorist a reason to file a citizen's complaint. If he has a bad attitude you did not cause, he may do that without any prompting from you. Do not try to compete. Such immaturity should never be a part of your own professional landscape. Treat each traffic stop, as if you might need that same motorist to save your very life, later the same day. The real question is, would he? Only you know the answer.

So whether you have to practice yoga, meditation, or some other way of snapping yourself out of bad moods, you must be in a good frame of mind, before you slide behind the steering wheel or handlebars, of your official police ride. Start the day with a smile. End it with an even bigger one.

Let me give you a real life example of how to do it. A longtime friend of mine, recently deceased from Agent Orange in Vietnam, was a station commander, when he retired. While still a road warrior, he was embroiled in a marriage from hell. Not even the most charitable of souls would have described it as pleasant. Calling his ex-wife crazy would not be inaccurate. By rights, he should have been virtually rabid every time he climbed into his patrol car.

Instead of letting her get under his skin, he was able to push that aside every working day. I have seen him in action on ride-alongs. His dog and pony show was the same every time he greeted the driver of any vehicle he had just stopped. In short, he worked hard to sell every citation he wrote. He smiled, kept his voice, low and friendly, and never acted judgmental.

By the time he was done issuing a citation, he probably could have sold the recipient a full set of encyclopedias, plus several magazine subscriptions. I never saw any motorist display resentment. Many motorists even thanked him. I heard it myself.

The likelihood is slim such a contented motorist will choose a trial, if acceptable alternatives exist. Motorists may even plead guilty, so they do not have to confront such a people-friendly LEO, in court. If my friend were still alive, he could be teaching a class called *Selling that Citation*. If I had my way? Each of you would be enrolled.

I just hope he passed along his personal pearls of wisdom to his own troops, at briefings and roll calls, before he retired. The man had a gift. This is not something he mastered his first day on the job. It takes practice. You can do the same thing. Remember, it is not automatic. You have to work at it, until you know what works, with the motorists you contact. Once you believe you have it polished, keep working on it, by writing citations, and selling each one, as if it's your very last.

In this chapter, you will learn possible alternatives to trial, you can offer motorists you cite, so both of you can bypass that experience. However, before you do so, please grasp part of your job is competent courtroom and administrative agency testimony. Like selling a citation. That, too, is perfected, only with practice.

Selling a citation, by offering a motorist alternatives to trial, is a necessary part of the experience you need. Do not overlook your need to obtain courtroom experience. No matter how hard you work to sell citations, there will always be drivers who insist on demanding a trial. Do not worry that going this route is going to deprive you of some courtroom action. And for that crowd, remember you need to be ready for them.

Alternatives to trial are nice because they offer motorists ways to resolve the matter, without having to take time away from work to go to court. They also allow you to remain in the field, rather than being tied up in court. While you are working to establish this part of your skill package do not neglect the part you will need, when you go to court.

Granted, the first few times you go to court, you will almost certainly be anxious. This is to be expected. Anyone who says they are not, at least a bit jittery, before they get their proverbial sea legs, in the courtroom, are probably prevaricating. Way too many cops have confidentially told me otherwise. What am I saying? You should not concentrate on one route, to the detriment of developing the other. Balance is the key.

Before we discuss the alternatives, let's consider the mechanics of how you should provide such information. Your approach needs to be as non-confrontational as possible. Not every traffic stop will permit you to treat the driver in a friendly fashion, for a variety of reasons. Some conclude with a motorist being arrested, possibly requiring varying degrees of force by you.

This does not mean you should not work daily at polishing your diplomatic skills. For example, doesn't it sound friendlier, to be able to talk a felon into a pair of handcuffs, rather than fighting the guy? Both of you could be transported to the ER? Before you get too dismissive, this happens. I have seen it. Therefore, unless you need to assert adequate command presence, to maintain control over an unruly motorist, keep your cool. Remember to keep selling that citation.

You can do this a number of different ways. First, do not forget to communicate. Take the time to explain why you made the vehicle stop. As an example, *"...sir/ma'am, the reason I stopped you is because you were exceeding the maximum 65 mph speed limit, by 15 miles per hour. You were doing 80, immediately before I activated my emergency lights..."*

This tells the motorist specifically why you stopped them, without making you sound disparaging. Once you explain why you stopped the motorist, explain how they can resolve the matter. Do not be argumentative. Do not be preachy. Chances are real high, despite protestations of innocence, or anger, to the contrary, virtually every motorist you stop knows why you stopped them.

Avoid editorial opinion. If you editorialize expect to see the motorist in court, complete with their own bad attitude. That's because they may believe they need to teach you a lesson. It may mean they want you to work for the conviction. Or they may merely wish to tell the judge you were less than kind, during your roadside encounter. Yes, I have heard that one a few times, as a Pro Tem. If you really tick them off, they may even beef you, to your brass.

Now let's consider some alternatives. Learn relevant laws. Find out what options are available, in your own jurisdiction. Be sure you are in compliance with any and all of your department's General Orders, policies, and procedures. If you are not sure, ask your supervisor for any needed direction.

Suggestions in this book are a bit more generic, than they would be, if it were written for officers in only one state. It has to be done this way. Otherwise, it would take too long to write, be too expensive, and be too heavy to carry.

Before we begin discussing specific alternatives, let's digress a moment, and grasp the fundamental importance of their proper use. They benefit the errant motorist. Why? They permit someone who has made a mistake, to be able to conclude an unpleasant experience, in a more dignified fashion, and hopefully become better educated about motoring safety.

If this happens, it means the citation can be resolved, without an unnecessary confrontation. So, hopefully, you see how offering such alternatives to trial, can also be beneficial to you, to your department, to the court, and to our collective tax dollars. Why?

Trials cost money. A full-fledged courtroom can cost around eight thousand dollars each day it's in operation. Personnel may include judge or commissioner, courtroom clerk, other staff in the clerk's office, bailiff, court reporter, and interpreter.

Add yourself to that mix, and the cost is even more prohibitive. Cost alone is not the sole factor that causes me to favor alternative routes of resolution, for traffic infractions. Once upon a time, police departments failed to grasp the need for positive and healthy public relations. Instead, a bunker type mentality seemed to permeate many departments. Us against them. Them against us. In a sense, it was good guys against other good guys.

Unfortunately, failure to differentiate this, into appropriate sub-categories, means errant motorists who are otherwise law abiding folks tend to be lumped in with common criminals. Yes, I know I've already said traffic violations are crimes. But there's a wide gulf between your garden variety felon, and the respected business owner you caught speeding, or not coming to a complete stop, before rolling the limit line.

This creates a separate host of problems. First, law enforcement agencies are tax-supported entities. This covers both personnel and equipment needs. So, if you conclude every minor traffic stop, with a combative stance, pitting you against the motorist, the likelihood of having a sympathetic ear from such a person, at budget time, is not going to be terribly high. That's especially so, if motorists complain to their relevant lawmakers, who control these purse strings.

This lack of connection, however, is even more significant, than factors such as, salaries and equipment replacement. For example, think of some of the auxiliary units, modernly supplementing the work performed by sworn officers, communications staff, and community service officers.

Depending on the department, this may include volunteer search and rescue units, reserve police officers, citizens on patrol, and citizen-police academy alumni organizations. Although such entities were hardly on the law enforcement radar screen, twenty-five years ago, talk to any police department today that relies on such citizen participation. Ask them how much they depend on these volunteers. If your department is anything like the ones I have worked alongside in my community, I would be shocked, if these volunteers are not an integral part of protecting their respective communities.

In short, a modern day law enforcement agency that lacks a healthy relationship, with the community it is sworn to protect and serve, simply is not doing its job. Let's face some basics. Although traffic enforcement does not generally fall into this category, police work at times can be necessarily brutal work.

Whenever an officer has to make an arrest, including placing a suspect into handcuffs, as we both know, there is the hard way to do it, and the easy way to do it. By the easy way, I am referring to the subject who simply submits to the authority of the arresting officer, and allows the officer to handcuff them.

I'm sure you can think of at least one such encounter you have had, or know of, involving a suspect who chose the wrong door. A case that vividly comes to mind is the Rodney King incident. That led to the career ruination of four LAPD officers, despite the fact the perpetrator continued to be arrested repeatedly during his lifetime. They were thrown under the bus.

Although my own research persuades me those men were in compliance, with departmental policies and procedures, the end result speaks for itself. So if you can utilize a methodology which *de*-escalates an encounter, rather than *escalates* it, doesn't it make sense to at least consider it as an available option?

Okay, now let's discuss possible alternatives to trial. If you are going to lecture a motorist, do so with the idea you are giving someone a warning, instead of a citation. If you lecture and cite, I can almost guarantee you'll see the same motorist, in court, maybe with a lawyer, leading interference. People do not like strangers, including cops, giving them unsolicited advice. I sure do not, and I trust you feel the same way. Before we get to the alternatives, what if the motorist asks how to contest the citation? Tell them. Don't take it personally.

But, whatever you do, make sure you avoid reciting any sections of law to the general public, irrespective of whether it is a statute or an appellate case. This information is solely for you. Providing such info, to the public, could place you in the untenable position of being accused of practicing law, without a license. Do not do it! In my state, that's a misdemeanor.

Alternatives to Trial

1. **Not Guilty Plea by Mail**: A cited motorist may be able to plead not guilty, by mailing a personal check, cashier's check, or money order to the court as bail, or by posting it online, depending on your state's laws, and local court rules. In California, this is permitted by Vehicle Code §40519(b), if a motorist wishes to contest the citation.

2. **In-Person Courtroom Trial**: The Sixth Amendment of the U.S. Constitution affords everyone accused of a crime the absolute right to make his accuser prove any criminal charges in a public courtroom.

a. Your own state's constitution, like California, should have a similar provision. Any motorist has the unconditional right to make his accuser prove he was correct in issuing a traffic citation.

3. Forfeiting Bail: In California, for example, Vehicle Code §40521 allows a motorist to send the bail amount, listed in the Courtesy Notice, to the court, without requesting a trial. This is essentially a guilty plea by mail.

4. Trial by Declaration: In California, Vehicle Code §40902 allows motorists to present their defense, by sending the court a declaration explaining why they believe they are not guilty.

The court generally requires the prior posting of bail. You, in turn, present a written declaration explaining why you issued the citation. If the court finds the motorist not guilty, the posted bail is returned.

If a motorist is found guilty, he can request a *trial de novo*. If the court allows this, a court appearance is required and a new trial, i.e., trial de novo, is held.

5. Traffic Violator School: In California, Vehicle Code §42005 allows a motorist to attend a traffic violator school, in lieu of pleading guilty, or going to trial. The defendant pays a fee to the court, and to the school. Proof of completion results in a dismissal. But this can only be done a maximum number of times in a given time frame. Approval of a request for traffic school is discretionary, with the court. I always confirm the motorist was not an Adam Henry at the scene of the T-stop, before I approve traffic school. Why waste tax dollars we can't afford to throw away?

Do not assume these options exist in your state, simply because I am listing them here, as examples from California's Vehicle Code. Buy your own state's book of traffic laws; buy a new one every year. Take the time to read it. Obviously, it will be too long to commit every section to memory. But familiarize yourself with it. Doing so will help you sell any citation to any motorist. If it fits, keep it in your posse box. Knowledge is power. Ignorance is *not* bliss.

Do not monopolize the conversation with motorists you stop. Let them talk. You may be amazed as to what you will hear. Let them tell you, if they believe they violated the section you observed them violate. And, if so, why.

Take the time to ask them questions. For example, ask *"...how fast do you think you were going?"* or *"...did you come to a complete stop at the limit line?"* etc.

You may be very surprised by some of the answers you obtain. By way of example, I heard a defendant in traffic court one day tell me, he did not think he deserved the citation. I asked what he meant. The defendant replied, *"The officer wrote I was going 78 mph and I wasn't going that fast."* I asked the defendant how fast he thought he was going. The defendant's reply? *"I was only going 72 mph."*

Hint, the speed limit was 65. The officer testified the guy was going 84 but he only wrote it for 78. The verdict? You guessed it, *guilty*. If you ask enough relevant roadside questions you are going to obtain admissions of wrongdoing. Make notes on the backside of your copy of the citation.

You may also receive denials of guilt, which are so ludicrous, even the motorist will know it. If that happens, you may avoid an unnecessary trip to court. So unless you are a glutton for overtime, or are morbidly fascinated by courtrooms, following these steps may save you some unnecessary wear and tear.

Chapter 11
Possible Administrative Actions

Various administrative actions may be available, for you to use, against errant motorists. I list ones in California to assist you, in determining, if similar ones are available, in your state. Let's discuss the status of a driver's license. California's Vehicle Code describes it as *a privilege to operate a motor vehicle*. Since it is not listed, as a described right in the U.S. Constitution, this means it is a driving privilege no matter what state you work in.

Although I certainly do not agree with everything lawmakers do, even if my wife was a Field Rep for the California Legislature for a number of years, this is one area in which we walk in lockstep.

I use California statutes for illustrative purposes only, and am certainly not suggesting what my state makes available for law enforcement, is available in your state. Know your state's traffic laws. Learn the scope of administrative remedies, at your disposal. Talk to one of your department's veteran traffic officers. Doing so should be illuminating. Be sure to follow up any discussion, by doing your own research.

Do not view traffic court, as the only option you have, to improve motoring skills. In addition to court, there may be a number of *administrative actions* you can employ, to more effectively help make this happen. They are outlined, in the veritable shopping list we will discuss below. One important thing, about these potential remedies, is the lesser standard of proof involved, compared to court. The burden of proof, in criminal court, is *beyond a reasonable doubt*. In the administrative arena, it's a mere *preponderance of the evidence.* And a hearing officer, rather than a jury, makes the decisions.

If you are required to appear in traffic court, to justify why you intruded into a particular driver's life, you must meet the highest standard of proof in the civilized world, to prove your allegations. As noted, this standard is called proof beyond a reasonable doubt; the same standard as in a murder case.

California Jury Instructions-Criminal, known to lawyers and judges as CAL-JIC (*now CAL-CRIM*) spells out what reasonable doubt is. It is that state of the case where you can say you have *an abiding conviction of the truth of the charges* the defendant faces. Even in traffic court, an abiding conviction of the truth of the charges, is a pretty tough mountain to climb. By contrast, administrative actions only require the same level of proof, as required in civil actions. To meet this standard, preponderance of the evidence, the trier of fact must determine it's more likely what you are trying to prove happened, than did not happen. Numerically, it's anything above 50 percent.

Is there another essential factor we need to consider, vis-à-vis the privilege to operate a motor vehicle? Yes. Your state's bureaucratic entity which issues drivers' licenses is also the sole body with legal authority to suspend or revoke that privilege, aside from legislatively-mandated suspensions that may occur, when a motorist is arrested for driving under the influence, etc.

Sometimes stronger medicine, than a conviction, is needed to heal a bad driver. This is what administrative actions are all about. Your state's version of California's DMV (*see State-by-State Information at the end of this book*) has the power to suspend or revoke one's privilege to operate a motor vehicle here in my state. That's because only the DMV is empowered to issue it.

This is true, irrespective of whether your state calls it the Department of Public Safety, Department of Transportation, Department of Finance and Administration, Department of Revenue, Division of Motor Vehicles, and so on. The basic concept is the same.

This entity also has the legal authority to suspend a driver's license, but may allow the offending motorist to keep the license, with a probationary status, including specific limiting terms and conditions. Your state's DMV-equivalent has precisely that sort of authority too. It may exercise it, following a number of administrative actions. We will discuss them below. These may include some, or all, of the following, which are listed alphabetically:

1. admin per se hearing
2. implied consent hearing
3. negligent operator hearing
4. re-examination hearing
5. refusal to take a preliminary alcohol screening (*PAS*) test hearing

Admin per se Hearings

An administrative hearing in California is commonly known as an *admin per se* hearing, pursuant to Vehicle Code §13353.2. In California, any motorist arrested for driving under the influence of alcohol, drugs, or a combination thereof, can have their privilege to operate a motor vehicle suspended forthwith.

The arresting officer can issue a temporary thirty (30) day license, while seizing the motorist's permanent license. The motorist can operate a motor vehicle, during that time period, until the order of suspension is issued, by the DMV. The order of suspension will give the effective date of the suspension.

Normally, for first time offenders, the suspension is for four (4) months. However, upon presenting proof to the DMV, of enrollment, in an approved driving under the influence program, and proof of financial responsibility, this may be shortened to thirty (30) days.

The arrestee may request the DMV to schedule an admin per se hearing, to challenge the legality of the arrest and license seizure. The completeness of your arrest report is important. Why? California DMV relies on it, to determine if the suspension should take effect. And, if the arrestee requests an admin per se hearing, you will need to rely on your report, in order to competently testify. Do not forget to take a copy with you to such a hearing.

Implied Consent Hearings

A type of administrative hearing you may be able to add to your set of traffic enforcement tools is the *implied consent* hearing. Implied consent appears to be the law throughout the entire country, according to my own research.

In California, for example, motorists are said to *impliedly consent*, to a sample of their blood or breath, upon the request of any peace officer, with reasonable suspicion to believe they are operating a motor vehicle, under the influence of alcohol, drugs, or a combination thereof. Urine used to be included until an appellate case nullified it. Why? Ask them.

If you advise motorists of their requirement to provide such a sample, pursuant to Vehicle Code §§13353 and 23157, and they refuse, or fail, to complete such a test, you can notify DMV. The driver faces license suspension, or possibly even revocation, depending on their driving history.

Upon you filing a sworn statement with the DMV, the suspension or revocation commences. As a part of this procedure you must serve the motorist, so affected, with a written order of suspension, or revocation. If the motorist requests an implied consent hearing, you must prove four elements at the hearing in order for license suspension or revocation to take effect:

1. you had reasonable cause to believe the motorist operated a motor vehicle, while under the influence
2. you placed the motorist under arrest for this
3. the motorist refused to submit to the required test
4. you adequately informed the motorist their driving privilege would be suspended, or revoked, if they refused to submit to, or failed to complete, such a test

If your state has a similar statutory provision to this one, take the time to fully acquaint yourself with what you have to do, in order to cause appropriate license suspensions, or revocations.

Obviously, it would be a shame to arrest someone, for driving under the influence of alcohol or drugs, and not have their license suspension or revocation occur, due to a technicality you personally caused, by failing to take all necessary steps. Therefore, remember, you have a multi-step process, to complete at your end. For example:

1. Do you have reasonable cause to believe the motorist violated the appropriate driving under the influence statute?
2. Did you place the person under arrest for doing this?
3. Did the motorist refuse to submit to such a chemical test or fail to complete one?
4. Did you clearly inform the arrestee their driving privilege would be suspended or revoked if he refused to submit to or failed to complete such a chemical test?

Negligent Operator Hearings

Pursuant to Vehicle Code §12810.5, a *negligent operator* hearing may be held, if a motorist's point count rises above a certain level, within a prescribed period of time. Convictions for moving violations, as well as every traffic collision deemed to be the driver's fault, normally count as one (1) point against that motorist's driving record.

Convictions for misdemeanors, such as evading a peace officer, driving under the influence, reckless driving, driving on a suspended license, and vehicular manslaughter generally count as two (2) points each. But as noted before, read your state's traffic statutes to be certain, as this can vary from state to state. Evading? In my humble opinion, that should be permanent suspension and vehicle impoundment. Second offense? Public auction of R/O's vehicle.

Using California, as an example once again, accumulation of four (4) points in a twelve (12) month, six (6) points in a twenty-four (24) month, or eight (8) points in a thirty-six (36) month period, by any California motorist qualifies them, as a *negligent operator*. Commercial drivers in California who accumulate six (6) points in a twelve (12) month, eight (8) points in a twenty-four (24) month, or ten (10) points in a thirty-six (36) month period, while driving commercially, can be labeled negligent operators.

Since they generally drive more miles, they need to accumulate more points, than their non-commercial cousins. Exceptions to general rules are a long standing part of the legal system. Not surprisingly, there are exceptions to commercial drivers' privilege, in California, to accumulate more points, during the same period of time, as non-commercial motorists, before they qualify as negligent operators. These exceptions are:

1. ambulance drivers
2. school bus drivers
3. farm labor vehicle drivers (*nine [9] passenger maximum limit*)
4. youth bus drivers (*other than a school bus, sixteen [16] passenger maximum limit*)
5. general public paratransit drivers (*twenty-four [24] passenger maximum limit*)
6. If you are one of the above-noted commercial drivers, your point count maximum is the same as for non-commercial California drivers. Please read your state's motoring statutes to see if a similar regulatory scheme exists, in your jurisdiction.
7. However, irrespective of where you go 10-8 as a traffic cop, should any motorist you T-stop qualify for negligent operator status with the citation you issue, I would suggest *not* giving them a break. Write it for what they did.
8. The governmental agency, that issues a driver's license, needs to be able to oversee the privilege to operate a motor vehicle, for public safety reasons. Such a motorist has more than demonstrated they probably should not be driving, for those very same public safety reasons.
9. In California, the DMV itself will automatically send the targeted motorist a written notice, informing them, they can request a hearing to try to convince the department's hearing officer they should retain their driver's license, without any required input from the issuing officer.
10. If you are in another state, please find out if your state's department that issues drivers' licenses does this differently.

Re-Examination Hearings

A *re-examination* hearing, pursuant to Vehicle Code §13800, et seq, is yet one more administrative action. In California, any peace officer who determines any motorist, within this state, should have their privilege to operate a motor vehicle revisited by the Department of Motor Vehicles, has the authority to act.

These can arise whenever a doubt exists, concerning the ability of a motorist to safely operate a motor vehicle. In general terms, the basic difference between this statute, and the preceding one? Negligent operator hearings happen because of one's point count. This one examines any motorist's privilege to operate a motor vehicle, based on driving competency.

If your state has a similar statute, please do not hesitate to use it. Public safety counts on trained observers, such as you, to do the right thing. Routinely, this happens whenever a traffic officer believes a motorist is incapable of safely operating a vehicle. Although the primary reason for arriving at such a conclusion may be the aging process, or the abuse of chemical body additives, do not limit your options, based on merely these as hypothetical choices.

The key is whether you are able to adequately articulate a valid reason why a motorist should not be legally driving a motor vehicle. So, for example, let's say you observe a driver operating a vehicle in such a fashion you believe they are likely to cause death or great bodily injury. Chances are slim-to-none a motorist will drive aberrationally reckless, only on the one day you happen to observe them. Conversely, I suspect this is closer to their normal driving pattern, than they would be willing to admit.

If I were a traffic officer making such an observation, I would err on the side of caution, and report the motorist to your state's driver's licensing authority. I'm not talking about mere excessive speed as a basis, either.

Below are examples of the types of driving I believe would qualify for re-examination. These include but are not limited to:

1. passing a multi-car line of vehicles, on a blind curve, over a set of double yellow lines
2. grossly exceeding the maximum speed limit
3. exhibiting road rage
4. driving so aggressively, other motorists pull to the side of the road
5. evading a peace officer displaying emergency lights and siren, aka high speed pursuits
6. driving the wrong way on a freeway
7. hit and run, following a traffic collision that causes great bodily injury, or death
8. driving a vehicle, after the court-ordered installation of an ignition interlock, with the device disabled

9. any other type of driving, you believe so qualifies the motorist for, such a hearing

Refusal to take Preliminary Alcohol Screening Test Hearings

Akin to implied consent hearings, in California there is now a lawful requirement that motorists submit to a *preliminary alcohol screening*, or PAS, test, upon the request of any peace officer, pursuant to Vehicle Code §13353.1. Failure to so submit creates consequences similar to the refusal, or failure to complete, a required blood or breath test. In other words, failure to submit may result in suspension, or revocation, of the motorist's privilege to operate a motor vehicle.

You must first articulate you have reasonable cause to believe a motorist is under the influence of alcohol, drugs, or a combination thereof, in a state with a statutory scheme, like California.

If so, next ask the motorist to take a PAS test. Their refusal to do so, or failure to complete it, can result in the suspension, or revocation of their driver's license, depending on their driving history.

Be sure to serve the motorist, with an order of suspension, if they refuse or fail, to complete this test. Do not forget to submit your sworn statement, attesting to the underlying relevant facts, to your state's driver's licensing agency.

As with the implied consent admonition, remember, you have a multi-step process to complete, at your end.

1. Do you have reasonable cause to believe the motorist violated the appropriate driving under the influence statute?
2. Did you place the person under arrest?
3. Did the motorist refuse to submit to, or fail to complete, such a test?
4. Did you clearly inform the arrestee their driving privilege would be suspended, or revoked, if they refused to submit to, or failed to complete, such a test?

Proper use of the administrative process is an ideal supplement to merely issuing an offending motorist a notice to appear in court, under appropriate circumstances. While the traffic court jurist can impose applicable fines and other penalties, the agency empowered by your state's legislative body to issue drivers' licenses is also the same entity vested with the exclusive power to suspend, or revoke, a motorist's privilege to operate a motor vehicle.

Therefore, if public safety dictates you take that extra step to help save lives, please take the time, and expend the energy, to do what is required. In certain circumstances you may actually help educate otherwise recalcitrant motorists, to become better drivers.

If they refuse to learn whatever lesson is provided, you have helped public safety, by removing their ability to lawfully operate motor vehicles. The next time a fellow peace officer stops one of them, from operating a vehicle, sans a valid driver's license, yet another tool exists to control them.

Motorists may go to jail, for driving on a suspended, or revoked, license, and vehicles may be impounded and stored, thanks to your taking the extra time to request an applicable administrative hearing. Take the time to use this administrative remedy. Protect public safety, just as you would employ any of the rest.

Chapter 12
The Importance of Good Notes

This chapter stresses the importance of taking good notes, for a number of reasons we will soon discuss. I was speaking with a buddy recently whom I have known for nearly twenty-seven years. He's a medically retired motor cop, from a department, in the same area, as Palm Springs. He collided with a palm tree, chasing armed robbery suspects, on his police motor, and lived to tell about it. That's why he's medically retired. The palm tree remains bent. The curb line is still missing the chunk of concrete his motorcycle tore out, at the point of impact.

He is still an expert in traffic law enforcement, even though he's been out of that particular loop for many years. We were discussing a veteran peace officer who recently had a couple of citations kicked back, by his sergeant. I inquired how anyone could have traffic citations rejected. He looked at me, grinned and said *"...figure it out..."*

I suggested four possible scenarios, listing the citations as either:

1. incorrect
2. incomplete
3. illegible
4. all of the above.

When I told him this, my friend nodded sagely and said, *Bingo!* The moral of this particular story? Take your time to fill out any citation, properly, competently, and completely. Make sure you provide all necessary information. Make sure any listed information is correct. Be sure you have completely filled it out. And fill it out, so anyone can easily read it. If you do not, expect to lose, assuming it even gets past your supervisor. It probably won't.

Let me give you a real life example of how important legibility is. I actually represented someone many years ago because she got a parking ticket. When I asked what violations were listed, I was told they could not read the citation. I instantly believed my client had a defense, and confirmed that, when I tried to read the citation. At my court appearance, the day of trial, I informed the judge I was moving to dismiss the citation, on constitutional grounds.

The judge did not know me. I did not know her. The reason? I was a DA, at the time, and the citation was in a neighboring county. No, I was not moonlighting. The recipient was my own daughter. The citation was just plain wrong. As her daddy, I had to act. Initially, the judge looked at me, as if I were a first-year law student. She asked me what I meant *by constitutional grounds*. I told her my client's Fifth Amendment Due Process rights and Sixth Amendment right to counsel, and a fair, impartial, speedy, and public trial were violated. Why? The citation was indecipherable.

Without any statutes or case citations to present, I noted I could not competently represent my client, because I did not know what she was accused of doing. Predictably, Her Honor was initially skeptical. I asked her to read my client's copy of the citation. She did so. She agreed with me, and immediately dismissed the case. Please understand something. This case was not dismissed because of factual innocence. My client was absolutely guilty of illegal parking. But that is not the point. Her case was dismissed because of embarrassingly sloppy work, by a parking enforcement officer.

If I were that guy's supervisor, such sloppiness would have translated into days off, without pay. It was that bad. And, it meant a guilty person beat the rap. Had I been able to decipher the citation, I would have simply advised my daughter to pay the fine. Had she been able to read it, she would have done the same thing on her own. But fair is fair.

Am I being hard-nosed about this? I do not believe so. It is axiomatic. Law enforcement professionals are public servants. As a prosecutor I prided myself on not wasting tax dollars. I worked hard to avoid doing this, on each and every case I prosecuted. I did so, when supervising other prosecutors, to make sure the cases they set for trial were not clunkers. You should treat every penny of the tax dollars, for which you are entrusted, as if it is your own money. And, it is.

But that is not the real reason why you need to excel. Most police departments have mottos or slogans which promise the public your agency exists *"To Protect and Serve,"* or words to that effect. It does not matter if you are arresting dangerous felons, or issuing parking citations. Always take pride in your work. Never settle for second best. If your job does not mean enough to do that, quit. I'm serious as a heart attack, when I say this. Remember, the brush you paint with, professionally, impacts every other member of your team, whether that is done positively, or negatively. The choice is yours.

As I attempted unsuccessfully to read the particular citation, it appeared to me the writer was in a big hurry. I do not know if he was near end of shift. Maybe he was simply in a hurry to write as many citations as possible that particular day. If the rest of his citations were written this poorly, his work was meaningless, and not deserving of a single penny of tax dollars. Maybe it was simply a matter of bad penmanship. Either way, it was sloppy and substandard work, unbecoming any member of the law enforcement team.

Do not let this happen to you. Same thing is true with your notes. If they are illegible, contain incorrect information, or are incomplete, you are on your way to a loss. Do not forget. The defendant has an absolute discovery right, to both review and obtain a copy of your notes, upon proper request. All that's required in my courtroom: *can I see that?* If your notes cannot be interpreted, because of careless handwriting, expect this to present what should be an unnecessary problem. This is also true if the information is incorrect or incomplete.

You are a trained observer. I have said this before, and suspect you will make professional observations many times during the course of your career, as a police officer. As such, you will be called upon, many times to recite events, in some sort of a hearing room. This may include courtrooms, depositions, arbitrations, mediations, or simply in some prosecutor's office, where you prepare a case for litigation. This will require you to relate past observations, in a manner that will take a finder of facts close enough to the event in question, to be able to make a correct decision, regarding those facts.

However, being a trained observer, does not mean you necessarily come equipped with a *photographic memory.* This means you need a proven methodology, to be able to recall events. Frankly, despite having experienced more than six decades of life, I'm not sure I really know what a photographic memory is.

I suspect it is one of those expressions, without a clear enough correlation to what it is supposed to describe, to be adequately definable. Let me try to be more specific. Just as there are differing degrees of strength, or intelligence, I believe that same concept applies to memory. Is it like a light switch, either in the on or the off position? Does every person who has a photographic memory have the same amount, or possess it in the same strength?

In other words, somewhat akin to the story of the seven wise blind men trying to describe an elephant, by touching it, this may depend on a person's perspective. Phrases such as photographic memory are too nebulous to rely on, whenever you are relating events, you are being paid to describe. I'm not sure how much faith I have in ivory tower types. Are such opinions based on reality? Or, are they merely the product of some textbook? I am unaware of any test that can establish you are capable of literally remembering everything. And even if such a test exists, stay away from this area as a potential witness. Meeting burdens of proof is difficult enough, without giving opposing counsel ammunition they do not deserve. Do not prove yourself wrong on the witness stand. If you do, it's an experience you will not forget.

If you want to mess up your case, six ways from Sunday, try telling the defense attorney, on cross-examination, the reason you failed to take any notes is because you possess natural total recall. However, unless the prosecutor is a complete imbecile, I doubt you will ever get that far. This is because a competent prosecutor will ascertain, if you have done your job, before the case is even filed. They will know, what you will say on the witness stand, before you do. If you try to convince the prosecutor, you rely exclusively on memory, I doubt you will even get near the courtroom.

In fact, chances are good your supervisor will not even send your case to the prosecuting attorney's office. If this really is your MO, do not be surprised if you wash out, while on probation. Therefore, no matter how good you personally believe your memory to be, stay away from this. Simply do things the old-fashioned, tried, and true way, officers, with lesser memories, do, *by taking good notes*.

You are not on the witness stand to merely impress anyone with how well you can remember. This is not some kind of contest. You are there to tell what happened. From the very first notes you take, get in the consistent habit of doing things the same way *every single time*. Develop a routine. LEOs use memory aids to refresh their recollection. They are called traffic citations and incident reports.

You should develop a routine for a couple of reasons. First, if you do this, in time, it will become an automatic way of gathering vitally necessary information. Secondly, if you get boxed into a corner by the defense, the prosecutor should be able to prove, your way of recording events establishes the admissibility of that evidence, if your state has a statute similar to California.

This is done, pursuant to the *Past Recollection Recorded* section of your state's Evidence Code. If your state does not have such a section, it certainly should. If it does, my hat is off to your lawmakers. If it does not, it means lawmakers are not doing their jobs, protecting public safety.

Past recollection recorded

Just because certain rules in a courtroom are black and white, this does not mean you should park your creativity, at the front door of the courthouse. As Mike Van Gorder so aptly demonstrates, he successfully convinced a traffic court commissioner to allow him to amend a citation, right there in the courtroom, because he discovered he cited a motorist for violating the wrong law.

The same is true with an evidentiary rule, known as *past recollection recorded*. Let's use the California Evidence Code, for illustrative purposes. The memory of any witness, can be refreshed, by any means necessary. The same should be true in your state. Please take the time to read your state's Evidence Code. See if a similar provision exists. In California, past recollection recorded is one of the ways to refresh the recollection of a witness.

Below is *Evidence Code §1237*:

"(a) Evidence of a statement previously made by a witness is not made inadmissible by the hearsay rule if the statement would have been admissible if made by him while testifying, the statement concerns a matter as to which the witness has insufficient present recollection to enable him to testify fully and accurately, and the statement is contained in a writing which:

(1) was made at a time when the fact recorded in the writing actually occurred or was fresh in the witness' memory;
(2) was made:
(i) by the witness himself or under his direction, or,
(ii) by some other person for the purpose of recording the witness' statement at the time it was made;
(3) is offered after the witness testifies that the statement he made was a true statement of such fact; and
(4) is offered after the writing is authenticated as an accurate record of the statement.
(b) the writing may be read into evidence, but the writing itself may not be received in evidence unless offered by an adverse party."

How does *Past Recollection Recorded* blend into your note taking? You write notes, on the back of your copy of each traffic citation you issue. The reason you write those notes is to refresh your recollection, when you go to court.

What if reading those notes does not refresh your recollection, adequately, to allow you to competently testify? I actually saw a situation, in traffic court, one day, where a particular officer's case was called. He stood up and informed the court he wished the matter dismissed. I asked why. He stated he could not identify the driver. I complied and dismissed the citation.

What if you could avoid this, by relying on past recollection recorded? If you were permitted to identify the motorist, you could read your notes into the court record verbatim, providing you complied with the following provisions:

1. you had first-hand knowledge of the act, condition or event at the time of its occurrence, but no present memory

2. the acts, conditions or events described were true and accurate at the time the notes were taken, and you can attest the notes are your normal habit, or practice, in order to refresh your recollection.

My longtime understanding of past recollection recorded is you are merely prohibited from offering the notes themselves into evidence. Only the opposing side can do that. I cannot think of any reason why you cannot testify as to the contents of your notes. Otherwise, why would lawmakers write such an evidentiary law in the first place?

Here are a couple of things to keep in mind. First, do not try this every time you go to traffic court. If you do, it will give the impression you are either being disingenuous, or so forgetful, you should not be a traffic officer. Do this sparingly. Secondly, does your department have a policy prohibiting your snapping a digital photograph of every motorist to whom you issue a citation?

If no such policy exists, please keep in mind, photographs can generally be used as past recollection recorded. The door is already open. Police departments routinely use in-car camcorders, surveillance cameras and body cams. Therefore, it's unlikely anyone can quarrel with your attempting to do so in a public place.

Since roadways are public places I do not see anyone legitimately raising privacy concerns, as a way of prohibiting your gathering such evidence. Had the above-described officer possessed such evidence, he would not have had to request a dismissal. And if you follow this suggestion, it is unlikely you will either. Over the course of time, this should also help to establish you are a professionally reliable person, photographic memory or not.

It has been my experience, no matter how large or small the area is where you work, the legal community tends to be rather intimate. By that, I mean the judges, prosecutors, and defense lawyers will know different police officers, and become acquainted rather quickly with the quality of your work, just as you are familiar with the quality of theirs. Get started on the right foot, but do not live on your past reputation. Work hard every day, at improving yourself, as a law enforcement professional.

Now, let us move on to the methodology of taking good notes.

Expect your work to be challenged

Just because you're a nice guy and are polite to every motorist you stop, this is certainly no guarantee your work will not be challenged, in court. The Sixth Amendment of the U.S. Constitution gives motorists the unabridged right to go to court, and force you to prove they did, what your citation says they did. Motorists who challenge you in court do so, because they can.

Some may do so because they really believe they did not commit the offense, even if your professional observations say otherwise. Others do so, because they believe you cannot prove they erred. Still others may do so, because they are gamblers. Their hope? You will not show up, in court, for their trial.

Most risk-takers wisely opt for traffic school, when you appear. Some may do this merely out of desperation. They have too high a point count, and figure they have nothing to lose, by going to trial. Finally, some demand a trial because they do not like the attitude you displayed. So remember, cite them or bite them. Never do both.

Do not editorialize

As we have discussed elsewhere, your job is to gather the facts. You do this, by being objective about everything you document, as a traffic officer. You also do this by not being conclusionary. You *are* conclusionary, when you describe a motorist as *drunk*. For one thing, most motorists who are detained are merely under the influence, rather than being full-fledged public drunks.

Whether they are or not, avoid being conclusionary. Take the time, instead, to include relevant facts, which lead any reasonable person to believe, they are what you say they are. Does your description include them displaying, making, or possessing:

1. red, watery, bloodshot eyes?
2. varying degrees of an odor of alcohol about their breath and person?
3. slurred speech?
4. unsteady gait?
5. stumbling?
6. falling down?
7. disheveled clothing?
8. soiled clothing?
9. an admission by them, they are drunk or under the influence?

10. open or closed alcoholic beverage containers?

11. remarkable driving patterns, consistent with alcohol-impaired motorists, including, but not limited to:

    a. unsafe speed for conditions (*both too fast and too slow*)?
    b. weaving, within their own lane?
    c. weaving, between lanes?
    d. tailgating?
    e. too wide a turning radius?
    f. slowing or stopping, for no apparent reason?
    g. failing to obey a red light, or a stop sign?
    h. failing to stop, at the limit line?
    i. (*per NHTSA*) do they *appear drunk*?

Be prepared

Taking good notes is a complete and total waste of your time, if you nonetheless come to court unprepared. Even if you do this one single time, that may be enough, in and of itself, to brand you as unprepared, for the rest of your career. Right or wrong, people form impressions. Some are not easily shaken, by the passage of time.

Keep something else in mind. Judges and commissioners talk among themselves, as do prosecutors, defense counsel, and LEOs. Do not give other folks the bullet they need to kill you professionally. Showing up for court unprepared, makes you look unprofessional. If such information is relayed to your supervisor, you may face disciplinary action, ranging from an oral reprimand, to even more severe punishment. On the witness stand, your lack of preparedness can easily be misinterpreted, as a lack of candor. I have seen that happen on my own watch.

Avoid getting beaten up, in court, by being sure you take good notes. Take the time to carefully review them, beforehand. This is true, irrespective of whether you are on duty, or on regular days off. Know what they say.

What is even worse, than being so embarrassed by defense counsel? One scenario that comes immediately to my mind would be experiencing such embarrassment, at the hands of a defendant, representing themselves. Either way, do not shoot yourself in the foot, by allowing this to happen.

Be specific

Keeping in line, with avoiding conclusionary verbiage, you also need to refrain, from being overly broad, with any description you provide. For example, it is not enough to merely say the motorist weaved in and out of a lane.

How many lanes did they traverse? Did they do so with, or without, signaling? Did it appear other drivers had to brake hard, to avoid colliding with them? Include all relevant details. Did a near collision occur? If so, what specifics led you to believe that? Be specific.

Did the violator cause anything remarkable to happen? For example, did the front end of another vehicle appear to dip, suddenly? Did that motorist sound their horn...flash their headlights...squeal their tires...or give any hand signals indicating displeasure? If so, spell this out specifically. Over what distance did all this activity take place? Did you observe other vehicles swerving, as the result of the violator's inattention? Do not forget to describe other involved vehicles, including their make, model, and color.

Although it is not likely you will be able to record every single license plate, or driver description, be sure to include as many relevant details, as you observed. Does your unit have a dash cam? If so, did it record any of this? If so, it might be worth the extra work, incorporating this, into your case, i.e., bring the video to court. If it's that significant, you should have already logged it into evidence.

Include all relevant information

The facts of every case you handle will be unique. Even though the basic violation may be the same, as ones you have previously issued citations for, this does not mean the facts are going to be identical. Differing factors may include time and date of incident, location, suspect, weather conditions, temperature, types and numbers of relevant vehicles, as well as the amount of your own growing professional experience.

Take the time to communicate with your percipient senses. What did you:

1. see?
2. hear?
3. smell?
4. touch?
5. feel?

I am purposely leaving out taste because real-life LEOs do not taste evidence. *This is not TV.* Using your senses properly, will make your job a lot easier. While I have told you to avoid being conclusionary, please do not confuse this, with the need to use descriptive language. Remember to be accurate. Avoid misspellings. If you do not do this, expect defense counsel to point this out, while you are on the witness stand, getting grilled. It happens.

In addition to accurately capturing relevant facts, do not ignore the law. Being intimately familiar, with the evidence germane to your case, will cost you dearly if you have not taken the time to be sure you are issuing a citation for the correct violation. A nice courtroom tactic you may wish to use is one successfully employed by expert traffic court veterans, such as Mike Van Gorder.

Here is how it works. Assume you issue a citation. But prior to your court appearance you discover you relied on the wrong statute. Is this fatal to your case? Not necessarily. Here's what Van Gorder does. When your case is called inform the court you wish to amend the citation, by interlineation, to replace the *incorrect* section with the *correct* one.

There is no guarantee the court will permit an amendment. If the jurist is doing their job, you should be allowed to amend. I would likely do so. Providing it is not deemed prejudicial to the defendant, prosecutors are allowed to routinely make such amendments, to their charging documents. So why shouldn't you be similarly allowed?

But, be aware this may also mean the defendant is entitled to a reasonable continuance, in order to amend their own defense. Such a timely amendment by you, will prevent the defense from creating reasonable doubt. If the defendant is represented by counsel, you will have the satisfaction of out-lawyering the defendant's lawyer, by doing this.

Never use words if you do not know what they mean

People wrongly criticize lawyers for their use of verbiage. Unfortunately, most critics are wrong. Lawyers are paid, to string words together, into meaningful sentences. A scalpel to a surgeon, as a total station to you, is the equivalent of appropriate verbiage, to a lawyer. The same is true with police officers. You must function accordingly. Practice makes perfect. Practice using verbiage, if you expect to consistently prevail in the courtroom. This includes what you write, as well as what you say.

Precision and economy of verbiage are as important to you, as they are to any lawyer. Be a wordsmith. As we have discussed elsewhere, if you do not know what a word means, do not use it.

If you cannot spell it, do what is necessary to make sure it is spelled correctly. Your computer's spellchecker is a handy tool. Also, take the time to acquaint yourself with a dictionary, and a thesaurus. The Internet is a treasure trove of information, including the definition of words. I have used each of these resources. It's more than worth the trouble.

Some helpful examples:

1. **Following too closely**

   a. What did the motorist do that led you to believe he was *tailgating*?

   b. Remember to describe it accurately. Be concise. Be descriptive.

   c. Did the motorist (*or was the motorist*):

      i. follow another vehicle at a speed of 60 mph?

      ii. closer than the legally required number of car lengths?

      iii. did they do this over a distance of approximately .5 of a mile, flash their headlights, and blow the horn?

      iv. swerve back and forth within a lane?

      v. exhibit rude or obscene gestures?

2. **Speeding**

   a. Describe what you observed accurately, concisely and descriptively.

   b. Did the motorist:

      i. pass six other vehicles in less than one half mile?

      ii. occupy all three westbound lanes, weaving from the #1 to the #2, then the #3 and back to the #1 again?

      iii. remain in the same lane with other speeding vehicles you were unable to stop?

      iv. exceed the posted speed limit for a distance of at least one mile?

         (a) if so, how did you measure the distance:

            (1) use of mile markers?

            (2) with your odometer?

               (i.) if so, can you provide competent evidence of calibration?

3. **Unsafe lane changes**

   a. Be accurate, descriptive and concise.

   b. Did you observe the offender:

      i. weave in and out of traffic from the #1 to the #2 lane and back?

      ii. cause other motorists to brake unnecessarily?

         (a) did the taillights illuminate?

         (b) did the turn signals flash?

         (c) can you describe traffic volume? Was it:

(1) light?
(2) moderate?
(3) heavy?
(4) bumper-to-bumper, rush-hour variety?

In any traffic stop, never neglect to obtain an admission of wrongdoing, if possible. It's really simple. Just ask. Begin with the magic words *"...do you know why I stopped you?"* A roadside encounter is considered a temporary detention, per *Berkemer*. Therefore, you do not have to Mirandize.

Mock foundational exercise

Let's run through a hypothetical courtroom scenario, wherein you attempt to convince the court to allow you to read the contents of your notes, verbatim, into evidence. In most circumstances, it would go something like this, assuming you were represented by a prosecutor. If not, just offer the court similar foundational verbiage.

Prosecutor: P

Traffic Officer: TO

P: "Officer Garcia, have you had an opportunity to review the notes from the backside of your citation?"

TO: "Yes, I have."

P: "Did you write those notes?"

TO: "I did."

P: "Were they written at, or near, the time you issued this citation?"

TO: "Yes."

P: "And, was the citation written, at or near, the time of the act, condition, or event, which led to your issuance of this citation?"

TO: "Yes, it was."

P: "When was that?"

TO: "Within a minute or two, of the time I made the traffic stop on the defendant."

P: "How do you know this?"

TO: "That's what I always do when I issue citations."

P: "I see what appear to be notes on the back side of that same citation. Do you recognize them?"

TO: "I do."

P: "How do you recognize them?"

TO: "Those are my notes. I recognize my handwriting."

P: "And, when did you write these notes?"

TO: "Within minutes of issuing the citation."

P: "Has your reading of these notes refreshed your recollection?"

TO: "No. Sadly, it has not."

P: "Is it the usual practice of your department, for such notes to be written, in the ordinary course of business?"

TO: "Yes ma'am."

P: "Can you explain that?"

TO: "Yes, this is how I was trained to be a traffic officer, and how my fellow traffic officers tell me they operate."*

P: "Were these notes written by you, in the ordinary course of business?"

TO: "Yes."

P: "Have they been under your sole care, custody, and control?"

TO: "Yes."

P: "Were they a true and correct representation, of the underlying facts, when you wrote them?"

TO: "Yes."

P: "Please read them into the record, verbatim."

Here's something you want to file away, for future reference, so it never ruins your case. Admissions are a two-way street. Just as any self-respecting cop, or prosecutor, will attempt to introduce admissions of wrongdoing, by the defendant, into evidence, as a way of sealing the lid on their proverbial coffin, expect turn around to be play, fair, or otherwise.

Where are we going with this, you ask? Do not develop roadside hoof and mouth disease that will allow a traffic offender, or their counsel, to use any editorial comments, from you, against you, in the courtroom. In line with the old adage, it's better to keep your mouth shut, and have someone label you a fool, than to open it and remove all doubt...especially if that doubt is *reasonable doubt*. Should that happen, you lose.

***Note**: California Evidence Code §1105 permits the introduction of evidence of a person's habit, or custom, to prove conduct on a specific date, if that conduct is in conformity, with his habit, or custom, to engage in a specific type of behavior. It reads: *"Any otherwise admissible evidence of habit or custom is admissible to prove conduct on a specified occasion in conformity with the habit or custom."*

Chapter 13
Corpus Delicti

In this chapter, we discuss the corpus delicti rule, and the role it plays, in your professional life. Law school comes complete, with a shopping list of Latin words and phrases. One of these is *corpus delicti*, aka *body of the crime*.

Do not mistakenly believe this rule applies only to homicide cases, because of the word *corpus*. It does not. In fact, nothing could be further from the truth. Every crime, irrespective of whether it's an infraction, a misdemeanor, or a felony, comes complete with its own corpus delicti, and attendant requirements.

Each crime is made up of its own specific elements, discussed elsewhere in this book. Every corpus is comprised of elements. Each crime has its own unique set of elements. Think of elements as the individual pieces to a jigsaw picture puzzle. Irrespective of what crime you are attempting to prove, the burden of proof is the same. The prosecution must convince, the trier of fact, guilt has been proved, beyond a reasonable doubt.

This is true, regardless of whether the fact finder is a judge, commissioner, or jury. And it's true irrespective of whether you are flying solo, or working with a prosecutor. Essentially, it is that state of the case, where a fact finder can say, they have an abiding conviction, of the truth of each charge.

Basically, this means being able to hypothetically wake up, at any future point, from the date such a decision is made, and still be able to say the decision was correct. The burden of proof is not, beyond all possible doubt. Nor is it, beyond any imaginary doubt, or any of that, beyond a shadow of a doubt, nonsense you hear TV talking heads blathering on about. It is simply that state of the case where the fact finder is convinced the crime has been proven. We will discuss this in more depth in Chapter 18. Now let's get back to corpus.

If the court is doing its job, it will be necessary for you to establish the presence of the corpus, before you can present any admissions, or confessions, made by the defendant. View the relationship of corpus to admissions, the same way you view your Sam Browne to the many accoutrements that routinely adorn it, such as holster and sidearm, Taser, handcuffs, and so on.

If the Sam Browne is not there, none of its normal gadgets will have anything, to which they can be connected. The same is true with an admission. If you do not first establish the corpus of the crime, in the courtroom, you will have nothing to hang any admissions on, you obtain from a suspect, in the field.

Therefore, do not waste your time trying to introduce an admission into evidence until you prove the corpus. Although the typical traffic court jurist is not going to be that nitpicky, unless so goaded, by a defense attorney, always plan for a worst case scenario. In other words, just because a judge does not do their job, does not mean you do not do yours.

You do not have to prove the corpus, beyond a reasonable doubt. Are you wondering how you present enough evidence of the existence of the crime's corpus, to convince the court, so you can offer the defendant's admission of wrongdoing? You do this by establishing all the elements of the crime of which the defendant stands accused. In other words, offer evidence of each element.

Each crime has its own exceptional elements. Since it is impossible for me to categorize, every offense, you will deal with, let us use California Vehicle Code §22350 which regulates basic speed laws in my state.

Vehicle Code §22350

"No person shall drive a vehicle upon a highway at a speed greater than is reasonable or prudent having due regard for weather, visibility, the traffic on, and the surface and width of, the highway, and in no event, at a speed which endangers the safety of persons or property."

In order to determine what we must prove, let us break this down into its basic elements:

1. "...(n)o person shall drive..."
2. "...a vehicle..."
3. "...upon a highway..."
4. "...at a speed, greater than is reasonable or prudent..."
5. "...having due regard for
   a. weather,
   b. visibility,

c. the traffic on, and,

d. the surface and width of, the highway, and,..."

e. "...in no event, at a speed, which endangers the safety of persons or property..."

Okay, the above gibberish is lawyer-speak. In plain language, did you catch the guy driving too fast to do so safely, for surrounding conditions? Once you determine how to establish the elements, of the particular offense you have to prove, organize your facts, in order to establish the corpus, prior to introducing any admission made by the defendant, during your roadside encounter.

Because the rules of evidence, in traffic court, generally are more relaxed, than the courtrooms where trial attorneys routinely work, the information I'm providing, will not necessarily be needed, in every traffic court case you handle. The reason I am taking these extraordinary steps? Defense counsel sometimes handle traffic court cases, including simple infractions. And, you need to be ready should that happen.

Expect defense counsel to formalize the experience. Remember, that is how I identified the problems I discovered, and why I wrote this book. I learned most traffic officers were not nearly as prepared for the courtroom experience as they should have been. I realize things are different today, with POST Radar classes, etc., But, is it wrong to be overly prepared? If the court does its job (*and if defense counsel does theirs, and, they will*), the defendant's lawyer will insist the formal rules of evidence apply.

The defense will do that by lodging objections to the introduction of evidence not permitted by your state's Evidence Code. This could happen with any of your cases. Defense counsel does not have to give you advance notice they will make an appearance for the guy you cited. Quite to the contrary, defense counsel love ambushes.

Even if there was such a requirement there is no guarantee a prosecutor will be there to rescue you from yourself. The judge may not do it *sua sponte*. Learn these lessons before you go to court. You can learn how right here. If you do your job you will be fine. Just do not let counsel rattle you. There is no reason to allow that if you are on top of your own game by being prepared.

Now let's apply corpus delicti rules to the facts of your particular case. In order to do this we will create what is called a hypothetical set of facts, akin to the same types of questions you may hear a lawyer ask an expert witness in court.

In order to introduce an expert's opinion, the lawyer must first set forth an arbitrary set of underlying facts upon which the opinion is based. Once that is done and only when that is done, can the expert offer his opinion. It does not matter if the lawyer is defense counsel or prosecutor.

With this in mind, let's make some illustrative assumptions:

1. *Assume* you cite a motorist for exceeding the posted 35 mph speed limit
2. *Assume* the posted limit is 25 mph, if children are present (*school zone*)
3. *Assume* the motorist admits going 45 mph
4. *Assume* you clocked the motorist at 54 mph
5. *Assume* the school is an elementary school, kindergarten through sixth grade
6. *Assume* children are on the street-adjacent sidewalk, in front of the school
7. *Assume* they are waiting to board the school bus or other rides home
8. *Assume* the motorist's identity is not an element of the offense
9. *Assume* you can prove identity, by an admission the motorist was operating the vehicle you observed them driving
10. *Assume* the motorist is not present at the trial

For purposes of this illustration, we will also dispense with how you determined the offending motorist's speed. In other words, it's irrelevant for the purposes of this hypothetical whether you used radar, bumper-paced the motorist, or otherwise determined the speed. All that matters is the measured speed, and the other underlying facts, set forth above. To make your job a bit easier, a prosecutor is present in court.

P: Prosecutor
TO: Traffic Officer
DC: Defense Counsel
C: Court

P: "Officer, by whom are you employed?"

TO: "Anytown Police Department."

P: "And in what capacity are you so employed?"

TO: "I am a traffic officer, assigned to my city's motorcycle division."

P: "Were you so employed, and assigned, on the date of this citation?"

TO: "I was." (You read the date of the citation)

P: "On (*the date of the citation*), did you observe a motorist, in front of Anytown Elementary School, to whom you later issued a citation?"

TO: "Yes, I did."

P: "What are the grades there?"

TO: "Kindergarten through sixth grade."

P: "What is the speed limit there?"

TO: "Thirty-five mph, but it drops to 25, if children are present."

P: "Were children present?"

TO: "Yes." (*Describes those present representing the ages of attending students*)

P: "So, for clarity, what did you believe the speed limit to be at that time?"

TO: "Twenty-five mph."

P: "Is the driver in court today?"

DC: "Stipulate to the identity of my client."

C: "People?"

P: "Yes."

C: "Stipulation accepted. Defendant is so identified."

TO: "Yes, he—"

DC: "Objection, we've stipulated to identity."

C: "That's true. Objection sustained. Proceed People."

P: "Did you determine the defendant's speed?"

TO: "I did."

P: "And what was that?"

TO: "54 mph."

P: "Did the motorist make any admissions to you?"

TO: "Yes sir."

P: "And was this before, or after, you determined his speed?"

TO: "Afterwards."

P: "What did he say?"

TO: "I asked him if he knew how fast he was going. He said *approximately 45 mph*."

P: "Did this happen in Anytown County?"

TO: "Yes."

P: "No further questions."

Has the motorist's identity been adequately proven? Remember, some judges are far more nitpicky than others. On the issue of identity, it may not be enough for you to know who you issued a citation to, if that person is not so identified in court. On traffic cases, it's common for defense counsel to appear for their clients, so they do not have to take time away from work to appear. I routinely did that for my former clients.

In California, a lawyer can appear for their client on infractions and misdemeanors, without the court's permission. Let us assume that is true elsewhere. Even on California felony matters, once a defendant appears in court, and signs a written appearance waiver, their lawyer can appear for them, on any additional appearance. This is a tremendous convenience for defendants, regardless of the nature of their cases. It can also be a tactical advantage. Do not be lulled into a false sense of security.

CAVEAT: *Be certain the above type of stipulation identifies the defendant, as the operator of the vehicle you stopped, and was the person to whom you issued the citation.*

If you do not do this, you may fail to prove identity. If this occurs, your case will be dismissed. Why? Without the defendant physically present, in court, you will have no one to identify, and no way of proving identity, of the perpetrator, of the crime you are there to testify about, absent a stipulation to the defendant's identity.

Even if a prosecutor is present, do not assume he will demand such a stipulation be entered into, by defense counsel. Please keep in mind you will encounter prosecutors with many different amounts of experience and common sense. Never assume your prosecutor is totally dialed in. Prosecutors may not be aware of this issue either. Err on the side of caution. Assume to the contrary.

If you do not hear the magic words, ask your sidekick in the courtroom, if the court is going to require a comprehensive stipulation, as to the defendant's identity, if you do not know, in advance, whether the judge will require this. You are not asking for a stipulation of guilt. All you need, is an agreement the missing defendant, is the guy you cited, and the one you accuse of committing a traffic violation. Fair is fair.

However, if you are familiar with the judge, and know a simple stipulation, as set forth in our hypothetical, is sufficient, that's okay. If you do not know, include the extra verbiage. Otherwise, you may have wasted your time even issuing the citation.

A stipulation, as noted above, is a simple procedure in any courtroom. Frankly, the mechanics are the same no matter if you are in Traffic Court, Superior Court, or U.S. District Court. Below is an example of how you do this.

P: "Your Honor, does defense counsel stipulate to the identity of their client, including operation of the described vehicle, and being issued the citation by this officer?"

DC: "So stipulated."

C: "So ordered."

Back to corpus. Once again, be ready to present evidence of the corpus delicti of the crime, you are attempting to prove, in court, before you introduce evidence, of any admissions of wrongdoing, by the defendant. Should you not take the time to do so, expect the court to tell you, your efforts to offer the admission, are premature.

Be aware of some pitfalls you may stumble over, if defense counsel is doing their job. This includes:

Avoiding speed traps

Are speed traps an issue, in your state? If they are, take the time to learn the relevant sections of your state's traffic laws. Although there is no way you will probably have the time to read every section, take the time to learn what sections you must know.

For example, as Sgt. Devinny notes, in Chapter 7, if you gather evidence of a motorist's speed, in violation of California speed trap laws, any evidence so acquired is inadmissible. Doing this means you have wasted your time.

In particular, be sure you have properly tested your radar unit, if this is how you determined a motorist's speed. Most motors I know do it, before and after, each shift. Is it factory calibrated? Is an ETS required? If so, be sure it's available, is current, and justifies the applicable posted limit. Also, be mindful of any other requirements, such as your need to: operate a distinctively marked police vehicle, wear a distinctive uniform, and display your name plate and badge.

Be sure your unit's speedometer is properly calibrated

Unless you are a certified mechanic, and are qualified to calibrate your patrol vehicle's speedometer, do not waste your time trying to calibrate it. And if you are not the person who did the calibration, do not waste your time trying to tell the judge it was properly calibrated, unless your state permits less formality, than my state.

This is true whether or not, it was properly calibrated. If everyone in the courtroom is doing their job it may be necessary for the calibrator to come to court to testify, they are qualified to do the calibration, and can tell the court they properly calibrated it. Err on the side of caution. Know your state's laws.

Identity of the defendant

Prove identity of the defendant, in a courtroom, one of three ways:

1. in-court testimony, you have personal knowledge the defendant committed the offense

2. the court accepts a stipulation, identifying the defendant, as the driver of the vehicle, to whom you issued the citation

3. the court accepts an admission, by the defendant, that he was the driver of the vehicle, to whom you issued the citation

Establish the corpus, prior to introducing evidence of any admissions

Remember, establish the corpus of the crime, before you attempt to introduce any admissions, of wrongdoing, by the defendant. If your traffic court does not routinely require such formality, that's icing on the cake for you. However, the fact your court is informal today does not mean a defense attorney cannot persuade the judge tomorrow the law requires what I am suggesting herein. It's better to be cautious.

Even if you do not routinely have to do so, be prepared to do so. If this is required by your traffic court, once you do, are you free to make such introductions? Just remember to do so, by establishing the corpus, element-by-element. If you take it slowly, and methodically, you should have no problem proving your case.

Chapter 14
Trial Preparation

Trials do not just happen. You must prepare for them. As we previously discussed, you make a T-stop because you observe a motorist violating some provision of your state's traffic laws. This does not mean the sole outcome is going to be a traffic citation. That may just be the beginning.

Your primary focus as a traffic officer is to prevent traffic collisions, right? Improve motoring safety? The end result of any T-stop is not something you can accurately predict, ahead of time. It may mean enforcement action will cause a motorist to sign the citation, you have written, for whatever infraction committed.

The motorist may pay the fine, demand a trial, or resolve it some other way. Or, you may issue a misdemeanor citation to appear in court. Since this carries a possible jail sentence, the motorist is guaranteed a lawyer. You may place the motorist under arrest, handcuff, and book them, instead of issuing a citation. A seemingly indistinguishable traffic stop may even lead, to the discovery of evidence, that results in a felony arrest.

Prior to a traffic stop, it's unlikely you know what the end result will be, unless you know one of the vehicle's occupants has an outstanding arrest warrant, or you learn the vehicle is stolen.

Assume you make a traffic stop. Assume further, as soon as you make initial contact, with a motorist, you immediately smell the odor of an alcoholic beverage, about their breath and person.

This fact, standing alone, still does not tell you what the end result will be. In other words, pending completion of an investigation, this objective symptom may, or may not, place the motorist in the backseat of a police car. But let's assume it does. In this day and age it still does not tell you what the final chapter is going to be.

What do I mean by this? Let's take a moment and analyze this. Let's use §18.2-266, from the Code of Virginia as our example, prohibiting driving motor vehicle, engine, etc., while intoxicated, etc. It reads verbatim:

"It shall be unlawful for any person to drive or operate any motor vehicle, engine or train (i) while such person has a blood alcohol concentration of 0.08 percent or more by weight by volume or 0.08 grams or more per 210 liters of breath as indicated by a chemical test administered as provided in this article, (ii) while such person is under the influence of alcohol, (iii) while such person is under the influence of any narcotic drug or any other self-administered intoxicant or drug of whatsoever nature, or any combination of such drugs, to a degree which impairs his ability to drive or operate any motor vehicle, engine or train safely, (iv) while such person is under the combined influence of alcohol and any drug or drugs to a degree which impairs his ability to drive or operate any motor vehicle, engine or train safely, or (v) while such person has a blood concentration of any of the following substances at a level that is equal to or greater than: (a) 0.02 milligrams of cocaine per liter of blood, (b) 0.1 milligrams of methamphetamine per liter of blood, (c) 0.01 milligrams of phencyclidine per liter of blood, or (d) 0.1 milligrams of 3,4-methylenedioxymethamphetamine per liter of blood. A charge alleging a violation of this section shall support a conviction under clauses (i), (ii), (iii), (iv), or (v).

For the purposes of this article, the term 'motor vehicle' includes mopeds, while operated on the public highways of this Commonwealth."

Let's plug in a few more facts. After you smell the odor of an intoxicating beverage, about the driver, you ask a few preliminary questions. *Berkemer* allows you to ask all of this, without having to Mirandize the suspect, assuming you do so, before placing the suspect under arrest. Therefore, you need to ask these questions as close to the beginning of the contact as possible. I would do a driving under the influence investigation, in this order:

1. observe driving that creates reasonable suspicion to detain
2. make traffic stop
3. contact motorist, and observe symptoms that create reasonable belief he is under the influence
4. request them to produce driver's license and vehicle registration
5. ask drinking history questions
6. conduct field sobriety tests
7. arrest and admonish re: choice of chemical test
8. Mirandize
9. transport to jail

10. re-ask drinking history questions (*to obtain prior inconsistent answers*)

The following are what I call *drinking history* questions; they include:

a. Have you consumed any alcoholic beverages? *(if yes)*

(1) When did you start?

(2) When did you stop?

(3) How many drinks did you consume?

(4) What were they? *(Beer, wine, hard liquor, etc.?)*

(5) Where did you do this?

(6) Did you do this alone or with others?

(a) Who, where, when, etc.?

b. Have you ingested any drugs? *(if yes)*

(1) What kind?

(2) What, where, when, how much, etc.?

(3) Did you do this alone or with others *(if so, who, where, when, etc.)*?

c. Has the consumption of alcohol affected your ability to safely operate a motor vehicle?

d Is anything mechanically wrong with your vehicle?

e. Are you sick or injured? *(if yes, please describe)*

f. Have you bumped your head?

g. When was the last time you had anything to eat?

h. When was the last time you slept?

Now, assume you have asked all these drinking history questions. Does it mean you know the end result yet? Of course not. Why? Because, at this point, all you know is what your percipient senses have told you. Your knowledge of the subject, at this point, is based on what you have observed.

In fact, pending receipt of the answers to your above-noted questions, you do not even know, yet, if you are going to ask the driver to step out of the vehicle. If the driver is not even out of the vehicle, this means you still do not know two additional facts:

1. Will the motorist be required to perform field sobriety tests? (FST; *also called field coordination tests, or FCT, in some jurisdictions)*

2. If you administer it, how will the subject perform?

But assuming you administer FST, what does this tell you, other than whether the suspect is going to jail? Frankly, not much. Among other question marks, you still do not know, if the blood alcohol level (BAL) is above the legal limit, set by your state, or whether the subject will provide a sample. Depending on the BAL, a higher level may increase the ultimate fine amount, or possible time in custody. This still does not complete the jigsaw picture puzzle you are trying to assemble.

This is because you have not had the opportunity yet, to run this person's criminal history, to determine if they have prior convictions. You should run their history, if you arrest them. You will run both their driving record and criminal identification and information index (CII). If your state is set up legislatively, like California, prior driving under the influence (DUI) convictions can be the difference between a misdemeanor and a felony. Back then, CA lawmakers still cared about public safety.

We still are not where we need to be. Not just yet. Let's assume you run the person's driving record. In California, we call this *running their DMV*. It does not matter what it's called in your state. The purpose is still the same.

Assume you determine the driver has enough prior DUI convictions within the correct window of time to qualify them for felony prosecution, if they are over the legal limit. Does this give you all the answers you need in order to properly prepare for a possible trial? *Sorry, but the answer is still no*. This is because you have not yet run the driver's CII. Assume you run it. Now, further assume, you discover they have two or more serious or violent felony convictions, such as robbery or residential burglary.

If you think this is not something you will ever have to deal with, as a traffic cop, think again. Many of the felony dope cases I dealt with, as a prosecutor, that CHP sent us, began life as simple infraction traffic stops. You will not know what you have, when you activate your emergency lights. What is the significance of this discovery?

If your state has a Three Strikes law, like my state once had, it creates a whole new scenario. When Three Strikes became law it meant anyone convicted of two or more serious felonies, two or more violent felonies, or one or more of each, qualified for prosecution as a Three Striker.

Note: In November 2012, California voters amended Three Strikes. Any third felony must now be either a Penal Code §1192.7 *serious* felony or a *§667.5 violent* felony, as opposed to any felony which the original law permitted. Nonetheless, I suggest you err on the side of caution, and still assume a motorist has committed such an offense.

This ups the odds considerably for the defendant and increases the significance for you too. A serious felony is defined in California Penal Code §1192.7. Examples are residential burglary or second degree robbery. A violent felony is defined in California Penal Code §667.5. Examples include first degree robbery, rape, arson, or murder.

Two prior Strike convictions cause a significant increase in potential penalties. Such cases carry life sentences. Two such prior convictions increase possible sentences to 25 years-to-life for each new felony a defendant faces. Such sentences are imposed consecutive to one another.

The Three Strikes law potentially takes a simple traffic stop, with a motorist committing a simple traffic infraction, in your presence, and instantly elevates it to a serious felony prosecution. The sentence can be potentially longer than one for murder.

Please understand how dramatic this can be. Back in the late '90s, I prosecuted a Three Striker who was arrested for possessing 2.89 grams of cocaine base for sale, possession of a stolen cellular phone, possession of a stolen handgun and because he was a convicted felon in possession of the same firearm.

His sentence was 75 years to life. Yes, he was convicted. And he will not be eligible for parole for at least 60 years from his sentencing. Without Three Strikes, his maximum sentence would have been seven years in prison, with eligibility for parole at the three and one-half year mark, less credit for time served in county jail, while awaiting prosecution and sentencing. In essence, Three Strikes takes a sandlot game of softball, and instantly elevates it to World Series status, with you facing the Yankees.

So be sure you never assume a traffic stop will simply conclude, with a motorist signing a citation, then driving away, especially if you work in a Three Strikes state like mine. You need to prepare for the unexpected. The detention, search, and arrest resulting in the above-noted Three Strikes case, that earned me Prosecutor of the Year, came from the grateful police department that made the arrest, started out as a traffic stop. Sure, it was a *felony* traffic stop. But it nonetheless began life as a T-stop.

So prepare for the unexpected. This may include you drafting a declaration, requesting either, or both of the following, if authorized by your state's lawmakers:

1. increase the bail amount for the arrestee
2. always request a significantly increased bail amount, if you reasonably believe either of the following exist:
    a. an increased public safety risk
    b. an increased risk of flight

The unique facts surrounding each case will dictate what you should do. Also, be prepared to draft a request for the judge to order a bail hold, if your state's laws authorize this. The purpose of this statutory public safety tool? Prevent a suspect from posting bail, if the likelihood exists any bail money may come from criminal enterprise. A hearing is held to determine if this is true.

Examples include drug dealers, burglars, robbers, car thieves, and identity thieves. However, do not let these all too brief examples limit your thinking. In deciding, if a bail hold is applicable, ask yourself if the suspect appears to make their living from criminal enterprise? If your answer is *yes*, then request a bail hold.

The burden of proof is not beyond a reasonable doubt. After all, this is only a bail hearing. And remember, the worst the judge can ever tell you is *no*. Like the good book says, *ask, and you shall receive*. While you may not prevail, every time, you never will, unless you ask. Expect the unexpected. Never presume.

A Three Strikes case means defense counsel is going to pull all the stops. They will zealously and vigorously represent their client, if they are doing their job. They will file every motion they can conceivably file. They will contest everything you do. Everything you touch will be subjected to intense scrutiny. Maybe it's not a bad idea to treat every traffic stop you make as a potential Three Strikes case.

I realize I use this expression a lot, vis-à-vis, *erring on the side of caution*. But, I do so, to drive the point home, why it is so important to be prepared. It's far better to plan on going to war, and not having to do that, than to not plan and end up getting your fanny handed to you, by the defense, in front of an appraising judge and jury.

Are you familiar with the expressions, *proactive* vs. *reactive* law enforcement? Proactive policing permits you to do some creative police work. It means you are out and about, looking for lawbreakers. Reactive, on the other hand, means you play the hand, you are dealt. The above Three Strikes case is an excellent example of proactive policing. This does not mean a parolee will not fall into your lap, as a Three Striker, when you are being reactive. Nonetheless, if that happens, you must know how to deal with it.

A simple traffic stop could go all the way to the U.S. Supreme Court. Such a trip could place your name, in the appellate books, forever. If you mess up, 300 million Americans could be watching. The end result could label you a hero, or a zero. Please be sure you carefully cross every T and diligently dot every I.

While the process of establishing the elements of the offense will be the same, irrespective of what the offense is, in most jurisdictions there should be a couple of additional critical differences between simple infractions vs. misdemeanors, and felonies.

As previously noted, one difference, is the likelihood a court-appointed attorney will represent the guy you arrested. The other variance, is the right to a jury trial. That's because infractions only carry the penalty of a fine, but misdemeanors and felonies will also carry the added penalty of possible custody.

A misdemeanor conviction can carry the penalty, of up to one year in county jail. A felony can carry the penalty of prison. A capital murder can carry a death sentence. Such increases, in potential penalties, mean you should also expect additional hoops you will have to jump through, before the defendant is convicted.

Let's take a moment, and dissect this further. If your T-stop results in the issuance of a citation, the normal course will be a simple court trial. No jury will be present. Unless the motorist has the money, or other motivation, to hire private counsel, chances are high, it will be just you and the defendant in court, with informal application of the rules of evidence by the court. Each of you will get to say what happened. You will have the first opportunity to testify, in a narrative fashion. You have the burden of proving guilt.

You may have some preliminary issues to deal with, particularly if the defendant is one of those folks who have read one or more of the traffic ticket defense books, floating around out there, usually written by former traffic cops.

Some may actually provide them with meaningful information. That will cause you to have to think. Others may contain drivel. That will merely annoy the judge and you. You may even have to deal with a motorist who has consulted with a lawyer, prior to coming to court. And yet again, other motorists may have engaged in no pretrial preparation whatsoever, thus relying on pure emotions.

Quite obviously, you will not know which category any motorist will fall into, before court. Even the super emotional guy you issued the citation to, may be well versed in court. You may not even be able to tell, once he shows up, and starts speaking. Assume any defendant has come prepared to do battle, even without benefit of courtroom counsel. Always expect your opponent to give you a worthy fight, and be pleasantly disappointed, to the contrary, not vice-versa. You can never be too ready for court.

I can tell you, from lots of battlefield time, this is a truism. No matter how many times I have tap-danced, in front of a jury box, I have yet to try a case where I have not privately complained to myself afterward, win or lose, that I forgot to do something, or should have done something differently. Expect no less from yourself. If you do not, you may well regret the decision.

Let's begin the process of preparation, by dealing with the first scenario, as an infraction trial. Rather than expecting the defendant to show up *In Propria Persona*, also known as *in pro per*, i.e., representing themselves, prepare as if the motorist will come to court, with competent and experienced counsel representing them.

Do not assume a simple little speeding ticket will not warrant a lawyer for the defendant. Remember my client, with the fast BMW, we discussed earlier? He drove a lot. And he drove too fast. He got lots of speeding tickets. I got paid to defend him. He paid well, and paid me often. And I went to court. This saddened lots of traffic cops. The sadder they got, the happier I was.

Necessity is the mother of invention. Such necessity commenced the forging of our professional relationship, which lasted for a number of productive years. It was productive for a couple of reasons. First, it allowed my client to continue racking up speeding tickets, with impunity. He was able to avoid convictions that, otherwise, would have been virtual certainties, eventually taking away his privilege to operate a motor vehicle, and, impacting his ability to earn a living.

From my side of the coin, it provided my growing law practice significant cash flow it would not have otherwise had. And, it gave me needed courtroom experience. Whenever he received yet another speeding ticket, he would immediately contact me. I would review the citation, and begin preparing for court. I smiled a lot in those days. And, I smile a lot anyhow.

For one of his many citations, he actually had his pilot fly me to Oakland, for trial. He also had his driver pick me up at the airport, drive me to court, and then drive me back to the airport afterward. Yes, the defense prevailed.

This time? The officer failed to appear. The reason for acquittal on that case is irrelevant, other than to demonstrate less than adequate officer preparation. If you cannot make the court appearance, do not issue the citation. Your reputation is on the line. Should you develop repute for not showing up for court, expect repercussions. Yes, I realize there will be times when you have a legitimate reason to not appear. Just do not make this a habit.

At the minimum, expect the judge to snitch you off to the brass in your agency if this happens more than once. Your failure to appear in court could result in some sort of disciplinary action. That could even cost you pay. Therefore, if something happens that will prevent you from making the court appearance, immediately contact the court clerk to inform the court. Let your supervisor know too. With e-mail, frankly, you can do this conveniently.

If you do not already have it, obtain the courtroom clerk's direct phone number at his desk. Keep that number with you. Put it in your cellular phone's address book. Do not bother calling unless you have the defendant's name and the citation number with you before you place the call. Although there is no guarantee this will happen, ask the clerk if the trial can be reset for a later date. Explain what the scheduling conflict is that prevents your appearance.

In California, for example, unless a defendant waives time, they have an absolute right to the trial of their infraction, within 45 days, from the date of their citation. Verify if your own state has the same timeframe, or a different one.

I realize circumstances will arise, you cannot anticipate, which will occasionally prevent you from fulfilling duties you otherwise have every intention of meeting. But bend over backward to make court appearances. Find a way to put whatever is in the way, on the back burner, unless it's something so significant it simply cannot be avoided.

If the case gets dismissed, it means an offending motorist beats the rap. The motorist avoids any negative consequences. They will not be held accountable for his misbehavior. This may well empower them to misbehave further.

Let's return to my former client, for a moment. Most of his driving was on California freeways. Therefore, most of his citations were issued by the California Highway Patrol. Frankly, I was shocked to learn how woefully unprepared so many CHP officers were back then. At the time, their title was State Traffic Officer.

This was especially true, when it came to understanding our state's Evidence Code. And in particular, a real glaring weakness was failing to grasp the essentials of *foundational* knowledge, such as calibration of devices, to measure speed. That was back when California's legislature did not see the need to permit CHP the luxury of using radar, to make speed law enforcement meaningful. In order to avoid the mistakes I routinely uncovered, let's discuss them.

My purpose in sharing this is not to embarrass the CHP. I have dealt with this excellent agency for a long time, and have the utmost respect for the organization, and its many dedicated officers. Some of whom, I have been on ride-alongs with. Many are still my friends. I am not trying to embarrass, but to educate. And, I hear many CHP traffic cases.

If you are going to testify, know in advance what you intend to say. Should you intend to testify, about a motorist's speed, be sure you can do that competently. If the citation you issued, was based on the use of radar, are you qualified to use that particular device? Did you test it yourself? Were you properly qualified to do that? If you are not, do not even waste your time issuing the citation. I am not aware of a single state that does not require every radar operator to successfully complete rigorous radar certification, before they are even so assigned.

What if the speed citation is based on a bumper pace, which will rely on the use of your vehicle's speedometer? The likelihood is slim, indeed, that you calibrated the speedometer. Chances are high the mechanic, your agency uses, is the guy who did the calibration. Can you testify, as to what that person did? In short, no, if the judge is following the law, regarding hearsay, unless your state allows you to take a shortcut, and present a speedometer calibration certification card as proof.

This is where many CHP officers goofed, concerning my BMW client. As we discussed a bit ago, this was back when CHP could not use radar, to enforce speed laws. This meant offending speed was determined by bumper-pacing, and observing a patrol unit's speedometer.

In case you are not aware of this, in California, measuring elapsed time, between two fixed points, to determine speed, is called *speed trap* evidence. Any evidence so gathered is *inadmissible*. This means you cannot use it. It has zero evidentiary value. Do not waste your time doing so. It may earn you a well-deserved lecture from the judge.

Interestingly, however, if you are a CHP officer who flies a fixed wing aircraft, for traffic law enforcement purposes, you are not capable of bumper-pacing a motorist, on the ground, because you are in the air. Therefore, despite contentions to the contrary, you are forced to rely on evidence, no doubt, labeled inadmissible speed trap evidence, if it were so gathered, by an officer operating a ground unit. The pilot measures speed between two fixed points.

Just as I correctly predicted an appellate case would one day limit the minimum elevation, in which air units could fly over crime scenes, such as suspected marijuana grows, to establish probable cause, to support the issuance of search warrants, I am making the same prediction about the use of aircraft to enforce posted speed laws. So if you are a traffic officer who sees potential violators, from this particular vantage point, expect one day to be successfully challenged, by an enterprising defense attorney. This, I predict.

Now, let's get back to speedometers. If you are not qualified to calibrate speedometers, you cannot perform the calibration. But what if you were present, when the calibration was done?

Are you qualified to say, under oath, the calibration was done properly? Are you a certified auto mechanic? If not, you will probably lack foundation. What if you were not present for the calibration, but the mechanic tells you he did the calibration? What that person tells you is called *hearsay*. Why? It's an out-of-court statement, by the mechanic, offered to prove the truth of the matter asserted, i.e., that he did the calibration properly, and was qualified to do so. Hearsay upon hearsay still equals inadmissible. It also lacks foundation.

Does this mean the acquisition of speedometer-based evidence, of a motorist's speed, is worthless? Not at all. If you face the same issues, I was able to exploit, with CHP speedometer-based citations, you simply have to do what your state's Evidence Code requires. There are a couple of ways you can solve this potential problem. If you do it right, you can probably do so, with the introduction of documents. It also means you have to first ascertain adequate preparation has been done.

Remember the earlier discussion we had, about ETS issues? Radar-based evidence of speed may be inadmissible, if written proof is not first presented, a timely ETS has been done, justifying the posted speed limit. This poses no problem, if the court accepts a certified copy of the document, as a public record, which requires no authentication.

Even if the document is technically hearsay, because it is an out-of-court statement, being offered, to prove the truth of the matter asserted, such a document is a recognized exception to the hearsay rule, and the evidence is therefore deemed admissible.

The same type of methodology can be used, with speedometer calibration. At some point, you may need to obtain a court determination the document you offer, in support of your contention, the speedometer was properly calibrated, is a business record exception, to the hearsay rule. Unlike a public record, however, the custodian of records would need to authenticate it, by testifying what it is, and why.

However, do not try this on your own. This is a job for an experienced trial lawyer, from your county or state prosecuting attorney's office. Once this has been done successfully, that should seal this issue, once and for all, in your jurisdiction if the document qualifies as a business record, adequately establishing the mechanic in question, is qualified to do the calibration, and the calibration was done properly.

If you obtain a written declaration, under penalty of perjury, from the mechanic, setting forth their qualifications, to calibrate speedometers, and they did so, on a given date, you may be able to offer such proof, as a business record, providing you qualify, as the custodian of records of that document.

This almost certainly means your department would need to designate each traffic officer, as the custodian of records, for such a document, for their assigned patrol vehicle. With proper training, each traffic officer should qualify, as the custodian of such a record, by showing all designated officers maintain the record the mechanic gives them, it was received, when the calibration was done, and all designated officers have maintained care, custody, and control of it, since they received it.

It should be an easy task for your department's lawyer, working in conjunction with the prosecutor, to prepare such a form declaration. The mechanic simply adds information such as their name, title, and the date and location of each calibration. Once this is done, and the court accepts it as valid evidence, it should simply become a standard part of your courtroom landscape.

Chapter 15
Courthouse Etiquette

Courthouse etiquette, involves two aspects: dress and demeanor. This will not vary, irrespective of whether the court appearance is for an infraction, a misdemeanor, or a felony.

Let's address these facets one-by-one. Dress involves the application of basic, good old-fashioned common sense. As a peace officer, you have two basic methods of dress for the courtroom. One is your uniform. The other is civilian clothes. I am not going to even try to tell you when you can and cannot wear your uniform. That is between you and your agency.

However, having said that, if wearing your uniform is authorized, my preference is you wear it. Assuming you are permitted to wear your uniform to court, you also need to consider whether it is appropriate. If you are working some special duty assignment, such as narcotics or gang investigation, wearing it is probably not doable. I'm old school. Uniform? Facial hair? Mustache.

Working the latter, you almost certainly do not present yourself in this role, the way you left the academy. In all likelihood, you now have visible facial hair, previously shaved close to the skin. You probably have long hair, or a shaved head, and may wear jewelry such as earrings. All this is part of the costume you wear as a dope cop or a gang cop. Such things just do not fit with your uniform. In other words, you look like a respectable dope cop.

You may be asking yourself why you would have long hair, and such other accoutrements, as a traffic officer. You would not. Keep in mind things happen. This may continue a case, far beyond the parameters of your actual length of duty, for a given assignment. Therefore, although you may have looked all spit and polish, when you issued a traffic citation you may not be appropriately coifed, to be in uniform, when it finally goes to court.

If I am describing your situation correctly, before your case goes to court, be sure you discuss this, with the prosecutor. Ask them to explain to any prospective jury, why you look the way you do, should the court appearance involve a misdemeanor or felony; in other words, a jury trial. An infraction should not present similar logistical issues. The judge understands professional rotation, just as you do.

My concern? Such an appearance, in a courtroom full of jurors, might otherwise have a negative impact on members of that venire. It only takes a few minutes, to deal with this properly. Doing so should remove any possible concerns a prospective juror might otherwise wonder why you look the way you now do. I had a defense attorney make a big deal out of a sockless dope cop.

I have also viewed that sort of reaction, when my wife used dope cops to help her present identity theft seminars, to that segment of the public she dealt with, as a legislative Field Rep. The initial negative reaction to such an appearance changed instantly, when she explained who the person was, and, more importantly, why he looked the way he did. It was like day and night.

Whether you are a male or a female, if you are not wearing a uniform to court, dress the way you normally would dress to attend religious services, or for a job interview. For either gender, a conservative suit always works. Men, be sure to add a tie. For women, a conservative dress, skirt, and blouse, or pants and blouse, will work fine. For women, I would skip the tie. Both genders, avoid excessive jewelry. Do not wear excessive amounts of aftershave, cologne, or perfume. Most people do not like inhaling someone's artificial smells, while trying to work at counsel table. Neither sex wants to come off appearing to play a professional role in the skin trades, either.

Women, please do not wear too much makeup. Remember, part of your job in the courtroom will be to assist the prosecutor, in convincing some potentially conservative jurors, *like me*, that your side of the case deserves to win.

Men, for goodness sake, please wear socks. The *Miami Vice* look has been dead for decades. For either gender, if you are all tatted up, be sure to not come off looking like a parolee. Cover up all your body art.

Proving a case is not done, solely with words. Actions truly can speak louder than words. If you do anything to irk even one single juror you may lose, whether it otherwise has nothing to do with the quality of your work.

Visualize how you will feel, if you technically do your job properly outside the courtroom to meet your burden of proof, only to lose the case, because a juror does not agree with something you subjectively did in court.

I'm not speaking in merely hypothetical terms here. Jurors will occasionally get burrs under their saddles, causing them to refuse to do their job properly. You do not need to give them any extra reasons to mess your case up.

Akin to California Evidence Code §780, expect your state to set out the parameters for the trier of fact to evaluate witnesses. This is not limited to defendants. It also includes you, the police officer. Let's take a look at §780.

"Except as otherwise provided by statute, the court or jury may consider in determining the credibility of a witness any matter that has any tendency in reason to prove or disprove the truthfulness of his testimony at the hearing, including but not limited to any of the following:

(a) His demeanor while testifying and the manner in which he testifies.

(b) The character of his testimony.

(c) The extent of his capacity to perceive, to recollect, or to communicate any matter about which he testifies.

(d) The extent of his opportunity to perceive any matter about which he testifies.

(e) His character for honesty or veracity or their opposites.

(f) The existence or nonexistence of a bias, interest, or other motive.

(g) A statement previously made by him that is consistent with his testimony at the hearing.

(h) A statement made by him that is inconsistent with any part of his testimony at the hearing.

(i) The existence or nonexistence of any fact testified to by him.

(j) His attitude toward the action in which he testifies or toward the giving of testimony.

(k) His admission of untruthfulness."

I believe §780 to be self-explanatory. Now let me give you a real life example of how easy it is for defense counsel to point a jury in the wrong direction. I should know. I have done that myself. I had to do so. It was my job.

Early in my career, I was appointed by the court to represent one of three young African-American males, charged with robbing a local convenience store. The victim, an on-duty clerk, testified through a Spanish-English interpreter.

In response to a question I posed, the clerk described the ethnicity of the suspects as *colored*, rather than *black*, the preferred ethnically-descriptive word, at the time. For some reason, the prosecutor did not catch this. Nor, did he attempt to do anything about it. I would have requested a recess and fixed it.

Actually, what the clerk said was *de color*, which translates to *of color*, not *colored*, but my job was not to educate the prosecutor. Why the interpreter decided to say colored, rather than of color, I will never know. I did not ask and did not care. Still don't. Wasn't my job. Ironically, the same expression is perfectly acceptable today; regularly used by persons of various ethnicities, when describing people who are not Caucasian. Not back then, however. Saying colored was clearly inappropriate, just as it is today, even though it previously was acceptable. A defense counsel prays for such opportunities. But, I digress.

In closing argument, I successfully used the tactic of arguing my case to the sole black juror, a curmudgeonly man, in his late '50s. My closing argument focused, not on the facts of the case, but by my pointing out the faux pas of the witness, and by uttering these tired old words: *how insulting...the only thing that witness didn't say was 'how should I know...they all look alike to me.'*

After three days of deliberation, a crestfallen foreman announced the jury was hopelessly deadlocked. The sole holdout for a not guilty verdict? You're correct. That very juror. Did his vote for acquittal have anything to do with the case's underlying facts? No.

His reason? According to the DA, he said: "I was slapped in the face by a white man at the age of ten and have never forgotten it." Interestingly, the prosecutor's case agent was an African-American veteran peace officer who, once again, had placed himself in harm's way to protect the lives and property of strangers, just as he'd done for many years. But, apparently, this did not resonate with that particular juror.

That officer's ethnicity and presence in the courtroom did nothing to calm the irrational anger of that particular juror. Yes, I agree, this is a bizarre reason to choose to acquit a defendant. The defendants were arrested by the police, approximately two blocks from the crime scene, just moments after the robbery. It was one of those *luck-out* arrests that do not happen very often. The crooks almost literally fell right into their laps.

The cops were in the right place, at the right time, and did their job the way they were supposed to do it. The jury should have promptly returned guilty verdicts against all three defendants. All three young men should have gone to prison. It was the sort of case any insider would call a *slam dunk.*

However, due to the volume of cases awaiting trial, the prosecutor had no choice but to offer a deal, allowing these three young thugs to get probation. I have tried lots and lots of cases before juries. This is one of those rare ones a prosecutor would also certainly describe, as I described it in the paragraph above.

The prosecutor was an excellent trial lawyer who later became an excellent trial court judge. Both defense and prosecution viewed him as such. He was acknowledged, far and wide, as a Fourth Amendment expert. I still respect him a lot. I always will.

There is no logical reason this jury should not have convicted all defendants. Justice was not dispensed in this case. Let this be a lesson to you. Do not ever tick off a juror. Rationality may play no role. This is a true story, not some hypothetical example. I still recall it vividly.

Do not labor, under the impression, courthouse etiquette applies only to the courtroom. I did not mistype when I used the word *courthouse*, rather than *courtroom*. I did so for a very fundamental reason. Anything you say, can, and probably will, be used against you, in the courtroom, from the moment you leave your patrol vehicle to issue the citation. Do not assume any word or phrase is too small, for a defense attorney to not glom onto, in a never-ending quest to prevail, with justice being damned in the process. Zealous representation carries a heavy price tag.

Never assume any bar is ever too low for a defense lawyer to wriggle under. Remember, the prosecutor's job, akin to your own, is to seek justice. A defense attorney's job is to seek victory. As long as they do not suborn perjury, or intentionally mislead the court, anything else is fair game. But it's more basic than that. Not only is anything fair game, defense attorneys are ethically expected to do just that. I know. That doesn't make sense. Complain to the American Bar Association. They write such ivory tower rules, not me.

Okay, it's time for another real life example of what not to do. This will take us back to days of yore, when many public defenders still wore corduroy coats to court, and just about any cop could be picked out of a crowd by the cheap, shiny polyester suit he wore.

Remember our earlier discussion, about my representation of the guy with the fast BMW? Well, he was not the only motorist who got speeding tickets, creating a need for me to be, in their life. Apparently, word of mouth advertising works.

In due course, I was also counsel to a number of long haul truckers who got citations for excessive speed. My standard practice was to appear, in court, without clients present, if they were not legally required to be there. Therefore, I always appeared in court, sans clients, on all infractions. Generally, their presence was a hindrance to me.

One such case took me to San Bernardino's main courthouse. As I strolled into the building, and approached the courtroom, I espied a man, sitting by himself, near the door. He was wearing a cheap-looking polyester suit. His hair was short, he was clean shaven and, well, he looked like a cop. Consistent with my informal manner, I jokingly replied to him *you look incognito out of uniform*, or words to that effect. The officer looked up at me, and responded *"you sure clean up nice in a suit too.*

My inference? He thought I was the trucker he had cited, wearing a dirty T-shirt and torn Levi's. I smiled, excused myself, and made a beeline to the courtroom, to find the DA, so I could share this close encounter, of the worst kind, for the officer. Moments later, the judge took the bench. One of the first cases called was my client's matter. I offered no objection to the prosecutor's motion to dismiss, based on his belief, reasonable doubt existed, as to my client's guilt. He simply accepted my representation. I would have been more skeptical.

The DA agreed the officer was not able to identify the person he had cited. Case dismissed. I promptly left, walking past the sitting officer to go to the parking lot. I was tempted to do so, without uttering as much as another word. I was not being rude. I did not need to say anything more. I had already done my job. I did not want to rub salt into his wounds. Telling him, he had just lost, was the prosecutor's job. Another example of an apparently overworked prosecutor.

Please understand something. The outcome of cases, often turns on simple issues like this. Do not expect the courtroom, which is really nothing more than an extension of your patrol beat, to mimic TV shows, like *Perry Mason* or *Law & Order*, pure fiction. That sort of drama is ordinarily not part of the landscape you will get used to seeing in court. In fact, let's take this situation a step further. Assume you have not been to court yet. When you first begin appearing in courtrooms, on the citations you issue, or the arrests you make, you probably will not know a soul.

You will not know any prosecutors, much less any defense attorneys. Nor will you be likely to know any judges, either. Conversely, none of them will likely know who you are yet. Because of the instant unfamiliarity, there will not be any guard for you to let down. However, you will reach a point where you will begin recognizing faces and names. Eventually, unless you are pathologically unsociable, you will get to know both prosecutors, and defense counsel. In some cases you will know them, on a first name basis. Many will also get to know you, with the same level of familiarity.

You will learn some defense counsel will view you, as the enemy, irrespective of how polite, how nice, and how professional you are. In some cases, that is just their nature as human beings. Real bunker mentalities. These folks do not take the time to talk with either cops, or prosecutors.

I suppose it is necessary for some of them to adopt this attitude, so they do not come off as appearing weak in front of their clients. With others, perhaps they were the victims of one too many punitive potty-training sessions? Or, maybe too many speeding tickets? Who knows?

But they are not the ones, of whom, you must be wary. Defense attorneys who seem hostile, probably are hostile, to law enforcement. These are the ones my favorite boss at the DA's office called true believers. It's them against the part of the world they do not like. One in Riverside, a long time ago, was notorious. As noted, they are not the ones you should watch out for. In fact, you can see them, and their attitude, coming, from a mile away. This group should leave you, with no illusion, they are ever to be trusted. It's not hostility either. It's something altogether different. They are ideologues.

The ones you need to be ever mindful of, are the ones, more garrulous, than they need to be. They are the glad-handers of the crowd. Do not be lulled into a false sense of security. Their ethical duty is to zealously represent their clients. Do not let their smile fool you, no matter how genuine it appears.

Their job is not to be your friend, even if they may act like they are. Rather, they seem to create this misperception. Just as, you never turn your back on a venomous reptile, be just as guarded with this variety of defense counsel. If you do not, it is quite likely you will say something, to one of them, in the hallway of a courthouse, that will come back to bite you, just as soon as you are on the witness stand. This is not hypothetical. It is raw fact.

This chapter is not meant to be a lesson in human psychology. First, I am not licensed to dispense such erudite advice. Even if I was, that is not the purpose of this particular chapter. I am not even suggesting all defense counsel, who seem overly friendly will ambush you, in the courtroom. I am merely trying to explain, your need to make sure, your own words, to a stranger will not attack you, when you are on the witness stand.

As you continue to get to know folks, you reach a point where you can make your own decisions, intelligently, and objectively, as to who you can trust, and who you cannot trust. The courtroom scene is no different.

The professional obligation of defense counsel is to walk out of each courtroom they enter a winner. If this means they make you appear to be a fool, or a liar, for them to get from point A to point B, their mission is accomplished. Be mindful of my tale about the unnecessarily deadlocked robbery jury. This happens. Sounds bizarre. But, it's ethical behavior. Mandated behavior.

To the extreme other side, let me acquaint you with a former low desert deputy public defender. He tried a lot of jury trials, as any aspiring new public sector lawyer does. For that I applaud him. But every case he tried, his MO was identical. That I will never applaud. His approach was fruitless, but nonetheless cheeky.

He had the chutzpah to tell nearly every jury his client was innocent, because all officers connected with that case, committed perjury. Didn't he realize hard-working cops take it personally, whenever some snotty-nosed defense lawyer calls them felons?

He was potentially destroying real people, with his zealotry. But his machinations found a happy ending. One Friday evening he foolishly decided to visit the local FOP, when he somehow learned his courtroom adversaries would be there, tipping a few brews. FOP, I'm told, is an acronym for drunken LEOs.

Despite his courtroom antics, he somehow naively assumed he was welcome there. He wasn't. But for, quick intervention, by a couple of big deputies, a grumpy and inebriated sergeant, approaching retirement, nearly throttled him. Soon thereafter, the lawyer got the message and left town.

Do not talk to strangers. I am not suggesting you act impolitely, or fail to respond to simple friendly greetings, from others. Good public relations are essential to the support you need, from the community you serve, if you are to do your job properly. In fact, that stranger you disrespect could very well be the juror you need, to convince in a future trial, your interpretation of the evidence is the correct one.

Do I sound as if I'm talking out of both sides of my mouth? I'm really not. Here's why. Conversing with others is fine, as long as you do not allow the conversation to get so personal, it allows the other person to gain an unfair, and otherwise unattainable, advantage over you, in the courtroom. Be polite. Even be genial. Just be circumspect.

Remember the example I previously shared, of the traffic officer who made the mistake of telling me, he thought, I was the trucker he cited? He shared something with me, in a courthouse hallway, he should have never shared. Innocent, but foolhardy. That could just as easily be you.

By doing what he did, he allowed me to realize reasonable doubt existed, even before I entered the courtroom. This caused a dismissal that probably would never have happened, otherwise. Had he not done that, I would have gone into court, and stipulated he cited my client for speeding. After all, my client was quite guilty, aside from his constitutional presumption of innocence.

Had he kept quiet, I would have walked into the courtroom, and stipulated the defendant was operating the vehicle. The officer would have testified, to his observations, which led to his issuance of the citation. I would have lodged my usual two objections, to wit: foundation and hearsay, and the court may, or may not, have found my client guilty.

Judges do not like to rule against traffic cops, on the underlying facts for a couple of reasons. First, the same cops have to appear in front of them, week after week after week. Judges or commissioners cannot afford to have traffic cops, bad-mouthing them, to their fellow officers, and to their departments. First, judges are political creatures. They do not want to risk, having your local POA back their challenger, in the next election.

Commissioners are selected by the judges of their jurisdiction. They, too, are political creatures. They need traffic cops stipulating they can hear traffic cases. This means they might otherwise be stuck hearing small claims, or family law matters instead of something interesting and fun, like traffic court.

Bad factual decisions, which acquit guilty motorists, may make this happen. The other reason traffic courts are not likely to acquit, based on factual disagreements, is to avoid opening the floodgates, where other motorists get the idea it is to their advantage to go to trial, rather than to accept traffic school, or plead guilty, to avoid trial. Do the math. Trials take far longer than guilty pleas or requests to go to traffic school. This is true, even with simple traffic trials.

I make a point of reminding traffic court defendants, in my courtroom, that CA appellate cases say traffic school is not a matter of right. Rather, it is up to the sound discretion of the trial court, to permit same. And, frankly, if a motorist is rude to the issuing officer, a snow ball has a much better chance of not melting in hell, than they have of getting into traffic school. Fair is fair.

The most salient reason to make sure the citations you issue, result in convictions, is to ensure offending motorists receive negative reinforcement, for violating the law. If the negative impact is not sufficient, they are not as likely to improve their driving. Paying a fine, and getting another point on their driving record, helps to emphasize that. Points also increase insurance premiums.

Are points the only reason particularly egregious drivers deserve citations? No. When a motorist commits a traffic violation, is it likely this is the only time they have done that? Of course not. Chances are, you caught them doing what they routinely do, i.e., violating the law. Flagrantly bad drivers generally have driven that way, for a long time.

Speeders, speed. Stop sign rollers, roll stop signs. Red light runners, run red lights. Tailgaters, tailgate. Illegal lane changers, change lanes illegally. You just happen to catch them doing what they so often do, the day you cite them. That cycle needs to be broken. If a motorist has to deal with a traffic stop, at a bare minimum, he is inconvenienced, by being temporarily detained.

If you issue citations, traffic offenders have to post bail. They can forfeit the bail, if they choose to not fight the ticket. This is costly, as they do not get their bail money back. It becomes a de facto guilty plea. Their bail becomes their fine. Even if they request traffic school or a trial, and their bail is returned, time is taken out of their busy lives.

Whether they choose to forfeit bail, or request a trial, they have to post bail money, to do either. Bail is returned, only if a case is dismissed. Should they opt for traffic school, they must incur two more costs: court costs and traffic school fees. Both are non-refundable. Traffic school may last a full day. So even if a case is dismissed, the offender has invested time and money.

Aside from the above-described inconveniences, let's take a moment, and discuss the point system. All of what we have just explored, deals with the inconvenience of lost time and money. Points, on the other hand, are a whole different situation. Each point is capable of raising a motorist's insurance rates. Assume one point is awarded to a motorist for each traffic collision, determined to be their fault, or for each traffic infraction of which they have been convicted. Points are also added, when a motorist pleads guilty or no contest, or is found guilty, by the court.

In California, a motorist is typically permitted no more than four (4) points in a consecutive twelve (12) month period, six (6) points in a consecutive twenty-four (24) month period, or eight (8) points in a consecutive thirty-six (36) month period, unless he is a commercial driver. Then, he is generally given more latitude.

Once those limits are reached, DMV deems the driver a *negligent operator*, pursuant to CVC §13800. When this happens, CVC §13801 kicks in, which reads, in pertinent part, the DMV "...may require the re-examination of the licensee, and shall give 10 days' written notice of the time and place thereof. If the licensee refuses or fails to submit to the re-examination, the department may peremptorily suspend the driving privilege of the person..."

Here's another example of what not to say. A friend was cited for exceeding the maximum speed limit. I agreed to represent her. When the LEO asked for her license, and registration, she cavalierly informed him *she* was a prosecutor. He merely reminded her to press hard, as she was signing a citation, with three copies. We've all heard of professional courtesy. But, we've also heard of humility and manners. Apparently, she missed that class.

I discovered the officer was someone I had previously dealt with, in traffic court. He had not learned anything from our previous encounter, so I made the same foundational objections, I made before. The court made the same rulings. I won. He grimaced again. I picked up my file from counsel table, and began walking out of the courtroom.

As I walked near her aisle seat, a deputy sheriff motioned to me. Since she was cute and I was single, I leaned toward her, curious if she was handing me her phone number. She whispered to me *"...I'm sure glad you weren't on my case..."*

Never do that! One of the worst things you can do, in any courtroom, is to display weakness. She did *exactly* that. Do not think for a blind second I would not take advantage of that, as defense counsel, on any of her cases. All's fair in love and war. If it does not need to be said, don't say it. Never lose, by saying too much. Be stoic. Even if you are scared, your mouth is dry, and your knees feel weak, always maintain a poker face. Give the enemy an unfair advantage? They will take advantage of you, every time. If you have nothing productive to say, do not speak. You will gain nothing, if you chose to violate this rule.

Chapter 16
Trial Strategy

This chapter deals with trial tactics. Before we delve into actual strategy, let's first make sure we are properly focused on trial procedure. Below is the chronological sequence of events you *might* expect to find in a traffic court trial.

1. Court calls case *(defendant's name and citation number)*
2. Both sides go to counsel table; officer closest to jury box.
3. Motion to exclude witnesses *(ask court if defense has any witnesses, other than defendant; if not, do not make motion)*
4. Opening Statements, if permitted; prosecution first *(*NOTE: *not usually done in traffic court)*
5. Prosecution testimony *(direct-examination)*
6. Defense cross-examination (NOTE: *not usually done in traffic court*)
7. Prosecution rests
8. Defense motions for dismissal *(*NOTE: *not usually done in traffic court)*
9. Defense testimony (*direct-examination*)
10. Prosecution cross-examination (NOTE: *not usually done in traffic court)*
11. Defense rests
12. Prosecution Closing Argument *(*NOTE*: not usually done in traffic court)*
13. Defense closing argument *(*NOTE: *not usually done in traffic court)*
14. Prosecution Final Argument *(*NOTE: *not usually done in traffic court)*
15. Court renders verdict
16. Any remaining defense motions are made now, including motion for new trial, etc. *(*NOTE: *not usually done in traffic court)*

17. Ruling by court on any defense motions.
18. Sentencing

Traffic court is generally far more abbreviated, than what I have described above. Generally, the court just calls the case. Defendant and officer proceed to counsel table. After taking the oath, they testify, usually at the top of the calendar. When the case is called, the officer says why they issued the citation. Defendant can say why they are not guilty. Court, thereafter, issues a verdict, after receipt of all evidence.

Counsel representing traffic court defendants may insist this format is followed, just as I did, when I was still extricating traffic scofflaws, from the agony, of yet another point, on their driving records. Trial strategy is a concept that will vary from case to case, dictated by relevant facts.

One big factor determining how you should proceed? Is a prosecutor assigned to traffic court? Personally, I believe a prosecutor should be, routinely assigned to traffic court, for a couple of reasons: (a) traffic cases deserve this, and, (b) the courtroom experience is helpful to newer prosecutors and cops.

The underlying facts will dictate what your preparation should entail. Therefore, no rigid blueprint is available to guide you. In an earlier chapter, we discussed the courtroom, as an extension of your patrol beat. Let's take that a step further. As a police officer, you get paid to think. The more experience you have under your belt, the better you become. Your ability to best control your beat, is tied to your ability, to fly by the seat of the pants. That's because you have to think on your feet.

I have learned, over and over again, from my many ride-alongs with officers, from all the agencies that sent us cases to prosecute, just how quickly police officers have to react. Observations easily overlooked by civilians, cannot be ignored by cops. That speaks volumes to experience gained by police officers. For example, suppose you see a vehicle, with two different license plates. This should tell you a felony is in progress. It's probably possession of a stolen vehicle. And, a felony vehicle stop is in the immediate offing.

Aside from such tense encounters that spring up with little or no warning, there are shopping lists, of other examples, of the many experiences you may deal with, on the same shift. Never assume you will handle only traffic matters, just because you are assigned to traffic enforcement.

What if communications reports a hostile encounter between adjoining neighbors, with no further information provided? As you arrive on scene, you have with no further facts. You must sort out what is relevant, by interviewing percipient witnesses. First, part of the decision making that takes place, is to determine if a crime has occurred. In other words, is this a civil dispute the parties may eventually resolve, by going to civil court, or entering mediation? Or has a crime actually occurred? Maybe, it's both. And if so, is it a felony, or a misdemeanor?

If it's the latter, since it did not occur in your presence, is the complaining party willing to make a citizen's arrest? Assuming the answer is yes, what's the next step? Will the victim do so? Once that threshold is crossed, will you simply issue the suspect a notice to appear in court? Or, will you take custody, and book the suspect into jail, pending release on bail, or their written promise to appear in court?

If an arrest is made, is a bail increase appropriate? If so, in what amount? Among other issues, this also means you must determine what the scheduled bail is, for such an offense. Does the subject have any outstanding warrants, which also must be addressed? And, is the nature of the suspect such, that a bail hold, or a no bail hold, should be placed?

In either of the latter situations, it will be necessary for you to complete a supporting declaration, and obtain a judge's authorization. This will probably also dictate a phone call to the on-call prosecutor, assigned to deal with such issues. This is not happening, in some sterile classroom exam. This is real life stuff. Perceived mistakes can result, in both you and your department becoming defendants, in a civil rights lawsuit, irrespective of whether you, or any other officers even did anything wrong. And aside from this, there are officer safety concerns.

Additionally, look at how overlapping police work can be. For example, I was on a ride-along, with a local PD, one Saturday. The officer, a traffic officer, normally rode motors, but obtained a traffic car specifically for my ride-along. We spent a good portion of that morning, parked alongside southbound Highway 111, running radar. As speeders coming into town would fly past us, we would instantly accelerate, from a dead stop, to a speed, which allowed us to overtake them, and make a traffic stop, and issue a citation, to each offender.

Upon doing so, we would return to our pre-designated spot, and await the next speeder. After doing this many times I was ready for new scenery. Frankly, I get bored easily. I'm a traffic court judge, not a traffic cop. The repetition had become thoroughly uninteresting.

Suddenly, dispatch directed us to investigate an illegally parked vehicle downtown. Not what I call terribly exciting police work. We had no sooner acknowledged the call, when things changed very quickly. Almost immediately, communications put out a *bolo* (aka *be on the lookout*) for a residential burglary, and a possible rape, just occurred. This quickly escalated. We soon spotted, thereafter pursued, and arrested the perpetrator, a parolee-at-large. So, as you probably already know, if you have any appreciable time, in the law enforcement saddle, a traffic assignment does not mean you should not be prepared to handle a potpourri of other possible violations of the law, including serious or violent felonies.

Going from garden variety speeders, to parking scofflaws, to dangerous felons, literally in a matter of moments, requires some quick mental adjustments. Assume the above-described felon was a Three Striker. Even more, fine-tuning, would have been required, including possible bail vs. no bail issues.

The same is true with the courtroom. Be prepared to shift gears, many times, during any court appearance. And, be prepared to do this, on a moment's notice. If you cannot do that, you will not prevail. While I would invite any prosecutor to try to match your ability on the street, you need to match them in the courtroom. Expect the unexpected. Surprises will happen, whether you anticipate them or not.

In my opinion, the safest way to prepare for traffic court, is based on the assumption no prosecutor will be assigned. You must be ready for any eventuality. One thing you need to be ever mindful of? The reliance any prosecutor will place, on the quality of your work, especially any work you have done, prior to coming to court. If you do your job, all the prosecutor can do, and has to do, is present the evidence you gathered, if they are doing their job.

If, for whatever reason, they fail to do their job, do not expect the trier of fact to agree with your interpretation of the evidence. But if you fail to gather adequate evidence, needed to prove guilt beyond a reasonable doubt, do not expect the prosecuting attorney to bail you out. Prosecutors are not magicians, nor miracle workers.

I repeatedly reminded my dope cops, I did little more than play the piano to accompany the lyrics they wrote to describe the bad guy's antics. The quality of their work, made me look like a rock star, in the courtroom. Had they not done their jobs, this would not have happened. Instead, I would have had no reason to even go to court. Traffic court is no different. If you do your job by properly issuing a citation, the end result should be a guilty verdict.

What are the primary issues, for which you need to prepare? These include:

1. Testimony
2. Documents
3. Photographs
4. Recordings
5. Diagrams
6. Physical evidence

Testimony

Before any witness testifies, an oath will first be administered. This is generally done by the courtroom clerk. However, I have occasionally seen the judge or commissioner administer the oath, even though I haven't done so myself. It does not matter, if this is done differently, in your jurisdiction. All witnesses, including police officers, must take an oath, before they can testify. Otherwise, such verbiage is not evidence.

You should never stop an arrestee from making a spontaneous statement. Conversely, your job is not to educate the opposition, with the exception of providing lawfully required discovery. By this, I mean, if a defendant, or any other defense witness attempts to tell the court their version of what happened, before they have been administered an oath, do not try to stop them. What they say will have zero evidentiary value. No oath? No testimony. It's as if, they never even spoke. In any event, control of the courtroom is the judge's job, not yours, unless you are invited to assist.

Documents

Documents are writings that cover any sort of topic imaginable. Some are ones you complete. Others are completed by other people. If you prepare them, you may do so, prior to going to court, in the courtroom, or commence completion, before court, and add additional information, in court. These papers may include diagrams of traffic collisions. It is common for the prosecution team to prepare basic layouts, such as street locations, in the prosecutor's office, and add details, in court, such as the locations of people, vehicles, and any fixed objects.

The most common way to do this, is by drawing the diagram, on a sheet of butcher paper, or cardboard. Another way is to draw a diagram, on the erasable whiteboard, found in most courtrooms today. For any case that may result in civil litigation, I suggest completing these, as hard copies, that can be marked as exhibits, and preserved.

We are quickly becoming a paperless society, in many ways. However, if I have to choose between butcher paper, and simply doing diagrams on erasable boards, with a grease pencil, I will always opt for the former. Here's why. Paper is more or less permanent. It is particularly more helpful, if the trial is before a jury, as it can go into the jury room, with the jurors, so they can study it adequately, during their deliberations. A jury cannot do that with a whiteboard or a blackboard, unless it isn't stationary.

Irrespective of which method you use, be mindful of issues, such as *authentication*, *best evidence rule*, and *hearsay*.

1. *Authentication* simply means you must prove who the author of a document is, including ones you personally create outside court. If you draft one, in open court, there should be no legitimate authentication issue. The judge or jury can watch you create it, right there in court. Your drafting it, in their presence, is the authentication.
2. The *Best Evidence Rule* requires the proponent of a document to produce the original, unless a valid evidentiary reason exists, as to why a copy is legally acceptable. Find out what your jurisdiction requires.
3. *Hearsay* is any out-of-court statement, being offered, to prove the truth of the matter asserted. However, because the hearsay rule has so many exceptions to it, this is best left to another time and place. If in doubt, ask a trusted prosecutor, in your jurisdiction, for direction. If prosecutors are leading interference for you, it is up to them to master the hearsay rule for you, not you for them.

We need to distinguish between documents requiring *authentication*, from those which are *self-authenticating*. Every day, run-of-the-mill documents must be authenticated. This is done, by providing foundational testimony, from a witness competent to testify to the document's authenticity. In other words, does he know what the document is? And if he does, how does he know this?

The witness is shown the document, and is asked, if they recognizes it. Has it has been under their care, custody, and control? If the answer is in the affirmative, then you next ask them to describe its mode of preparation. Once this is done, next ask the witness to describe the document. Upon doing this, it is authenticated.

Self-authenticating documents do not require any foundational testimony, prior to their introduction, into evidence. Examples of public records include:

1. Birth certificates
2. Death certificates
3. Other documents, from public entities

As an example of this sort of document, let's use an ETS. If your jurisdiction requires you to introduce an ETS, in traffic court, offer the original, or a certified copy. That should overcome any evidentiary concerns. On the other hand, if you simply offer a non-certified copy, then you may encounter some issues. For example, what if the defense challenges the legitimacy of some portion of the document, such as a signature or lack thereof?

If that happens, you may have to offer testimony, from the custodian of records, or other qualified witness, who can attest to the genuineness of that part of the document. In order to avoid these sorts of problems, before your first court appearance, take the time to learn what you need to do, to avoid such issues. Once you learn how to do this, there should not be any repeated concerns. Even if defense counsel raises such objections on any future cases, the court should overrule them.

Photographs

Photographs are documents, with pictures, instead of text. Generally, you will offer only an original in evidence. However, irrespective of whether you introduce an original photo, or a copy, plan to have a witness available, competent to provide the court any necessary foundational testimony.

Ideally, this should be the person who took the picture. However, someone who witnessed the taking of the picture, should be able to authenticate it. Avoid using someone's hearsay to do this. It's an out of court statement, being offered, to prove the truth of the matter asserted. One of the nice things about digital cameras is their ability to imprint times and dates on pictures, if the camera has been properly programmed. This is especially helpful, if the witness you plan to use, is someone, other than the photographer.

If the date and time on the photograph is consistent with dates and times, on any other document a witness created, the court will be able to compare them, and should be able to quickly determine, if adequate foundation has been laid.

Let's say you took a picture of acceleration marks, left by the vehicle driven by the offender you cited for exhibition of speed, or a speed contest. This will greatly assist your attempts to convince the court you have met your burden of proof. If your digital camera has captured acceleration marks left by the two vehicles, driven side-by-side, by the two motorists you cited, this should be particularly incriminating evidence. Log the memory card into evidence.

Recordings

There are two types of recordings to consider. One is audio. The other is video. Modernly, your recording device may have both features. Tape recorders are quickly being replaced by digital recorders. Be prepared to overcome the same issues, you must overcome with photographs, such as authentication, best evidence rule, and hearsay. You should have your own digital recorder, if your department has not purchased one for you. Before you open your wallet, see if any grant money is available through

Department of Homeland Security, NHTSA, or any other governmental agency.

Here's an experience, from one of my cases, involving a tape recording, when I was still Deputy-in-Charge of Indio Municipal Court. A rookie CHP officer brought me a case to review, following his arrest of a DUI suspect. He appeared troubled by something. At first blush, nothing in his report appeared remarkable. I completed reviewing it, so I could assign the case to one of my trial deputies for trial.

In the property portion of his report, I saw the phrase "One (1) cassette tape." I asked what this meant. There was no reference to any recording, in his narrative. Nor did it contain any transcript. He informed me the suspect offered him a $100 bribe, to drive her to her expensive country club home, rather than him taking her to jail. He captured this, with his pocket recorder. I asked why this was not in the narrative.

He shrugged. His FTO told him it had no evidentiary value, as this was a DUI investigation, not a corruption case. We listened to his cassette tape. We both heard the offered bribe. I explained, while this was a DUI, it was also a corruption case. His FTO needed a tune-up. He appeared confused. My input was at odds, with what his FTO said. I informed him I was amending the complaint to add an additional count of attempted bribery. I also ordered a copy of the recording for defense counsel, and directed this raw rookie to write a supplemental report, describing the inappropriate offer of money, and log the tape into evidence. In due course, the matter went to trial.

The trial prosecutor later informed me the jury, somehow, returned *not* guilty verdicts on both DUI counts, but found the defendant guilty of attempted bribery. The importance of using a recorder to gather possible evidence speaks for itself. Capture the moment, by recording what otherwise will not be seized. Had he not recorded the attempted bribe, a criminal would have gotten away with her crime. Let's just observe his FTO and I had words, and let it go at that. Now, she was convicted of a moral turpitude offense. I don't mean to disparage FTO's. But, this sort of tutelage is sorely lacking.

Diagrams

Akin to photographs, you will normally offer only originals, of diagrams, into evidence. Customarily, diagrams will be prepared, right in the courtroom, as you, or another witness, testifies. However, as noted earlier, the prosecutor may have you draw the basic framework in his office, such as streets and roadways, and have you fill in the details, in court. The easel, it will be displayed on, should be near the witness stand.

If you do not see it, do not be shy about asking the prosecutor, or the judge, where it is. Alternatively, courtroom butcher paper may be on, or near, the erasable whiteboard. Do not rush to judgment on this. If someone is asking you to prepare the diagram, be patient. Wait for instructions. Expect the prosecutor, or defense counsel, to ask you to first draw the relevant streets or roadways, on the diagram. Next, you will probably be asked to name each, and indicate north, by printing a capital letter **N** with an arrow pointing toward it.

Once you have done this, you will probably be directed, to next draw relevant fixed and movable objects, such as:

1. buildings
2. stop signs
3. traffic signals
4. vehicles
5. people

If you are instructed to prepare a diagram, prior to going to court, the prosecutor will ask you to provide foundational testimony, from the witness stand, to properly authenticate it, for the judge or jury, by adding the above details. Once you have done so, you will be asked to provide descriptive testimony. What if you are in court, sans prosecutorial assistance? This does not mean you cannot draw diagrams. If you believe it is necessary, to help you meet your burden of proof, with the court's permission, draw the diagram. Make sure each and every diagram you produce is clear, legible, and understandable.

<u>Physical evidence</u>

Physical evidence includes virtually any item that can be brought into court, and offered into evidence. I cannot even begin to list all the items you might describe, as physical evidence. A representative sampling of them includes, but is not limited to:

1. empty alcoholic beverage containers
2. firearms
3. knives
4. nunchakus
5. billy clubs
6. narcotics
7. cell phones
8. pagers
9. pay-owe sheets

10. scales
11. dinner plate (*heroin being cut on it, during service of search warrant*)
12. packaging material
13. rubber boots
14. rubber gloves
15. rubber aprons

There is no limit to the number of items you may label *physical evidence*. These may include license plates, vehicle parts, bodily fluids, body parts, and so on. If you believe it has evidentiary value treat it as such, log it into evidence, and maintain a clean, unbroken chain of evidence, from the place where it was located, all the way to the courtroom.

Examples of seemingly bizarre items of evidence I've ordered seized during search warrant executions? These include a bloody mattress, a discarded, bloody disposable diaper, the trash can it was found, and a bedroom door with the perfect imprint of a two-year old, baby's body. She later died from chronic physical and sexual abuse, at the hands of her mother's live-in boyfriend, now doing a life sentence for his crimes.

If it needs to be scientifically preserved, such as being refrigerated, do what you have to do. If in doubt, ask your supervisor, or local prosecutor. If in doubt, seize it, and log it into evidence. If the prosecutor says it’s no necessary, that is their call.

ELMO

In courtrooms today, you may find an analog, or digital, visual presenter commonly called an ELMO. The courtrooms where I worked as a DA each had one. It's manufactured by ELMO USA Corporation and displays documents, on a network of in-court television screens. You simply place each document you wish to display on its top glass, much as you might, with a document, on your home photocopier, turn on its light for illumination, and turn on the television monitors.

Any document can be simultaneously displayed, so everyone in the courtroom can view it. This speeds up the process significantly, because you do not have to take the time to show each document individually. If you need to use one, but do not know how, just ask for directions.

Remember to maintain the chain of evidence. If you are not able to convince the court a piece of evidence has been under your constructive care, custody, and control, from the time you initially discovered it, you may have difficulty introducing it into evidence. You can prevent this from being a problem, by doing a couple of things. First, be sure you adequately describe each item of evidence, listed in your reports. Describe it in both your narrative and property list.

Affix a property tag to any item, too large, to fit individually, into one of the brown paper evidence bags, your department uses. If you are depositing evidence, into an evidence bag, note the date and time, at the top of the bag. Then initial, and seal it, following your department's policies and procedures.

Remember to ask the court to exclude any witnesses, who are not going to testify immediately. If the opposition has more than one witness, ask the court to admonish each witness, to not discuss their testimony with anyone, other than counsel, or the court. Once your case concludes, gather whatever documents you brought to court, and exit, as soon as you have been excused, as a witness, by the court, and have no further business to attend to, on this case. But, make sure they have not been marked as exhibits. Those stay in court.

If you are the case agent, wait for the prosecutor to excuse you, if they participated in your case. Leave when they do. Once you can leave, you gain nothing, by hanging around the courthouse. You may risk dealing with an irate motorist, if they are found guilty, or a pompous one, if they are not.

Here's some extra information you may find helpful. As noted earlier, you may occasionally cite the wrong code section, when you issue a citation. Your department may have an amendment of charge form, you can submit to the court. Submitting a completed form allows you to amend the citation, assuming you learn the need to do so, prior to court. This will do two things:

1. It will put the court, and defendant, on notice of the requested amendment.
2. It will allow the defendant to request a continuance.

However, there will be times, when you cannot complete such a form, in a timely fashion. Should this happen, do what Mike Van Gorder suggests, in Chapter 8. Be prepared to provide an adequate reason why you are asking to amend, at the last possible moment. If the defense requests a continuance, expect the court to grant it. Assuming such a request is made, and is granted by the court, do not bother objecting. It will only make you look unreasonable. Plus, if you're on days off, you may get paid twice.

Chapter 17

Overcoming Speedometer Foundational Issues

Do foundational issues prevent you, from introducing evidence, of the calibration of your speedometer, in order to prove a motorist was speeding? If so, this chapter should provide the solution. Modernly, most traffic officers measure the speed of motorists, by use of radar or lidar. Part of a radar unit's testing, involves reviewing the speed displayed, by your unit's speedometer, discussed earlier herein. If your speedometer is not properly calibrated, evidence you gather using radar, will be similarly suspect.

The primary purpose of this chapter is to show you, how to prove, in court, your unit's speedometer correctly measures speed. If you have not faced any speedometer calibration issues, this does not necessarily mean you won't. Defense counsel's job is to find the weak spots, and exploit them into an acquittal for their client. More acquittals. More new clients.

Defense counsel's shortest route to victory, is to knock out your case, by convincing the court, it lacks adequate foundation. The defense does not have to prove innocence. It just needs to show reasonable doubt. If it does, the prosecution loses, with, or without, a prosecutor present. Therefore, if the defense prevents the introduction of enough relevant evidence of guilt, it will win. You will be barred, from presenting any incriminating evidence. Guilt or innocence is not even considered. Did the motorist commit the violation? Doesn't matter.

Your department should have a written policy that determines how often, you are supposed to test the factory-calibrated radar unit, you use to determine speed. In my area, that is done daily. Your department should also have a written policy, dealing with how often speedometers must be calibrated, by the assigned mechanic.

When you testify, at a radar-based speeding citation trial, you should be the only required witness. That's because you personally did the testing. Appellate courts have ruled radar is *presumptively reliable*, if the operator is qualified, and proper procedures are followed. Therefore, does it make sense, multiple witnesses are required, if the device used is a speedometer?

If calibration tracking documents are properly maintained, proving a speeder's guilt should only require the issuing officer's testimony, both as to the speed gathered, and the authentication of any required documents. This is true, even in a state like California, that tends to legislatively micromanage the introduction of traffic court evidence. If other states' lawmakers accept speedometer calibration certification cards, my state's legislature should be a follower, not a leader. (*Hint, hint, Sacramento.*)

It appears to me two simple ways exist, to adequately introduce proof, the speedometer of any traffic unit was properly calibrated. In California, this is done, by offering such proof as either a business record, pursuant to Evidence Code §1271, or an official record, pursuant to Evidence Code §1280.

Before we get into the mechanics of this, immediately below, please find both code sections verbatim. If this procedure works in my state, it should work anywhere. I cannot think of a reason why it will not work in California. Either Evidence Code section appears to be a proper vehicle, with which to do this, providing the underlying facts support it. I will show you why I believe it's an official record.

Business Record, Evidence Code §1271

Evidence of a writing made as a record of an act, condition, or event is not made inadmissible by the hearsay rule when offered to prove the act, condition, or event if:

1. the writing was made, in the regular course of a business;
2. the writing was made, at or near, the time of the act, condition, or event;
3. the custodian or other qualified witness testifies to its identity, and the mode of its preparation; and
4. the sources of information, and method and time of preparation, were such as to indicate its trustworthiness.

Introduction of calibration evidence as a *business record* requires (1) the record was made in the regular course of business, (2) it was done, at or near, the time of the calibration, (3) either the custodian, or some other qualified witness, identifies it, and explains how it was prepared, and, (4) the source of such information, method, and time of its preparation, shows it is trustworthy. This means any officer, providing foundational testimony for the introduction of this document, must be able to authenticate it. The officer must testify it is the certification form, the calibrator completed, and how they know that.

Official Record, Evidence Code §1280

Evidence of a writing, made as a record of an act, condition, or event is not made inadmissible, by the hearsay rule, when offered, in any civil or criminal proceeding, to prove the act, condition, or event if all the following applies:

1. the writing was made, by and within the scope of duty of, a public employee.\
2. the writing was made, at or near, the time of the act, condition, or event.
3. the sources of information, and method and time of preparation, were such as to indicate its trustworthiness.

Introduction of calibration evidence as an official record requires (1) it was made by a public employee, within the scope of their duties, (2) was done at, or near, the time of the calibration, and, (3) the source of such information, method, and time of its preparation shows it is trustworthy, just like a business record. For this document to be admissible, the mechanic must be a public employee doing the calibration, within the course and scope of those duties, not a private sector employee.

The case that appears to put this issue to rest is *Bhatt v. Dept of Health Services* (2005) 133 Cal. App. 4th 923. *Bhatt* relies on Evidence Code §195, which defines a public employee, and concludes the Administrative Law Judge properly received a document, as an official record, pursuant to Evidence Code §1280. I have always believed in the old adage that warns against not reinventing wheels. If the court in *Bhatt* is satisfied an agent can be properly described as a public employee, I am comfortable such legal reasoning works in any other state.

Does your state require the person, who did the calibration, to prove the speedometer was working accurately, when you used it? If so, that person may need to testify to the calibration they did, and can do so as the custodian of records, pursuant to your state's version of §1271. However, if your traffic court judges follow the reasoning of *Bhatt*, then any calibration records generated, should be viewed, as official records requiring no authenticating testimony. All you will need to do is bring a certified copy of the document.

There are appellate cases trial court judges must follow, irrespective of whether they agree with the ruling or not. There are also cases trial court judges may follow, but are not mandated to follow, if they believe the ruling is legally sound, providing no contrary case overrules them.

Such is the case with one I often cite, whenever the issue is bumper-pacing. Should you not be familiar with this term, it's used often, in my state, whenever an officer uses their patrol vehicle's speedometer to determine a motorist's speed, by matching their speed, and observing what speed the patrol vehicle's speedometer indicates.

The case in question is *People v. Lowe*, (2002) 105 CA 4th Supp 1, decided by the Appellate Division of San Bernardino Superior Court. *Lowe* stands for the proposition, police vehicle speedometers are presumptively reliable, because they are calibrated frequently. This means motorists who challenge such evidence, in court, must present evidence establishing such a device was not functioning properly on the day, at the time, and at the location, where it was used to determine their speed.

I find *Lowe* compelling for two reasons: (a) its legal reasoning is solid, and, (b) it relies on the rulings of appellate cases, from several other states, to arrive at its conclusion. I find its reasoning solid, because it is consistent with the calibration records I have repeatedly reviewed in traffic court, presented by officers, from a wide variety of departments.

I have never found any discrepancy, in such records, greater than two miles per hour, between indicated speed, and actual speed, measured by any speedometer, from 30 miles per hour, all the way up to 110 miles per hour. The normal variance is 1 mile per hour, with actual vs. indicated speeds, just as often identical. Plus, whenever such a case cites decisions from several other states, I'm persuaded traffic courts, in other states, are functioning similarly to my own.

But even though I believe any traffic court jurist can comfortably rely on the readings of police vehicle speedometers, at a minimum, it is helpful to review calibration records for such devices, to be sure guilt is proven beyond a reasonable doubt.

Therefore, the next question to be answered is what type of record is it? Is it a business record, or an official record? In California, a business record is described, by Evidence Code §1271, and an official record, by §1280. If it's a business record, a custodian of records will need to lay foundation, for it to be admissible. An official record is considered self-authenticating. That means certified copies of such a document require no testimony to be authenticated.

If the judge determines it to be a business record, and the calibrator does not testify, expect the judge will exclude such evidence. Alternatively, does your state permit a certification card, or other type of documentary proof to suffice, in lieu of testimony, by the person who did the actual calibration? Remember, if appropriate, try to convince the judge the document is a self-authenticating official record, if that's reasonable. This always is more of an issue, if the motorist you cited is represented in traffic court by a lawyer.

Following, please find two hypothetical samples of direct testimony you may provide, with the assistance of a prosecutor. The first example is your testimony for a *speedometer-based* citation. The next one is your testimony for a *radar-based* citation. Both examples are offered in connection with certified copies of documents, pursuant to *Bhatt* (*supra*).

Speedometer-based Citation

P: "Officer, by whom are you employed?

TO: "I'm employed by Anytown Police Department, and am assigned to their traffic division."

P: "How long have you been so employed?"

TO: "Nine years."

P: "On the date of this citation, were you so employed, on duty, in uniform, driving a distinctively marked police vehicle, and assigned primarily to traffic duty?"

DC: "Objection, compound."

C: "Technically, that's true. Those are multiple questions within the same question. But it's preliminary, and the court doesn't want this matter to become a marathon. Overruled."

TO: "I was."

P: "Officer, have you brought any documents that show your patrol vehicle's speedometer was properly calibrated, on the date you issued this citation?"

TO: "Yes sir."

P: "Is it the practice of your department to prepare, or maintain, these documents, in the ordinary course of business?"

TO: "Yes."

P: "Have these documents been under your exclusive care, custody, and control?"

TO: "Since I received them, as I routinely do, yes."

DC: "Objection. Vague as to time."

C: "Look counsel, I said I didn't want a marathon, and I meant it. Officer, please explain."

TO: "Our department's certified calibration form (*displaying to court*) is completed by the people who perform the calibration, as soon as they do that. Then, the completed document is sent to our department. As you can see, the unit number of the patrol vehicle is listed, on the calibration form, which reflects the indicated, and actual, speeds, reflected by the speedometer, once the calibration is done, from 0 mph, up to and including, 150 mph."

C: "Clear as a bell to me. Overruled. You may proceed."

P: (*Gesturing*) "How did you obtain this document?"

TO: "As I just explained to the judge, it was completed, then certified, as a true and correct copy, which, in turn, is sent to our department."

DC: "Objection, no foundation. Lack of personal knowledge."

C: "Sustained."

P: "Do you know how your department received the certified copy of the calibration?"

TO: "I do."

P: "Explain."

TO: "In order to prevent problems like this from happening, both the calibration team, and officers involved, are trained how to do this. The training includes a walk-through of the calibration, completion of the certificate, and the process that sends it to us."

DC: "Objection, irrelevant."

C: "Is this procedure done like this every single time?"

TO: "Yes sir. This is why we are trained to do it like this, so we don't run into problems, in court. There can be no variation from this. Failure to comply is insubordination."

C: "Overruled. Please proceed."

P: (*Obtains document and shows it to defense counsel*) "Your Honor, I am offering this document as People's first in order. It's a one page document entitled Calibration Certificate of John Doe, dated _______________ 2015."

DC: "I object. Hearsay and Best Evidence Rule."

C: "It's admissible, pursuant to California Evidence Code §1280, as an official record. Pursuant to Evidence Code §1500, it's admissible as best evidence, too. It's an original document. Also, pursuant to *Bhatt*, the court is further satisfied the person who did the calibration is a public employee, within the meaning of Evidence Code §195, per the court's previous receipt of testimony from John Doe, as to his role, in the calibration of speedometers, as an agent for Anytown Police Department. Objection overruled. It's received as People's 1."

(*Note: Counsel for the prosecution has just successfully laid foundation to establish the method of determining speed was appropriate.)*

P: "Officer, directing your attention to the date of the citation, did you observe a vehicle being driven in a fashion that resulted in you issuing the citation, in this case?"

TO: "Yes, I did."

P: "Describe the driving you observed."

TO: "I saw what appeared to be a bright red mid-'90s Chevrolet Corvette, in the number 1 lane. It was passing other traffic. I visually estimated its speed to be 100 mph."

(*Note: A foundational objection is made, the officer is not qualified to estimate speed. The prosecutor is allowed to voir dire the officer, who testifies they successfully completed a 24-hour POST radar class, which requires visual estimation of speed of 100 vehicles, with 50 from a stationary position and 50 while mobile, with an accuracy of 5 mph per vehicle. The court finds the officer is an expert and overrules the objection.*)

P: "Which lane is the number 1?"

TO: "That's the one, left of all the other lanes."

P: "What did you do next?"

TO: "I looked at my own vehicle's speedometer. It showed my vehicle's speed to be 80 mph."

P: "What did you do next?"

TO: "I looked again at the Corvette, and noticed it was pulling away from my vehicle."

P: "Then what?"

TO: "I accelerated up to 90 mph, but saw the 'Vette was still pulling away from me, so I accelerated up to 120 mph, and appeared to slowly begin catching the vehicle. Then, I was able to match the pace of the vehicle when I slowed my speed to 100 mph."

P: "You're still referring to the red Corvette?"

TO: "Yes sir."

P: "Was anything obstructing your line of vision?"

TO: "No sir. We were both in the number 1 lane at this point, with no vehicles between us."

P: "What happened next?"

TO: "I activated my overhead emergency lights."

P: "Did the driver yield?"

TO: "Not immediately. It took approximately one-half mile, before the driver appeared to acknowledge me, and began pulling to the right side of the freeway, eventually coming to a complete stop."

P: "Did you contact the driver?"

TO: "Yes."

P: "Were there any passengers in the vehicle?"

TO: "Only the driver."

P: "Do you see that person in court today?"

TO: "I do."

P: "Can you identify that person, by telling the court where they are located, and what they are wearing?"

TO: "Sitting next to defense counsel, wearing a black golf shirt and tan slacks."

C: "Indicating the defendant."

P: "Did you ask the defendant anything, after making contact?"

TO: "Yes, I asked him how fast he thought he was traveling."

P: "What did he say?"

TO: *Around 80 mph.*

P: "Did you issue him the citation, which is before the court in this matter?"

TO: "I did."

P: (*Showing officer document*) "And is this the citation?"

TO: "Yes, it is. That's the court's copy."

P: "And, did all these events occur in ________________ County?"

TO: "Yes."

P: "No further questions."

Radar-based Citation

P: "Officer, by whom are you employed?"

TO: "I'm employed by Anytown Police Department, and am assigned to their traffic division."

P: "How long have you been so employed?"

TO: "Nine years."

P: "On the date of this citation, were you so employed, on duty, in uniform, driving a distinctively marked police vehicle, and assigned primarily to traffic duty that day?"

DC: "Objection, compound."

C: "Technically, that's true. But it's preliminary, and the court doesn't want this matter to turn into a marathon. Overruled."

TO: "I was."

P: "Officer, was the police vehicle you were driving that day, equipped with an in-car radar unit?"

TO: "Yes."

P: "Did you calibrate that radar unit at the beginning of your shift?"

TO: "No sir. Only the manufacturer calibrates. All I do, as the officer who operates the device, is to test it. I do so, at the beginning, and end, of each shift."

P: "I stand corrected. And can you describe how you did that test, please?"

TO: "Yes, I did so, using a tuning fork test."

P: "Please describe what you mean by this."

TO: "The tuning fork, when lightly tapped, produces a fixed harmonic tone. This harmonic tone influences the transmitted radar signal, resulting in a predictable, and uniform, speed reading, by the radar device."

P: "Please describe how the tuning fork works, as a radar testing device."

TO: "All tuning forks are produced for individual bands of radar, and must be used with the same radar bands. A tuning fork may have a tolerance, of plus or minus 1 mph."

P: "Do you also calibrate the tuning fork?"

TO: "Yes, tuning forks are calibrated, rather than tested. They should be calibrated, and kept with the radar device they are used to test. They should not be interchanged, with other radar units."

P: "Please tell the court how you calibrate the tuning fork."

TO: "I gently tap the fork ends against a surface, causing the tuning fork to generate a harmonic tone. Then, holding the tuning fork upright, I align the forks, anywhere from one-half inch to two inches, from the radar antenna, and activate the radar device."

P: "What happens, when you do that?"

TO: "The tuning fork should cause the radar device, to immediately produce a speed on the display. If the radar device display speed, is within plus or minus 1 mph of the tuning fork speed, then it has passed the test."

DC: "Objection, no foundation as to qualifications to competently perform the calibration."

P: "Excuse me, Your Honor. Is counsel referring to the tuning fork, or radar device, when he says calibrate? The officer has testified he only *tests* the radar device. It is *calibrated*, only by the *manufacturer*."

DC: "I misspoke. I meant *test*."

C: "Sustained."

P: "Prior to the date of this citation, have you received any training, on how to properly test the radar device you used, to issue this citation?"

TO: "Yes."

P: "Please describe that."

TO: (*Describes training, including 24-hour POST radar class*)

P: "Officer, did you test the radar device, you used on the date of this citation, in the same fashion you have described, the manner in which, you have been trained?"

TO: "Yes sir."

P: "Your Honor, I ask the court to find the device was properly tested on the relevant date, this officer was qualified to do so, and used it properly, as well."

C: "The court so finds."

P: "Officer, directing your attention to the date of the citation, did you observe a vehicle being driven in a fashion that resulted in you issuing the citation in this case?"

TO: "Yes, I did."

P: "Describe the driving you believed to be remarkable."

TO: "I saw what appeared to be a bright red mid-'90s Chevrolet Corvette in the number 1 lane. It was passing other traffic."

P: "Which lane is the number 1?"

TO: "That's the one left of all the other lanes."

P: "What did you do next?"

(*Note: Officer describes visual estimation of speed. As with speedometer hypothetical, court finds officer an expert on the visual estimation of speed and overrules objection*)

TO: "I looked at the digital display, on my patrol vehicle's radar unit, and observed it to show the other vehicle's speed, at 80 mph."

P: "What did you observe next?"

TO: "I looked again at the Corvette, and noticed it was pulling away from my vehicle."

P: "Then what?"

TO: "I accelerated up to 90 mph, but saw the 'Vette was still pulling away from me, so I accelerated up to 100 mph, and once again, observed my radar unit which showed the suspect vehicle's speed to be locked in, at 99 mph."

P: "You're still referring to the red Corvette?"

TO: "Yes sir."

P: "Was anything obstructing your line of vision?"

TO: "No sir. We were both in the number 1 lane at this point, with no vehicles between us."

P: "What happened next?"

TO: "I activated my overhead emergency lights."

P: "Did the driver yield to you?"

TO: "Not immediately. It took approximately one-half mile, before the driver appeared to acknowledge me, and began pulling to the right side of the freeway, eventually coming to a complete stop."

P: "Did you contact the driver?"

TO: "Yes."

P: "Were there any passengers in the vehicle?"

TO: "Only the driver."

P: "Do you see that person in court today?"

TO: "I do."

P: "Can you identify that person, by telling the court where they are located, and what they are wearing?"

TO: "Sitting next to defense counsel, wearing a black golf shirt, and tan slacks."

C: "Indicating the defendant."

P: "Did you ask the defendant anything, after making contact?"

TO: "Yes, I asked him how fast he thought he was traveling."

P: "What did he say?"

TO: *Around 80 mph.*

P: "Did you issue him the citation, which is before the court, in this matter?"

TO: "I did."

P: (*Showing officer document*) "And is this the citation?"

TO: "Yes, it is. That's the court's copy."

P: "And did all these events occur in _______________ County?"

TO: "Yes, they did."

P: "No further questions."

One note of caution. Although we have discussed the need for the production of ETS, in the courtroom, if your jurisdiction requires such production, to avoid the gathering of evidence of speed being labeled as, speed trap evidence, let's talk about that again here.

If your jurisdiction requires the production of an ETS, which justifies the posted speed limit, every so many years, remember to include that as part of your courtroom evidence production. Since the governmental entity charged with care, custody, and control of it is not likely to surrender the original, be sure the copy you obtain is certified.

If you do not, all your other hard work and training will be in vain. If your traffic assignment is other than my state, you probably not only will not have an ETS to concern yourself with, you can probably establish speedometer calibration with a simple certification card. Common sense vs ivory tower thinking.

Chapter 18
Burden of Proof

Throughout this chapter, we shall discuss the legal concept commonly known as *burden of proof*. Per California Evidence Code §115: "Burden of proof means the obligation of a party to establish by evidence a requisite degree of belief concerning a fact in the mind of the trier of fact or the court. The burden of proof may require a party to raise a reasonable doubt concerning the existence or nonexistence of a fact or that he establish the existence or nonexistence of a fact by a *preponderance of the evidence*, by *clear and convincing proof*, or by *proof beyond a reasonable doubt*. Except as otherwise provided by law, the burden of proof requires proof by a preponderance of the evidence." (*Emphasis added*)

As we have discussed elsewhere, the burden of proof in any criminal case is on the prosecution. So, if you have a prosecutor, with you at counsel table, you both share that same burden. However, if you are in court, without a prosecutor's assistance, this means you shoulder that burden, exclusively. Either way, the defense has no burden of doing anything, other than to create reasonable doubt. In other words, you peddle the bicycle. The defense tries to cram a stick between the spokes of your front wheel.

If defense counsel can do that, they not only do their job better than you did yours, they win. Therefore, here's how I believe you prevent that miscarriage of justice from happening. We both know you do not purposely cite innocent motorists. (*But, if you do, adios amigo.*)

<u>California Evidence Code §500</u>:

"Except as otherwise provided by law, a party has the burden of proof as to each fact the existence or nonexistence of which is essential to the claim for relief or defense he is asserting. Each party is entitled to the benefit of all the evidence, including the evidence produced by an adversary." Williams v. Barnett (1955) 135 Cal App 2d 607.

First, meeting your burden of proof, does not begin in the courtroom. And, it does not begin, at the door to the courthouse, either. It begins before you even turn on your *excuse me* lights. At the risk of sounding preachy, your job is to protect the lives and property of strangers. You do this by knowing the relevant laws, and applying them to every factual situation you face, as a traffic officer.

This means you must become an expert, on any and all traffic issues you deal with, as a law enforcement professional. You must know the law better than the defense lawyer does. And, you should also know the law better than the prosecutor you will occasionally team up with, in court. Same rules apply for the judges. They, too, are human. Mistakes happen. Judges are not infallible.

Both rookie cops and prosecutors labor under the same misperception. Never expect the prosecutor to know the law well enough, to bail you out of an inextricable situation. In other words, if you bring the prosecutor a screwed up case, do not expect them to fix it for you. They probably cannot. The corollary of the time-tested adage *if it ain't broke don't fix it*? *If it's broken, by the time the prosecutor gets it, it probably isn't fixable*. But, it gets even more basic than this. Occasionally, expect to teach the prosecutor the law that makes the underlying facts of your case relevant. Cops taught me. Teach your own prosecutors.

Do not expect the prosecutor to know more about traffic law than you do, simply because they may have more formal education than you. All it means is they have more seat time in classrooms, than you have. But you have more seat time in a patrol vehicle. That's what counts. So, realize this. You may have to educate any prosecutor, with whom you work. This happened to me regularly, whenever I would sit down with the police officer, who had put the case together, I was asked to review.

Do not put any of the professionals you deal with on a pedestal. I do not care who they are. At the risk of sounding totally cliché, everybody puts their pants on, one leg at a time, whether it's a prosecutor, private attorney, public defender, judge, or commissioner. Prosecutors? It means they were able to convince panels of interviewers they were less harmful to the operation, than they would be, as an enemy combatant. Private defense counsel? They probably were not able to convince anyone to hire them for public sector jobs. If they are deputy public defenders, all it means is, they *may be* true believers.

Judges? They convinced enough people, to convince the governor, to appoint them to a position, someone else may not have wanted anymore, or they convinced enough voters to select them, on a ballot. Commissioners? Again, they were able to convince enough judges, to hire them, to be part of their team. Let me be clear here. I am not saying there are not honest-to-goodness stars in any of these various groups.

There certainly are. I am privileged to have worked with, or against enough of these folks, to be confident about what I'm saying. It does not automatically mean any folks from this crowd have any expertise whatsoever, in traffic matters. I still recall a Commissioner, from my DA days, who regularly stopped me, on my way back from court, to pick my brain on traffic issues. You better have expertise. You are a traffic cop. Working the streets and observing the violators is what you do. We're counting on you to carry the mail.

Earlier, we talked about the differences between reasonable suspicion to detain, probable cause to search or arrest, and proof of guilt beyond a reasonable doubt to convict. Granted, your burden of proof to make a T-stop is a mere *reasonable suspicion* you believe a crime either has been, or is being committed. And, you only require probable cause you believe a crime has been committed, or is being committed, before you ask a motorist to autograph the citation you have just completed.

However, my suggestion, in line with my repeated suggestion to always err on the side of caution? Be ready to prove guilt beyond a reasonable doubt *before* you flip on your emergency lights. That's because you do not turn them on until you observe a provable violation. If you are not sure, do not even hit the switch.

Let's start, by talking about the presumption of innocence. In my own state, California Jury Instructions-Criminal, also known as CAL-JIC (*now CALCRIM*) explains this presumption, in CAL-JIC 2.90. "A defendant in a criminal action is presumed to be innocent until the contrary is proven, and in case of a reasonable doubt, whether his doubt is satisfactorily shown, he is entitled to a verdict of not guilty."

Wording may differ from state to state, but not the concept. Each state requires the prosecution to meet the same lofty standard, in order to remove the presumption of innocence. So let's take a moment, and get acquainted with the different burdens of proof you will deal with, as a traffic officer.

First, as you already know, the designation traffic officer does not mean you only chase taillights, and write citations for traffic infractions. You have to be prepared for virtually any eventuality.

This includes notices to appear you may issue for either infractions or misdemeanors. These may include a wide variety of offenses, ranging from speeding, to driving on a suspended, or revoked driving privilege.

Therefore, I believe it's prudent for us to revisit the various burdens of proof, and take one more look, at the types of situations they may cover:

1. Consensual encounters

a. None required [*U.S. v. Williams*] (*supra*)

b. Encounter must end, when subject says so, unless adequate justification exists to elevate this, to either a temporary detention, or an arrest.

2. Reasonable suspicion

a. Temporary detentions:

i. vehicle stops

ii. pedestrian detentions, aka ped checks

As we have already discussed, elsewhere in this book, your burden of proof to make a traffic stop, or any other kind of temporary detention is to articulate reasonable suspicion, you believe a crime has been committed, or is being committed. Temporary detentions are considered seizures, within the meaning of the Fourth Amendment of the U.S. Constitution. Let's revisit the relevant cases.

1. [*Alabama v. White*] (*supra*) "Reasonable suspicion can arise from information that is less reliable than that required to show probable cause."

2. [*U.S. v. Sokolow*] *(supra)* "That level of suspicion is considerably less than proof of wrongdoing by a preponderance of the evidence."

3. [*INS v. Delgado*] (*supra*) "Some 'minimal level of objective justification' for the stop."

4. [*U.S. v. Arvizu*] *(supra)* "When discussing how reviewing courts should make reasonable suspicion determinations, we have said repeatedly that they must look at the totality of the circumstances of each case to see whether the detaining officer has a particularized and objective basis for suspecting legal wrongdoing."

5. [*Ornelas v. U.S.*] (*supra*) "Although an officer's reliance on a mere hunch is insufficient to justify a stop, the likelihood of criminal activity need not rise to the level required for probable cause, and it falls considerably short of satisfying a preponderance of the evidence standard."

6. [*Terry v. Ohio*] (*supra*) "The officer in Terry observed the petitioner and his companions repeatedly walk back and forth, look into a store window, and confer with one another. Although each of the series of acts was perhaps innocent in itself, we held that, taken together, they warranted further investigation."

3. Probable cause (*to search or arrest*)

Arrests and searches require a higher burden of proof, than that required for temporary detentions. As with a temporary detention, an arrest is a seizure, within the meaning of the Fourth Amendment. In order for you to justify an arrest, you must be able to articulate probable cause establishes the suspect, either has committed a crime, or is committing a crime. Your legal authority to search is limited to:

a. voluntary consent
b. search warrant
c. probable cause
d. exigent circumstances
e. incident to lawful arrest
   (1) Arrests may include:
      (a) handcuffing and subsequent booking at jail
      (b) issuance of traffic citations

1. *Beck v. Ohio* (supra) Probable cause exists when: "...the facts and circumstances within (one's) knowledge and of which (one has) reasonably trustworthy information were sufficient to warrant a prudent man in believing that the (defendant has) committed or was committing an offense."
2. *People v. Gonzales* (supra) In order to determine if your arrest has adequate probable cause, the court is required to measure you "...under a standard of objective reasonableness without regard to (your) underlying intent or motivation..."
3. *People v. Ingle* (supra) Probable cause is defined as "...having more evidence for than against...evidence which inclines the mind to believe, but leaves some room for doubt..."
4. *Illinois v. Gates* (supra) "Probable cause requires only a probability or substantial chance of criminal activity, not an actual showing of such activity. By hypothesis, therefore, innocent behavior frequently will provide the basis for a showing of probable cause; to require otherwise would be to sub silentio impose a drastically more rigorous definition of probable cause than the security of our citizens demands...In making a determination of probable cause the relevant inquiry is not whether particular conduct is 'innocent or guilty,' but the degree of suspicion that attaches to particular types of non-criminal conduct."

   a. Searches and seizures may include:
      (1) persons
      (2) vehicles under a person's control
      (3) residences under a person's control
      (4) garages under a person's control
      (5) yards under a person's control
      (6) storage facilities under a person's control

   b. Searches and seizures may be accomplished legally by any of the following:

4. **Consent**

a. Consent searches are constitutionally acceptable, provided the consent you obtain is freely, voluntarily, and knowingly given, by the target of the search. *People v. James* (1977) 19 C3d 99; *People v. Reyes* (1974) 12 C3d 486. Suspect need not be advised of ability to refuse consent, in order for consent to be valid *James* (supra). Suspect need not be Mirandized, in order for consent to be valid *Schneckcloth v. Bustamonte* (1973) 412 U.S. 218.

5. **Search warrants**

a. Automobile exception to search warrant requirement

The landmark U.S. Supreme Court case that established the automobile exception, to the usual requirement of obtaining a search warrant, for a search to be lawful is *Carroll v. U.S.* (1921) 267 U.S. 132. *Carroll* (supra) dealt with the illegal transportation of contraband liquor; holding law enforcement could lawfully search a vehicle, for contraband, without the requirement of first securing a search warrant, if the officer could articulate probable cause to do so. A significant factor *Carroll* considered was the mobile nature of motor vehicles:

"On reason and authority the true rule is that if the search without a warrant is made upon probable cause, that is, upon a belief, reasonably arising out of circumstances known to the seizing officer, that an automobile or other vehicle contains that which by law is subject to seizure and destruction, the search and seizure are valid."

In *Chambers v. Maroney* (1970) 399 U.S. 42, the Supreme Court took *Carroll* a step further by extending the warrantless vehicle search to the police station:

"The principal questions in this case concern the admissibility of evidence seized from an automobile, in which petitioner was riding at the time of his arrest, after the automobile was taken to a police station and was there thoroughly searched without a warrant. The Court of Appeals for the Third Circuit found no violation of petitioner's Fourth Amendment rights. We affirm."

A number of other cases expanded the original ruling of *Carroll.* They include:

- *Texas v. White* (1975) 423 U.S. 67, which reaffirmed its holding in *Maroney*, by noting "...(i)n Chambers v. Maroney we held that police officers with probable cause to search an automobile on the scene where it was stopped could constitutionally do so later at the station house without first obtaining a warrant."

- *U.S. v. Ross* (1982) 456 U.S. 798 reaffirmed the court's original holding in *Carroll* by stating, "In Carroll v. United States, (supra), the Court held that a warrantless search of an automobile stopped by police officers who had probable cause to believe the vehicle contained contraband was not unreasonable within the meaning of the Fourth Amendment. The Court in Carroll did not explicitly address the scope of the search that is permissible. In this case, we consider the extent to which police officers-who have legitimately stopped an automobile and who have probable cause to believe that contraband is concealed somewhere within it-may conduct a probing search of compartments and containers within the vehicle whose contents are not in plain view. We hold that they may conduct a search of the vehicle that is as thorough as a magistrate could authorize in a warrant 'particularly describing the place to be searched.'"

- *Michigan v. Thomas* (1982) 458 U.S. 259 reaffirmed the court's prior ruling in *Maroney*. "In Chambers v. Maroney, (supra), we held that when police officers have probable cause to believe there is contraband inside an automobile that has been stopped on the road, the officer may conduct a warrantless search of the vehicle, even after it has been impounded and is in police custody. We firmly reiterated this holding in Texas v. White, (supra), See also U.S. v. Ross, (supra). It is thus clear that the justification to conduct such a warrantless search does not vanish once the car has been immobilized; nor does it depend upon a reviewing court's assessment of the likelihood in each particular case that the car would have been driven away, or that its contents would have been tampered with, during the period required for the police to obtain a warrant."

- *Florida v. Meyers* (1984) 466 U.S. 380 involved a car that had been searched roadside, then towed to, and secured, in a wrecking yard. The Supreme Court overruled the Florida District Court of Appeal for the Fourth District, which erroneously distinguished this case from the holding in *Maroney*, by finding the fact the vehicle had been secured, removed the element of mobility. The court pointedly noted "...(t)he District Court of Appeal either misunderstood or ignored our prior rulings with respect to the constitutionality of the warrantless search of an impounded automobile. In *Michigan v. Thomas*, (*supra*) we upheld a warrantless search of an automobile even though the inventory search had already been made. That ruling controls the disposition of this case. In Thomas, we expressly rejected the argument accepted by the District Court of Appeal in the present case, noting that the search upheld in Chambers was conducted 'after [the automobile was] impounded and [was] in police custody' and emphasizing that the justification to conduct such a warrantless search does not vanish once the car has been immobilized. The District Court of Appeal's ruling that the subsequent search in this case was invalid because the car had been impounded is clearly inconsistent with Thomas and Chambers. The petition for certiorari is therefore granted, the judgment of the District Court of Appeal is reversed, and the case is remanded to that court for further proceedings not inconsistent with this opinion. It is so ordered."

- *U.S. v. Johns* (1985) 469 U.S. 478 expanded the automobile exception, by holding a warrantless search of packages, taken from within a vehicle, done three days, after the vehicle was stopped, was lawful. The court said "(i)n U.S. v. Ross, (supra), the Court held that if police officers have probable cause to search a lawfully stopped vehicle, they may conduct a warrantless search of any containers found inside that may conceal the object of the search. The issue in the present case is whether Ross authorizes a warrantless search of packages several days after they have been removed from vehicles that police officers had probable cause to believe contained contraband (b)ecause the Customs officer had probable cause to believe that the pickup trucks contained contraband, any expectation of privacy in the vehicles or their contents was subject to the authority of the officers to conduct a warrantless search."

6. Probable cause

Please refer to the numerous cases, cited in this chapter, under the heading *automobile exception to search warrant requirement*, as well as other references in Chapter 4.

7. Parole searches

Parole searches can be conducted lawfully, without the parolee's consent, and without a search warrant, either by the parole agent, or someone authorized by that agent, to conduct the search. One's status as a parolee cannot be used as a pretext to search. The standard considered acceptable, if the parole agent were conducting the search, is reasonable suspicion of criminal activity. *People v. Burgener* (1986) 41 C3d 505.

8. Probation searches

Most probationers have a search term, or condition, as a part of their probation. I frequently created this investigative tool on misdemeanor cases.

I did so, by agreeing to no jail time, if the defendant had no prior convictions, in return for requiring search terms of their person, residence, vehicle, garage, yard, or any storage facility, under their control, any time of the day or night, with or without a search warrant, and with or without probable cause, as a part of their probation. Doing this elevated traffic stops, and consensual encounters, to warrantless searches, occasionally leading to the discovery of contraband that might not have been located, otherwise.

A search term permits a search, pursuant to the specified terms and conditions of the search, without the probationer's consent, and without a search warrant. *People v. Mason* (1971) 5 C3d 759. However, be mindful a probation search cannot be undertaken, for harassment, or for arbitrary or capricious reasons. *People v. Bravo* (1987) 43 C3d 600.

9. Exigent circumstances

As the term implies, to conduct a lawful search, using this particular rubric, you must be able to articulate *an actual emergency*. Since your traffic duties will more than likely only include you searching vehicles, it is not likely this scenario will present itself to you. However, if appropriate facts present themselves, here are a few tidbits you should file away, just in case. Remember to be objectively creative.

An emergency, or other exigent set of circumstances, will permit you to lawfully enter a residence, and conduct a partial search. *People v. Hill* (1974) 12 C3d 731; *Carrington v. Superior Court* (1973) 31 Cal App 3d 635.

There are no black and white guidelines that spell out what an exigency is. This boils down to the use of your own judgment, based on your training and experience. The key is to articulate why you lack adequate time to obtain a search warrant. To assist you, here are a number of cases, with their unique underlying facts.

1. *People v. Curley* (1970) 12 Cal App 3d 732: preserving evidence of an arson
2. *People v. Scheib* (1979) 98 Cal App 3d 820: presence of explosives
3. *People v. Ammons* (1980) 103 Cal App 3d 20: a wildly barking dog
4. *People v. Soldoff* (1980) 112 Cal App 3d 1: possible shooting victim, with evidence of bullet holes and blood

10. Incident to an arrest

Federal case law permits you to search someone you have arrested. The rationale is simple. The arrestee is going to be fully searched, at the time of booking, at the jail. Therefore, you are not going to be any more invasive, than jail personnel, who conduct the actual booking search. *U.S. v. Robinson* (1973) 414 U.S. 218; *Gustafson v. Florida* (1973) 414 U.S. 260.

By way of example, California cases permit full searches of pockets, including arrests for public intoxication. *People v. Sanchez* (1985) 174 Cal App 3d 343; *People v. Dennis* (1985) 172 Cal App 3d 287. Check with your own prosecutor, for further guidance, on the legality of this, in your own state.

Preponderance of the evidence

Preponderance of the evidence means proof something is *more likely true than not true.* California Civil Jury Instructions (*CACI*) §200. The general rule of law in California is "...issues of fact in civil cases are determined by a preponderance of the testimony."

"A party must persuade you, by the evidence presented in court, that what he or she is required to prove is more likely to be true than not true. This is referred to as 'the burden of proof.'

After weighing all of the evidence, if you cannot decide something is more likely to be true, than not true, you must conclude the party did not prove it. You should consider all the evidence, no matter which party produced the evidence. In criminal trials, the prosecution must prove the defendant is guilty, beyond a reasonable doubt. But, in civil trials, such as this one, the party who is required to prove something, need prove only, it is more likely to be true, than not true." CACI

1. *Weiner v. Fleischman* (1991) 54 Cal 3d 476. To establish preponderance of the evidence, it *"...simply requires the trier of fact to believe that the existence of a fact is more probable than its nonexistence."*
2. *In re Angelica P.* (1981) 28 Cal 3d 908. Preponderance of the evidence "...means what it says, viz, the evidence on one side outweighs, preponderates over, is more than, the evidence on the other side, not necessarily in number of witnesses or quantity, but in its effect on those to whom it is addressed." *Glage v. Hawes Firearms Co.* (1990) 226 Cal App 3d 314; *People v. Miller* (1916) 171 Cal 649.

Examples of hearings where preponderance of the evidence is the standard include:

1. Violation of probation hearings
2. Administrative hearings

Clear and convincing evidence

Clear and convincing evidence is a higher standard, than preponderance but lower than proof beyond a reasonable doubt. To meet this burden of proof, you are required to prove something is *more likely true*. California Civil Jury Instructions (*CACI*) §201. Who comes up with this stuff?

"Proof by clear and convincing evidence is required 'where particularly important individual interests or rights are at stake,' such as termination of parental rights, involuntary commitment, or deportation. However, 'imposition of even severe civil sanctions that do not implicate such interests has been permitted after proof by a preponderance of the evidence.'" *Fleischman* (supra); *Herman & MacLean v. Huddleston* (1983) 459 U.S. 375.

Other issues decided by clear and convincing evidence include:

1. Termination of parental rights
2. Involuntary commitments
3. Deportations

Beyond a reasonable doubt

California Jury Instructions-Criminal defines *reasonable doubt* as: "... not a mere possible doubt; because everything relating to human affairs is open to some possible or imaginary doubt. It is that state of the case which, after the entire comparison and consideration of all the evidence, leaves the minds of the jurors in that condition that they cannot say they feel an abiding conviction of the truth of the charge."

- Criminal trials include:
-

a. Felonies
b. Misdemeanors
c. Infractions

In short, prepare for the type of hearing you are required to attend, by taking the time to know what burden of proof you must meet. Unless you are a lawyer, I do not expect you to function at that particular level of expertise, any more than I expect lawyers to be able to function at your level of expertise, in the field, unless they also have the training and have gained the experience you have received, e.g. *Blue Bloods'* Jamie Reagan. Know your battlefield.

Chapter 19

Meeting and Overcoming Objections

The purpose of this chapter is to teach you how to meet, and overcome, defense objections, when you present evidence. Your state's Evidence Code will determine what evidence is admissible, and what evidence is not. The only way you will truly know what the parameters of admissibility are, is to read the relevant statutes. There are no shortcuts, irrespective of what you may hear to the contrary.

Like your academy, except for none of the demanding physical stuff, law school is flat brutal. A student can easily pour hours of study, into each day they are in school. But, in retrospect, that sort of indoctrination, at the beginning of one's career, only makes sense. For one thing, we develop a work ethic we might not otherwise have. And in order to succeed, either as a LEO or a prosecutor, you need to be willing to work hard, and work long hours, generally doing so without any pats on the back. So, without such a beginning, we might not develop the stamina we need to take care of business.

This chapter is designed to prepare you for traffic court, particularly when defense counsel represents the motorist you cited, so they can try to cram a monkey wrench, into the gears of your machinery. Remember, their job is not to help you present your evidence. It's to keep you from doing it.

Irrespective of how many times, you hear defense counsel tell a jury, a trial is a search for the truth? That is nothing but a boatload of fertilizer. How they can say that, with a straight face, is amazing. It's never a search for the truth, from any defense perspective. That's because their ethical duties mandate they do the exact opposite. They are not under oath, when they say such outlandish things. Why do they do this? Because they can.

It's tantamount to hearing political office candidates telling you what they are going to do, when they get elected, then comparing those with any results, at the end of their first term. Perhaps, if they were required to take an oath, as you do, before you get to talk in the courtroom, it would improve the quality of their verbiage. Perhaps, perpetrating a fraud on the court, should include doing this to unsuspecting jurors.

I heard similar statements ad infinitum, ad nauseum, over my career, as a prosecutor. Let's be honest here. Defense counsel's job is to ingratiate themselves with jurors, as much as they can get away with, so they can get away with torpedoing, what you are trying to do.

In a perfect world, a defense attorney representing the guy you cited should see a prosecutor leading you through your own courtroom paces, akin to one of the immutable laws of physics that declares *for every action there is an equal and opposite reaction*. But thanks to budgetary considerations, most prosecuting attorneys' offices do not provide prosecutors for traffic court, unless a jury hears the evidence. I never had traffic court duty as a DA.

What is the significance, of the evidence you have already collected, concerning the offending motorist, you are preparing to deal with, in court? For one thing, it is utterly meaningless, if you are not able to present it, to the trier of fact persuasively enough, to allow you, to meet your burden of proof.

Irrespective of whether the trier of fact is a judge, commissioner, judge pro tempore, or jury, your burden of proof, in any criminal courtroom, is proof of guilt, beyond a reasonable doubt. This includes traffic citations. That will not vary either, regardless of whether the crime you are there to testify about is an infraction, misdemeanor, or felony. If it's one of the two latter classes of crimes, a jury will be present, unless the defendant and prosecution both agree to *waive jury*. A jury trial means defense counsel gets to misbehave far more, than they would, if only a judge was deciding guilt or innocence.

If a jury is waived, and a court trial is selected, both sides agree a jurist, in black robes, can hear the case, rather than the defendant's fate being decided, by a jury of his peers. However, this chapter focuses primarily on infraction cases. That means you are in court, without the assistance of a prosecutor, leading interference for you.

Should this happen, and the defendant is nonetheless represented by counsel, the normally informal rules of evidence we discussed, in Chapter 16, will probably be enforced far more strictly, by the court, than they normally would be. In this chapter, we try to somewhat level the playing field, without masquerading it, as a quick substitute, for a law school evidence class.

In order for you to meet your burden of proof, you must present sufficient evidence to replace the constitutional presumption of innocence, with proof of guilt, beyond a reasonable doubt. At the other side of counsel table the only burden the defense has, is to create the very reasonable doubt you are working hard to erase. If they do so, it's a good day's work for them. Meanwhile, you are proverbially writing TRUTH, in big bold letters, on the white board. And, they are diligently trying to obliterate it. Don't let them.

The huge difference between your burden of proof and theirs is fundamental. You have to present evidence to do so. They do not. All the defense must do, in order to meet their burden of proof, is to keep you from meeting yours. They can do so, without producing a single defense witness, sworn to an oath, and without presenting any document, photograph, or any other evidence whatsoever.

They do this, by making *timely and proper objections* to the evidence you seek to introduce. In lay terminology, timely means defense counsel must inform the court they object to you attempting to introduce evidence, before you do so. Proper simply means telling the court what section of your state's Evidence Code they rely on, when they so object. For example, expect to hear: *objection, Your Honor, foundation, hearsay*, and so on. Keep something firmly implanted at the very front of your brain. If the defense is going to knock your case out of the batter's box, before you even get a good pitch to swing at, *it will probably be on foundational grounds*.

Speedometer-based speeding citations

I know this to be true, because I did it way too many times, as a defense attorney, to not believe. This will happen, primarily on speeding tickets. If you measured an offending motorist's speed, by bumper-pacing them, and reading your patrol unit's speedometer, they will try to derail you, by objecting, each time, you attempt to tell the court what your patrol unit's speedometer said their client's speed was.

First and foremost, the objection raised, is foundational. The defense will raise this objection, because someone, other than you, did the calibration, unless you beat them to the punch, and adequately provide that foundation, before you try talking about their client's speed, as we discussed in the previous chapter.

Let's break this down. Doing it the wrong way, you attempt to tell the court *Joe the mechanic* told you he calibrated your unit's speedometer, two days before you issued the citation that brings you to court, on this case.

Therefore, you are relying on what Joe told you, so you can convince the court the speedometer displayed a given speed. That is irrelevant, unless you can first prove the speedometer was properly calibrated. That's called *hearsay*. It's an out-of-court statement, being offered by you, to prove the truth of the matter being asserted, i.e., the speedometer was properly calibrated. In other words, you are attempting to tell the court the speed you measured was true and correct, because your department's mechanic told you he calibrated the speedometer, and it accurately measured *X* mph at *Y* mph. This allowed you to correctly determine an offending motorist's speed. Close? No cigar.

However, if you follow my suggested approach, in Chapter 17, even in California, you should not be side-tracked. That's because you rely on the Evidence Code to present proper foundation that allows you to talk about the real issue. That is how fast the motorist was traveling, when you made the observation for which he was cited.

A collateral problem you face, in such situations, is an additional foundational issue. Joe's calibration is meaningless, even if he appears, in person, to testify, unless he was properly trained to do the calibration, in the first place. Once that issue is put to rest, and the court accepts what Joe says, as credible, you can confidently go to court, and not worry about being ambushed.

This is not rocket science. It's simply a matter of taking the time to do the work, in the courtroom, you so painstakingly, and routinely, do in the field. You just need to understand the essentials. As noted previously, do not count on the judge helping you, if you do not first help yourself, by doing your job properly. The fact you are a nice guy means nothing.

Radar-based speeding citations

The same basic scenario exists, with speeding citations you issue, when you have measured speed with radar. First, you must show you know how to properly test your radar device, including calibrating the tuning fork, you did both, as required, and properly used the device, to measure the motorist's speed.

Let's say you are a California LEO. This means you must be prepared to do more, than simply give testimony about any relevant training and experience you obtained, prior to your issuance of the citation, in question. But, on the issue of proving your qualifications, this is why creating, and maintaining, an updated hero sheet is so important. And, akin to bringing the citation, or incident report, with you, always bring your updated résumé to the witness stand.

Never try to rely on your memory to do this. This also looks impressive, especially in front of a jury, when you place it in front of you and ask: "...Your Honor, may I refer to my résumé to refresh my recollection, as to my relevant training and experience?" In fact, such attention to detail, even impresses cynical folks like most judges, and me. Never forget a significant part of your job is selling the sizzle that accompanies the steak.

Assume you overcome any foundational hurdles, laid by the defense, that claim you were not adequately trained, nor sufficiently experienced, to test or use the radar device. Instead, let's say you successfully convince the judge you know how to test the radar device that determined an offending motorist's speed, know how to use it, properly tested it, and properly used it.

Does this mean you are out of the woods? Not yet. Remember, for purposes of this lesson, you are in my state. This means, the defense should also object, if they are doing their job, you have not presented adequate evidence of a timely ETS that justifies the posted speed limit.

Before you get to court, you need to determine whether your jurisdiction even requires proof of a proper ETS, on radar citations. If it does, the next question is whether you are expected to produce the ETS in court, or if the court maintains it, as part of its duties. As to the first issue, the answer is in your state's book on traffic laws. Please read it. Doing so will tell you, if you have to be concerned with speed traps. In other words, does your state forbid them in connection with gathering evidence of speed?

You can always ask your supervisor for guidance. But my respectful suggestion is to do the digging yourself. For one thing, your supervisor may not have the answer. Or, they may give you incorrect information.

Some superiors do not take kindly to being bothered, with such a request, irrespective of whether they wear chevrons on their sleeves, or metal bars on their collars. If you find the answer yourself, you can impress your supervisor, and others, you took the time to do so, and know how to find such information.

Erring on the side of caution, unless you conclusively know differently, assume it will be your job to produce the ETS in court. If so, four issues present themselves:

1. Is an ETS required, for the stretch of roadway, where you issued a radar-based citation?
2. Has it been done recently enough, to comply with your state's statutory requirements?
3. Does it justify the posted limit?
4. Is the Best Evidence Rule an issue?

If this applies in your jurisdiction, the Best Evidence Rule requires production of an original document, or a certified copy, unless you can provide the court with an adequate reason why you are not doing this.

Exceptions? Here are a couple of examples of why you are not able to offer the original, or a certified copy, of a document you are attempting to introduce into evidence:

1. The defense has not returned the original, or certified copy, you lent them
2. The custodian of records cannot find the original, and cannot provide you a certified copy

Evidence may be deemed inadmissible for different reasons. Is it inadmissible, because your state's Evidence Code says so, such as ETS non-compliance? Or, is it inadmissible, because the court finds it was illegally seized, in violation of the Fourth Amendment to the U.S. Constitution?

Evidence, in the former category, is inadmissible for statutory reasons. But, evidence, in the latter group, is inadmissible, because such a seizure violates constitutional principles. Never be surprised to hear defense counsel ask the court to do something, the law does not authorize.

In other words, if their request to suppress evidence, on statutory grounds, is not successful, they may shift gears, and tell the court they are now renewing the same motion on common law grounds. Ask your local prosecutor if such grounds exist in your state. Always expect the unexpected, including defense nonsense.

In California, Penal Code §1538.5 is the statute used to allege evidence was not seized properly, from a constitutional standpoint, i.e., the Fourth Amendment. Evidence Code §402 is used, if evidence lacks foundation.

These statutory vehicles are used, if the defense attempts to bar introduction of evidence they claim was seized illegally either because of a purported Fourth Amendment issue, or because proper foundation allegedly was not laid.

But just because the motion is made does not mean it has substance. Failure to do this can mean counsel is accused of not adequately representing their client. So, being cautious, many more motions are filed, than are granted. We must be aware of a fundamental concept concerning defense counsel's job. The fact they state something does not make it a fact. Usually, defense counsel is merely protecting their own hide, whether they are public sector lawyers, or private counsel.

Remember the example I used in Chapter 4 about the deputy public defender moving to suppress evidence, calling a plain sight observation, an illegal search? If you have not been to court yet, expect to see such attempts, done repeatedly, to keep you from doing your job, even on infractions. I know. I have done this, as a defense attorney, and had to oppose it, as a DA.

So, just because you hear defense counsel loudly claiming you did not do your job, does not mean you did anything wrong. But, conversely, it does not mean you did not do anything wrong. Sometimes evidence will be suppressed because you made a mistake. Ergo, avoid making them.

In either scenario, the underlying facts should speak for themselves. If it's a case the prosecutor must approve, before it gets to court, it probably will *not* get there, if you make such a fundamental mistake. Therefore, if it is in court, and defense counsel is caterwauling, it probably means they are simply meeting their ethical obligations. If you are new to the courtroom, do not panic, whenever you hear a defense attorney making such a fuss. They are just doing their job, even if some do it more vociferously, than others.

Let's deal with another hypothetical. Assume you show up, for what you believe, is a routine traffic matter, and discover defense counsel is asking the judge to dismiss the case, claiming you illegally seized evidence, and it should be suppressed.

They probably are claiming you violated their client's Fourth Amendment rights. Therefore, let me ask you this. Did they serve you with a written notice of their intention to seek suppression of evidence? If they did not, you are entitled to a continuance. I would immediately ask for one and, as soon as the judge sets the matter for a new date, make a beeline to your local prosecutor's office for help.

In order for evidence to be admissible, the court must view it as *relevant*. According to Black's Law Dictionary, relevant means *applicable, pertinent, significant, directly related, and connected to the subject*. In lay terminology, if it has nothing to do with the price of eggs, do not waste your time talking about omelets. If it does, talk. And, be sure to make yourself perfectly clear.

California Evidence Code §210 defines *relevant evidence*: "Relevant evidence means evidence including evidence relevant to the credibility of a witness or hearsay declarant having any tendency, in reason to prove or disprove any disputed fact, of consequence to the determination of the action."

However, relevance alone will not guarantee the court will admit your proffered evidence, if your state also has an Evidence Code provision, similar to California's. This will probably apply, only if, you are dealing with a jury trial. If so, it's likely the prosecutor will take care of this, without your assistance. But this does not mean you should not understand the concept, even in traffic court. Defense counsel sure does. Don't be outgunned.

Probative Value vs. Prejudicial Effect

In California, Evidence Code §352 may bar introduction of otherwise relevant evidence, if the court finds the prejudicial effect of the proffered evidence, outweighs its probative value. Let's take a moment to analyze this. Before we review §352, we need to familiarize ourselves with Evidence Code §351, which reads, in pertinent part: "(e)xcept as otherwise provided by statute, all relevant evidence is admissible."

When §351 talks about *otherwise*, it refers to §352. Expect to find similar evidentiary requirements in your own state.

What is the difference between an objection and a motion to strike? An objection is made, before the question is answered, by the witness. A motion to strike is made, if the question has been answered, before counsel is able to lodge an objection. Earlier, we discussed how an objection must be timely and proper, in order to be correctly ruled upon by the court.

Let's examine Evidence Code §352, so you can compare it to your own state's version, assuming you live and work elsewhere. "The court in its discretion may exclude evidence if its probative value is substantially outweighed by the probability that its admission will (a) necessitate undue consumption of time or (b) create substantial *danger of undue prejudice, of confusing the issues, or of misleading the jury."* (*Emphasis added)*

This means, even if the evidence you present is relevant, the judge can nonetheless exclude it if they find:

The court does not have to wait for either lawyer to make such a request. In order to exercise control of a proceeding, the court can do this, totally on its own, with the court exercising its discretion *sua sponte*, i.e., on the court's own motion.

Objections vs. Motions to Strike

1. Its probative value is substantially outweighed by the probability its admission will:

   a. necessitate undue consumption of time
   b. create substantial danger of:
      (1) undue prejudice
      (2) confusing the issues
      (3) misleading the jury

In other words, proper means you must tell the court why the question violates some provision of your state's Evidence Code. Timely merely means the objection must be made, before the answer, to the question, is given. So if an objection cannot be done timely, counsel must use a motion to strike. Even if counsel is paying attention the witness may answer too quickly, before counsel can object. Considering how much multi-tasking trial attorneys must do, counsel may simply have not been paying close enough attention, in order to make a timely objection. They may have been ogling the cute court reporter. Ergo, the motion to strike.

Such motions are requests to the court to remove unexpectedly quick answers to questions, non-responsive answers, or spontaneous statements volunteered by a witness, even if no question is pending. However, you must follow general rules. The motion must be specific. Overly broad motions will not be granted.

Motions to strike apply to issues, other than evidentiary rulings, during trial. They may be made, in connection with, a variety of other topics, such as pleadings and transcripts. Counsel simply asks the court to remove the objectionable verbiage.

Although these subjects have no other relevance in this chapter, I want to be sure you do not mistakenly believe these motions, only pertain to the deletion of unwanted testimony. Like any other trial lawyer, I prefer lodging an objection, to a motion to strike, especially in a jury trial. The jury may be inappropriately influenced, because jurors have already heard testimony the judge is now telling them to ignore. (*Think about any color, but blue*.)

Now, let's discuss the various grounds for making objections. As with other examples herein, I will list the California statute, governing my state, and remind you to review the applicable section, if you are in another state.

Hearsay

California Evidence Code §1200 governs hearsay. Hearsay is any out of court statement its proponents are offering, to prove the truth, of whatever they are attempting to assert. If hearsay does not fit into any of the statutory exceptions, it is inadmissible.

"(a) Hearsay evidence is evidence of a statement that was made other than by a witness while testifying at the hearing and that is offered to prove the truth of the matter stated.

(b) Except as provided by law, hearsay evidence is inadmissible.

(c) This section shall be known and may be cited as the hearsay rule."

Please note subsection (b). The final four words in it read: *"hearsay evidence is inadmissible."* That is the general rule concerning hearsay. However, the preceding five words, *"(e)xcept as provided by law,"* is the exception, to the general inadmissibility of hearsay. In law school, I remember one of my professors wryly noting, some general rules have so many exceptions, they virtually swallow up the general rule itself. I believe it was my evidence professor who said this. No doubt, he was talking about hearsay. Here are some of the common exceptions, to the hearsay rule, which otherwise dictate inadmissibility of such evidence.

Exceptions to Hearsay Rule

1. Admissions and Confessions

a. Admissions

Section 1220 refers to what is commonly called *an admission.* To be admissible, it must be made by a party, to an action, such as a defendant in a criminal matter, rather than made by a third party, in the defendant's behalf. An example? A shooter admitting they shot their victim.

Evidence Code §1220: "Evidence of a statement is not made inadmissible by the hearsay rule when offered against the declarant in an action to which he is a party in either his individual or representative capacity, regardless of whether the statement was made in his individual or representative capacity."

Section 1221 refers to what is commonly called an *adoptive* admission, and is admissible, against a party to an action, providing the party's words or conduct indicate they personally believe in the truth of the statement made. An example would be the same shooter, described above, shrugging, when asked if he shot the victim, thus indicating he did.

Evidence Code §1221: "Evidence of a statement offered against a party is not made inadmissible by the hearsay rule if the statement is one of which the party, with knowledge of the content thereof, has by words or other conduct manifested his adoption or his belief in its truth."

Section 1222 refers to what is commonly called *an admission authorized by a party to an action.* The party must authorize another person, to make the admission, in their behalf. An example would be two fellow arsonists leaving the scene of the fire. One admits lighting the fire. The other indicates they approve of the admission.

Evidence Code §1222: "Evidence of a statement offered against a party is not made inadmissible by the hearsay rule if:

(a) The statement was made by a person authorized by the party to make a statement or statements for him concerning the subject matter of the statement; and,

(b) The evidence is offered either after admission of evidence sufficient to sustain a finding of such authority or, in the court's discretion as to the order of proof, subject to the admission of such evidence."

Section 1223 refers to what is commonly called *an admission of a co-conspirator.* To be admissible, it must be made, while the conspiracy is still pending. An example would be a gang-banger making a statement, on behalf of other members of the same criminal enterprise.

Basically, an admission is a statement by a party, acknowledging a fact, or statement, relevant to the case, to which they are a party, is true. The statement may or may not be made to law enforcement personnel. The statement may or may not be spontaneous.

Evidence Code §1223: "Evidence of a statement offered against a party is not made inadmissible by the hearsay rule if:
(a) The statement was made by the declarant while participating in a conspiracy to commit a crime or civil wrong and in furtherance of the objective of that conspiracy;
(b) The statement was made prior to or during the time that the party was participating in that conspiracy; and,
(c) The evidence is offered either after admission of evidence sufficient to sustain a finding of the facts specified in subdivisions (a) and (b) or, in the court's discretion as to the order of proof, subject to the admission of such evidence."

How do admissions differ from confessions? Think of admissions as partial confessions, by the person making them. By that, I mean such statements lack one or more of the elements of the crime, of which such a person stands accused.

Confessions, on the other hand, contain full detailed renditions of what happened. They routinely include each and every element of whatever crime they stand accused of committing. Generally they include minute details known only to the actual perpetrator, and are made to relevant law enforcement personnel.

Confession

Evidence Code §1228: "Notwithstanding any other provision of law, for the purpose of establishing the elements of the crime in order to admit as evidence the confession of a person accused of violating Section 261, 264.1, 285, 286, 288, 288a, 289, or 647a of the Penal Code, a court, in its discretion, may determine that a statement of the complaining witness is not made inadmissible by the hearsay rule if it finds all of the following:
(a) The statement was made by a minor child under the age of 12, and the contents of the statement were included in a written report of a law enforcement official or an employee of a county welfare department.
(b) The statement describes the minor child as a victim of sexual abuse.
(c) The statement was made prior to the defendant's confession.
The court shall view with caution the testimony of a person recounting hearsay where there is evidence of personal bias or prejudice.

(d) There are no circumstances, such as significant inconsistencies between the confession and the statement concerning material facts establishing any element of the crime or the identification of the defendant that would render the statement unreliable.
(e) The minor child is found to be unavailable pursuant to paragraph (2) or (3) of subdivision (a) of Section 240 or refuses to testify.
(f) The confession was memorialized in a trustworthy fashion by a law enforcement official.

If the prosecution intends to offer a statement of the complaining witness pursuant to this section, the prosecution shall serve a written notice upon the defendant at least 10 days prior to the hearing or trial at which the prosecution intends to offer the statement.

If the statement is offered during trial, the court's determination shall be made out of the presence of the jury. If the statement is found to be admissible pursuant to this section, it shall be admitted out of the presence of the jury and solely for the purpose of determining the admissibility of the confession of the defendant."

Since the typical confession is obtained from a suspect, who is not free to leave your immediate presence, prior to any questioning of them, remember to read them their Miranda rights, from the departmental-issued Miranda advisement card, you should routinely carry, if this is the situation. This applies if they are:

1. a suspect in a crime
2. not free to leave the presence of any LEO
3. about to be asked questions which may lead to incriminating answers

Read the admonition, verbatim. Make certain the suspect has acknowledged they understand their rights, by executing the waiver form provided them, by your department.

Even if you are a veteran officer, who has long before committed the verbiage to memory, as we discussed earlier, please read it from the card verbatim. You do not want to give a defense attorney a foothold they do not deserve. It is too easy for them to convince a jury you misspoke, even when you did not. If you read it from the card, you decrease the likelihood the defense will get any traction. Remember, the job of defense counsel is to create reasonable doubt. Do not inadvertently help them, by getting unnecessarily creative.

Any Miranda admonition must inform any suspect of their right to remain silent:

1. anything they say can, and will, be used against them in court
2. their right to counsel, without any charge to them

If you are in a jurisdiction that requires you to also obtain a waiver that the suspect not only waives his Miranda rights, but also is willing to answer your questions, be sure to include this in any waiver you obtain, written or oral.

Miranda Admonition

1. You have the right to remain silent
2. Anything you say can, and will, be used against you, in a court of law
3. You have the right to an attorney
4. If you cannot afford an attorney, one will be appointed for you, at no cost to you

Waiver

1. Do you understand the rights I have just read to you?
2. Do you wish to give up, or waive, those rights, so you can talk to me?

Declarations against Penal Interest

Evidence Code §1230: "Evidence of a statement by a declarant having sufficient knowledge of the subject is not made inadmissible by the hearsay rule if the declarant is unavailable as a witness and the statement, when made, was so far contrary to the declarant's pecuniary or proprietary interest, or so far subjected him to the risk of civil or criminal liability, or so far tended to render invalid a claim by him against another, or created such a risk of making him an object of hatred, ridicule, or social disgrace in the community, that a reasonable man in his position would not have made the statement unless he believed it to be true."

A declaration against penal interest is deemed to be admissible because it is "...so far contrary to the declarant's pecuniary or proprietary interest, or so far subject(s) him to the risk of civil or criminal liability, or so far tend(s) to render invalid a claim by him against another, or create(s) such a risk of making him an object of hatred, ridicule or social disgrace in the community...", a reasonable person would not make such a statement, unless they believed it to be true.

Prior inconsistent statements

Evidence Code §1235: "Evidence of a statement made by a witness is not made inadmissible by the hearsay rule if the statement is inconsistent with his testimony at the hearing and is offered in compliance with Section 770."

By using a *prior inconsistent statement*, you are attempting to impeach the credibility of a witness, by showing they previously said something, not consistent with their testimony, at your trial, or at whatever other hearing they are testifying.

This is not limited to courtroom proceedings. If you are participating in an administrative hearing, or anywhere else an adverse witness is testifying, after taking an oath, you can attempt to discredit the witness by showing they have previously testified inconsistently, with their instant testimony. Please compare your own state's Evidence Code, to confirm its language is consistent with §1235.

Prior consistent statements

Evidence Code §1236: "Evidence of a statement previously made by a witness is not made inadmissible by the hearsay rule if the statement is consistent with his testimony at the hearing and is offered in compliance with Section 791."

Prior *consistent* statements are the opposite of prior *inconsistent* statements, and are used to show one of your own witnesses is being credible, when challenged, by the opposition. You do this by showing a witness previously made the same or a similar statement, and therefore is to be believed now because they are essentially saying the same thing they have already said, outside court. The prior statement does not have to be made under oath.

Past recollection recorded

Evidence Code §1237: (a) "Evidence of a statement previously made by a witness is not made inadmissible by the hearsay rule if the statement would have been admissible if made by him while testifying, the statement concerns a matter as to which the witness has insufficient present recollection to enable him to testify fully and accurately, and the statement is contained in a writing which:
(1) was made at a time when the fact recorded in the writing actually occurred or was fresh in the witness' memory;
(2) was made (i) by the witness himself or under his direction or (ii) by some other person for the purpose of recording the witness' statement at the time it was made;

(3) is offered after the witness testifies that the statement he made was a true statement of such fact; and,
(4) is offered after the writing is authenticated as an accurate record of the statement.
(b) the writing may be read into evidence, but the writing itself may not be received in evidence unless offered by an adverse party."

Past recollection recorded can be used, whenever a witness testifies they are unable to remember, fully and accurately, a prior event. If you have a document, you can use to refresh their recollection, but are unsuccessful in doing so, by using it. Once you establish the preliminary facts, i.e., the witness does not recall the event and reviewing the document does not refresh his recollection, show the witness the document, and:

1. ask if the document was made, when the event was still fresh in their mind
2. ask if they either personally made the document, or personally directed someone else to do so, in order to record someone's statement
3. ask if the statement in the document is true
4. ask if the document is an accurate record of the statement
5. ask to read the document, verbatim, into the court's record

CAVEAT: *Only an adverse party can offer the actual writing into evidence.* In other words, only your courtroom opponent can do this. If the witness is yours, you are limited to having them read the content of the writing, into evidence. However, they can read the contents of it, verbatim. If you do this, take the time to insure it is read, slowly enough, the trier of fact is able to clearly hear the evidence, whether that is the judge or a jury.

Spontaneous statements

Evidence Code §1240: "Evidence of a statement is not made inadmissible by the hearsay rule if the statement:
(a) purports to narrate, describe, or explain an act, condition, or event perceived by the declarant; and
(b) was made spontaneously while the declarant was under the stress of excitement caused by such perception."

Spontaneous statements are also known as *excited utterances*. They are admissible, only if they are made, by the declarant, reacting to the stress of whatever excitement caused them to speak, as they did.

Evidence Code §1241: "Evidence of a statement is not made inadmissible by the hearsay rule, if the statement:
(a) is offered to explain, qualify, or make understandable, conduct of the declarant; and

(b) was made, while the declarant was engaged, in such conduct."

A spontaneous statement is used to explain, qualify, or make understandable, the conduct of the declarant, i.e., the person who made the statement. An example could be one made by an eyewitness to a shooting, e.g., "...he just shot that guy..."

Dying declarations

Evidence Code §1242: "Evidence of a statement made by a dying person respecting the cause and circumstances of his death is not made inadmissible by the hearsay rule if the statement was made upon his personal knowledge and under a sense of immediately impending death."

A dying declaration is offered, on behalf of a person who believes they face imminent death, when they make a statement incriminating the person they believe is the perpetrator. They do not have to die for the statement to be admissible. They only have to believe they are facing imminent death. For example, if you find a stabbing victim who appears near death, and ask who did it, if the victim replies: "...Joe Smith did this...", or words to that effect, you can offer it into evidence as a dying declaration despite the fact it is unmistakable hearsay,. Even if the victim survives, it's still admissible.

Statements about a declarant's mental or physical health

Evidence Code §1250: "(a) Subject to Section 1252, evidence of a statement of the declarant's then existing state of mind, emotion, or physical sensation (including a statement of intent, plan, motive, design, mental feeling, pain, or bodily health) is not made inadmissible by the hearsay rule when:

(1) the evidence is offered to prove the declarant's state of mind, emotion, or physical sensation at that time or at any other time when it is itself an issue in the action; or,

(2) the evidence is offered to prove or explain acts or conduct of the declarant.

(b) this section does not make admissible evidence of a statement of memory or belief to prove the fact remembered or believed."

Evidence Code §1251: "Subject to Section 1252, evidence of a statement of the declarant's state of mind, emotion, or physical sensation (including a statement of intent, plan, motive, design, mental feeling, pain, or bodily health) at a time prior to the statement is not made inadmissible by the hearsay rule if:

(a) the declarant is unavailable as a witness; and

(b) the evidence is offered to prove such prior state of mind, emotion, or physical sensation when it is itself an issue in the action and the evidence is not offered to prove any fact other than such state of mind, emotion, or physical sensation."

Evidence Code §1252: "Evidence of a statement is inadmissible under this article if the statement was made under circumstances such as to indicate its lack of trustworthiness."

Evidence Code §1253: "Subject to Section 1252, evidence of a statement is not made inadmissible by the hearsay rule if the statement was made for purposes of medical diagnosis or treatment and describes medical history, or past or present symptoms, pain, or sensations, or the inception or general character of the cause or external source thereof insofar as reasonably pertinent to diagnosis or treatment. This section applies only to a statement made by a victim who is a minor at the time of the proceedings, provided the statement was made when the victim was under the age of 12 describing any act, or attempted act, of child abuse or neglect. 'Child abuse' and 'child neglect,' for purposes of this section, have the meanings provided in subdivision (c) of Section 1360. In addition, 'child abuse' means any act proscribed by Chapter 5 (commencing with Section 281) of Title 9 of Part 1 of the Penal Code committed against a minor."

As with a dying declaration, a statement about a declarant's mental or physical health is offered to prove how they felt when they made the statement, providing the declarant is unavailable as a witness.

Business records

Evidence Code §1270: "As used in this article, 'a business' includes every kind of business, governmental activity, profession, occupation, calling, or operation of institutions, whether carried on for profit or not."

Evidence Code §1271: (please see **Chapter 18** for verbatim version, and author's comments)

Evidence Code §1272: "Evidence of the absence from the records of a business of a record of an asserted act, condition, or event is not made inadmissible by the hearsay rule when offered to prove the nonoccurrence of the act or event, or the nonexistence of the condition, if:
(a) it was the regular course of that business to make records of all such acts, conditions, or events at or near the time of the act, condition, or event and to preserve them; and,

(b) the sources of information and method and time of preparation of the records of that business were such that the absence of a record of an act, condition, or event is a trustworthy indication that the act or event did not occur or the condition did not exist."

Public records

Evidence Code §1280: (*please see Chapter 18 for verbatim version and my comments*)

Relevancy

Evidence Code §210: "'Relevant evidence'" means evidence, including evidence relevant to the credibility of a witness or hearsay declarant, having any tendency in reason to prove or disprove any disputed fact that is of consequence to the determination of the action."

Relevant simply means the proffered, i.e., offered, evidence has any tendency in reason to prove or disprove any disputed fact needed to prove your case or disprove the opposition's case.

Best Evidence Rule

Evidence Code §1520: "The content of a writing may be proved by an otherwise admissible original."

Evidence Code §1521: "(a) The content of a writing may be proved by otherwise admissible secondary evidence. The court shall exclude secondary evidence of the content of writing if the court determines either of the following:
(1) a genuine dispute exists concerning material terms of the writing and justice requires the exclusion.
(2) admission of the secondary evidence would be unfair.
(b) nothing in this section makes admissible oral testimony to prove the content of a writing if the testimony is inadmissible under Section 1523 (oral testimony of the content of a writing).
(c) nothing in this section excuses compliance with Section 1401 (requiring authentication).
(d) This section shall be known as the 'Secondary Evidence Rule'."

Evidence Code section 1522: "(a) In addition to the grounds for exclusion authorized by Section 1521, in a criminal action the court shall exclude secondary evidence of the content of a writing if the court determines that the original is in the proponent's possession, custody, or control, and the proponent has not made the original reasonably available for inspection at or before trial. This section does not apply to any of the following:

(1) a duplicate as defined in Section 260.

(2) a writing that is not closely related to the controlling issues in the action.

(3) a copy of a writing in the custody of a public entity.

(4) a copy of a writing that is recorded in the public records, if the record or a certified copy of it is made evidence of the writing by statute.

(b) In a criminal action, a request to exclude secondary evidence of the content of a writing, under this section or any other law, shall not be made in the presence of the jury."

Evidence Code section 1523: "(a) Except as otherwise provided by statute, oral testimony is not admissible to prove the content of a writing.

(b) Oral testimony of the content of a writing is not made inadmissible by subdivision (a) if the proponent does not have possession or control of a copy of the writing and the original is lost or has been destroyed without fraudulent intent on the part of the proponent of the evidence.

(c) Oral testimony of the content of a writing is not made inadmissible by subdivision (a) if the proponent does not have possession or control of the original or a copy of the writing and either of the following conditions is satisfied:

(1) neither the writing nor a copy of the writing was reasonably procurable by the proponent by use of the court's process or by other available means.

(2) the writing is not closely related to the controlling issues and it would be inexpedient to require its production.

(d) Oral testimony of the content of a writing is not made inadmissible by subdivision (a) if the writing consists of numerous accounts or other writings that cannot be examined in court without great loss of time, and the evidence sought from them is only the general result of the whole."

The *Best Evidence Rule* has been significantly relaxed, in California, during the period of time I have been a lawyer. When I first began practicing law, the general rule concerning admissibility of evidence, was a requirement, the proponent of any document had, to produce the original document, unless a statutory exception, for its production, in court, was established.

The primary reason, for the existence of this rule, is to prevent doctored, i.e., bogus, documents from being introduced, instead of the genuine document. But the passage of time has created so many exceptions, to the requirement the original be produced, the original rule has virtually been swallowed up by them.

They include:

1. certain duplicate copies
2. writings not closely related to the relevant issues in the case
3. copies of original documents, in the custody of public entities
4. copies of original documents, in the custody of public entities, if the original, or a certified copy, is viewed as evidence, by statute

Authentication

Evidence Code §1400: "Authentication of a writing means (a) the introduction of evidence sufficient to sustain a finding that it is the writing that the proponent of the evidence claims it is or (b) the establishment of such facts by any other means provided by law."

Evidence Code §1401: "(a) Authentication of a writing is required before it may be received in evidence.
(b) Authentication of a writing is required before secondary evidence of its content may be received in evidence."

Evidence Code §1402: "The party producing a writing as genuine which has been altered, or appears to have been altered, after its execution, in a part material to the question in dispute, must account for the alteration or appearance thereof. He may show that the alteration was made by another, without his concurrence, or was made with the consent of the parties affected by it, or otherwise properly or innocently made, or that the alteration did not change the meaning or language of the instrument. If he does that, he may give the writing in evidence, but not otherwise."

As noted previously, *authentication* of any document is nothing more, than producing evidence to establish the document in question, is genuine. This is generally done by offering foundational testimony from the custodian of records. Keep in mind, the information provided in this chapter is offered to prepare you to both deal with objections made by your opposition in court, and to understand the mechanics of objecting to the introduction of evidence.

Chapter 20
Examination of Witnesses

This chapter deals with the questioning of witnesses, under oath. California Evidence Code §772 spells out the manner in which examination of witnesses is done:

"(a) The examination of a witness shall proceed in the following phases: direct-examination, cross-examination, redirect-examination, recross-examination, and continuing thereafter by redirect and recross-examination.

(b) Unless for good cause the court otherwise directs, each phase of the examination of a witness must be concluded before the succeeding phase begins.

(c) Subject to subdivision (d), a party may, in the discretion of the court, interrupt his cross-examination, redirect-examination, or recross-examination of a witness, in order to examine the witness upon a matter not within the scope of a previous examination of the witness.

(d) If the witness is the defendant in a criminal action, the witness may not, without his consent, be examined under direct-examination by another party."

Following, you will find the various facets of testimony, including an explanation of what each segment involves.

1. Direct-examination
2. Cross-examination
3. Redirect-examination
4. Recross-examination
5. Rebuttal (*if permitted by court*)
6. Surrebuttal (*if permitted by court*)

Direct-examination

Examination is the questioning of witnesses, usually by a lawyer. *Direct-examination* of witnesses obtains initial testimony, by one's own attorney. If a witness is without counsel, their initial testimony is still called *direct.* The normal narrative you offer, in traffic court, to explain what a motorist did that merited their receipt of the citation you issued, is your direct testimony.

The word examination is synonymous with *questioning*, as in an inspection. The questioner inspects, or examines, the witness. Whenever I offer the direct-examination of one of my own witnesses, which is done in a question and answer format, as is any exchange between counsel and witness, I am eliciting testimony, so they can tell the trier of fact what I have subpoenaed them to share, under oath.

This is true whether the trier of fact is a judge, or a jury. A witness either testifies to something they observed with their percipient senses, such as witnessing a traffic collision, or as an expert, so they can offer their opinion, on an ultimate issue in a case. An example of an expert would be the criminalist who testifies to the significance of the significance of a .15 percent blood alcohol level blood sample.

On direct-examination, although the witness is not generally permitted to give a narrative answer, the questioning is designed to provide witnesses, with more freedom to answer questions, than is permitted on cross-examination.

A leading question, on the other hand, is designed to severely limit the witness' ability to answer it. Such a question normally calls for a yes or no answer. Asking a witness, for example, if they are still beating their spouse is a leading question. They can answer it, with a yes or a no.

The examiner, aka questioner, is not permitted to ask a witness a leading question on direct or redirect, unless otherwise permitted to do so, pursuant to California Evidence Code §767, which reads:

"(a) Except under special circumstances where the interests of justice otherwise require:

(1) a leading question may not be asked of a witness on direct or redirect-examination.

(2) a leading question may be asked of a witness on cross-examination or recross-examination.

(b) The court may, in the interests of justice permit a leading question to be asked of a child under 10 years of age or a dependent person with a substantial cognitive impairment in a case involving a prosecution under Section 273a, 273d, 288.5, 368, or any of the acts described in Section 11165.1 or 11165.2 of the Penal Code."

Cross-examination

Cross-examination occurs immediately after direct-examination. Depending on the nature of the proceeding, direct-examination will either be a question and answer scenario, or a narrative version of a factual situation, upon approval by the court, as described earlier, illustrating your normal traffic court presentation.

Although narrative answers are generally not permitted, if the formal rules of evidence are being followed, sans counsel, this is normally permitted by both sides, in traffic court. When you are questioning, or *examining*, a witness, irrespective of whether this is a prosecution or defense witness, never forget this cardinal rule. *never ask a question, unless you first know the answer.*

This is particularly crucial, if the witness is a defense witness. The reason for this, is very simple and basic. Once you ask the question, you are pretty much stuck with the answer. That's because you asked the question.

You cannot erase it, by asking the judge to strike it either. You asked it. You are stuck with it. In fact, if you ask the judge to strike it, expect them to bluntly tell you why that will not happen in their courtroom. Try this in mine.

I can assure you, from first-hand experience, this is not a mistake you will want to repeat. However, as indicated earlier, you are permitted to ask leading questions on cross. In fact, you are expected to do this. The reason? It allows you to obtain testimony from an adverse witness that is going to be more helpful to your side of the case, than it would be, if you were limited to asking questions that would allow the witness to elaborate.

Redirect-examination

Redirect-examination is nothing more than questioning your own witnesses in order to clear up any ambiguities, created by their testimony on cross-examination. You are limited, with redirect, to the scope of cross-examination. In other words, do not ask questions that do not deal with what was discussed *exclusively* on cross.

This is not an automatic thing. In other words, if opposing counsel did not do any damage to any of your own witnesses on cross, there is no reason to waste time and energy redirect examining them.

Recross-examination

R*ecross-examination* is meant to clear up questions raised, as the result of the testimony, of any witness, on redirect. Like being limited to the scope of cross-examination, during your recross, you are similarly limited, on recross, to the scope of redirect. If opposing counsel did not ask questions about it on redirect, you are barred from asking questions about it, on recross. Even if opposing counsel asked about it on redirect, but did no damage to your case, do not waste your time talking about it on recross.

In order to give everyone, final bites of the apple, the questioner is also permitted to ask questions of the witness on rebuttal, limited to the scope of redirect. In conclusion, the opposing side can present evidence on Surrebuttal, limited to the scope of rebuttal. However, I have never personally seen examinations go this far. Surrebuttal, in essence, is used to rebut what was presented on rebuttal.

My respectful suggestion? Don't get carried away, asking any more questions, than necessary. Jurors tend to get bored. If it does not need to be asked, do not ask it. I am not saying opposing counsel should be permitted to mislead a jury, with answers they may twist, from a witness' mouth. Just be sure to take the time to see how the jury is doing. If jurors appear bored, they probably are.

As we discussed elsewhere, all evidence is admissible, but for a timely and proper objection. This is reasonably well spelled out in California Evidence Code §351, which reads: "Except as otherwise provided by statute, all relevant evidence is admissible," and should apply similarly, if you work in another state. Just check your state's Evidence Code to be sure. Rely on your local prosecutors. They do it daily. Ask and ye shall receive.

As previously discussed, your state should have a comparable section. Therefore, this particular sword cuts both ways. It allows you to testify to the underlying facts of your case, unless the opposition objects, before you say something under oath. However, the opposition must also base its objection, on the proper ground, found in your state's Evidence Code. If the opposition does not do that timely, they must make a motion to strike, relying on the same evidentiary grounds.

So, what if you are in traffic court, without the assistance of a prosecutor? Conversely, it may also mean you can prevent the other side's witness, from offering inadmissible testimony, or proffering any other forms of inadmissible evidence.

You will not have an unlimited range of cross-examination. Irrespective of your state, expect cross-examination to be limited, to the scope of direct-examination. For example, per California Evidence Code §773:

"a) A witness examined by one party may be cross-examined upon any matter within the scope of the direct-examination by each other party to the action in such order as the court directs.

(b)The cross-examination of a witness by any party whose interest is not adverse to the party calling him is subject to the same rules that are applicable to the direct-examination."

Civil and Administrative Matters

Although California Evidence Code §776, or your state's equivalent, will not work in criminal matters it's a nice tool to use, in civil or administrative matters. It will not work in criminal matters because a criminal defendant has the absolute right to not testify, unless he so chooses. However, in civil or administrative matters, unless defendants are otherwise able to assert their Fifth Amendment privilege against self-incrimination, this section works nicely.

I used it regularly in matters heard by Administrative Law Judges from the Office of Administrative Hearings, when I was a DMV Staff Counsel. What's the real beauty of this section? It allows you to call the subject of the hearing as your first witness, even if they are an opposition witness. If they are not expecting you to call them, as your first witness, it tends to rattle them, if nothing else. It also gives you the opportunity to begin presenting your case quickly, through the mouth of the very target of the hearing. See if your state has a similar statute.

California Evidence Code §776 reads:

"(a) A party to the record of any civil action, or a person identified with such a party, may be called and examined as if under cross-examination by any adverse party at any time during the presentation of evidence by the party calling the witness.

(b) A witness examined by a party under this section may be cross-examined by all other parties to the action in such order as the court directs; but, subject to subdivision (e), the witness may be examined only as if under redirect-examination by:

(1) in the case of a witness who is a party, his own counsel and counsel for a party who is not adverse to the witness.

(2) in the case of a witness who is not a party, counsel for the party with whom the witness is identified and counsel for a party who is not adverse to the party with whom the witness is identified.

(c) For the purpose of this section, parties represented by the same counsel are deemed to be a single party.

(d) For the purpose of this section, a person is identified with a party if he is:

(1) a person for whose immediate benefit the action is prosecuted or defended by the party.

(2) a director, officer, superintendent, member, agent, employee, or managing agent of the party or of a person specified in paragraph (1), or any public employee of a public entity when such public entity is the party.

(3) a person who was in any of the relationships specified in paragraph (2) at the time of the act or omission giving rise to the cause of action.

(4) a person who was in any of the relationships specified in paragraph (2) at the time he obtained knowledge of the matter concerning which he is sought to be examined under this section.

(e) Paragraph (2) of subdivision (b) does not require counsel for the party with whom the witness is identified and counsel for a party who is not adverse to the party with whom the witness is identified to examine the witness as if under redirect-examination if the party who called the witness for examination under this section:

(1) is also a person identified with the same party with whom the witness is identified.

(2) is the personal representative, heir, successor, or assignee of a person identified with the same party with whom the witness is identified."

Putting all the legalese aside, this section basically says you may call any adverse witness, to the witness stand, as your witness, and ask them leading questions, just like you can otherwise do, when you cross-examine opposing witnesses. As a rule of thumb, I found administrative law boring, but §776 certainly added some excitement, otherwise absent.

Credibility of Witnesses

Credibility of witnesses is critically important. If the trier of fact does not believe a witness, you are wasting your time, offering their testimony. By way of example, I knew of a police officer, decades ago, who had a horrible reputation for perceived dishonesty. I'm told the senior judge at the Municipal Court where he often appeared on traffic matters contacted the man's sergeant.

In no uncertain terms, His Honor said to not waste the court's time anymore, with any of his cases. Talk about a career ender. Let me explain why this is so important so there is no confusion. I cannot stress enough how important it is to not get painted with this particular brush.

An immediate problem for any LEO who is accused of professional dishonesty is the impact *Brady* has on their career. A LEO in my state, labeled dishonest is finished. Such a situation means the DA is ethically obligated to voluntarily disclose that information to the defense, on any case that officer appears. This is best case scenario, which is not going to happen anyhow.

Hypothetically, any defense attorney obtaining such information would be derelict in their duties, if they did not use that for whatever benefit they could acquire, if that officer was on the witness stand. Not only would that be embarrassing for the officer, to have to answer such questions in a public courtroom, but it also would instantly be quite career limiting.

Here is what would really happen. If such a predicament developed, the prosecuting attorney's office would begin resolving any of that officer's cases. If any of those cases were still pending, the prosecutor would not take them to trial. This means defendants would get lenient sentences they did not deserve.

Any new cases handled by that officer would almost certainly be rejected by the prosecutor, due to the *Brady* baggage that officer would now be carrying. And since dishonesty would quite likely result in disciplinary action by that officer's department, it would not surprise me a bit, if the officer would eventually be terminated for that very reason.

So jealously guard your reputation for honesty, by always telling the truth. If you cannot do that, you are in the wrong line of work. If that's true, please start job hunting now.

In my state, you may even impeach the credibility of your own witness, according to California Evidence Code §785, which reads: "The credibility of a witness may be attacked or supported by any party, including the party calling them."

A number of factors will dictate how you are perceived, from the witness stand. They include the following factors:

1. your demeanor while testifying, and the manner in which you do this.
    a. in other words, do you come across as sincere?
    b. or, do you appear evasive and untruthful?
        (1) if so, why?
2. the character of your testimony.
3. what is the quality of your testimony?
4. the extent of your capacity to perceive, to recall, or to tell the trier of fact the factual scenario, you are attempting to convey.
    a. were you able to adequately tell the trier of fact what your percipient senses perceived? Were you able to recall relevant facts?
5. the extent of your opportunity to perceive underlying facts connected to the case.

a. were you in a position to really perceive what you say you observed?

(1) your character for honesty, veracity, or the opposite.

b. do people who know you see you as truthful or as a liar?

c. do you have a bias, interest or other motive that colors your testimony?

d. is there anything about your view of this case that tends to make your testimony appear suspect?

e. for example, did you say anything to the motorist, during the T-stop that makes it appear you have any special bias against this type of offense, more so than other offenses?

f. or, did the motorist say anything to you that causes you to reasonably believe that motorist has a bias against the enforcement of the code section you believe he violated?

(1) did you say anything previously consistent with your testimony?

(2) did you say anything previously inconsistent with your testimony?

(3) do the facts, as testified to by you, really exist?

(4) what is your attitude concerning the case or your own testimony?

(a) do you come across as:

i. hostile?

ii. reluctant?

iii. untruthful?

(a) have you admitted telling a lie?

California Evidence Code §780 deals with the credibility of witnesses:

"Except as otherwise provided by statute, the court or jury may consider in determining the credibility of a witness any matter that has any tendency in reason to prove or disprove the truthfulness of his testimony at the hearing, including but not limited to any of the following:

(a) his demeanor while testifying and the manner in which he testifies.

(b) the character of his testimony.

(c) the extent of his capacity to perceive, to recollect, or to communicate any matter about which he testifies.

(d) the extent of his opportunity to perceive any matter about which he testifies.

(e) his character for honesty or veracity or their opposites.

(f) the existence or nonexistence of a bias, interest, or other motive.

(g) a statement previously made by him that is consistent with his testimony at the hearing.
(h) a statement made by him that is inconsistent with any part of his testimony at the hearing.
(i) the existence or nonexistence of any fact testified to by him.
(j) his attitude toward the action in which he testifies or toward the giving of testimony.
(k) his admission of untruthfulness."

In other words, irrespective of whose witness it is, if a party, to any action, in a California courtroom, disagrees with what he heard a witness say he has the ability to impeach that witness. The same vehicle should be available in your own state.

This can be done a number of ways. One way is to offer testimony, from another witness. A witness can also be impeached by confronting them, with a prior inconsistent statement they have made. If the court permits argument, following the presentation of evidence, this would be the time to point out, to the court, anything remarkable about the testimony of any defense witness that should make their believability suspect.

Do not be surprised, if a defendant tells the court the reason he is not guilty, is because you are a liar. However, unless you have a well-deserved reputation for dishonesty, expect the court to put this issue to rest quickly, if the jurist is doing their job. It's been my personal experience traffic court judges tend to be rather protective of the traffic cops they deal with regularly. Do the math.

Compound Questions

Compound questions are to be avoided. A compound question is one that asks more than one question, in the same sentence. They are actually multiple questions wrapped up, in a single question. Think of the kind of questions you hear TV talking heads routinely asking their guests, even if they are lawyers.

Each question should never call for more than one answer. As a practical matter, compound questions are confusing. It is unfair to ask witnesses to remember a shopping list of questions, they are supposed to answer, without a recorder available, to capture it, and play them back one-by-one. Here is why I personally dislike compound questions. Even if they were legally permitted, how is a witness expected to remember every sub-question the compound question tosses at them? To my way of thinking, compound questions are just fundamentally unfair. Never try to answer one. And, never ask any.

Leading Questions

As previously discussed, a big benefit cross-examination has over direct-examination? You are permitted to ask leading questions of opposing witnesses. A leading question is one that suggests the answer, or contains the information you are seeking.

An example of a leading question would be to ask a witness if he is still selling dope. As you can see, even if the witness is not a dope dealer, such a question tends to make them appear so, irrespective of their answer.

Leading questions are objectionable, unless they are asked on cross-examination, or meet other limited exceptions to this requirement. A leading question is one that essentially calls for an affirmative or negative answer, i.e., a yes or a no. Please consult your own state's Evidence Code for guidance.

Some Testimonial Do's and Don'ts

Here are some *do's* and *don'ts* you must absorb, and remember, in connection with your role as a witness. They are not limited to traffic court. They apply to your role as a witness, in any type of proceeding, whether it's in a court of law, an administrative proceeding, or elsewhere, such as arbitration or mediation.

In other words, if you are required to speak, after taking an oath, and perjury is the felony you face, if you are caught lying, the following suggestions I wholeheartedly recommend. They are comprehensive, common sense, and they work. I call them the *Ten Commandments of Testifying*.

Ten Commandments of Testifying

1. Wait for the Question

A common mistake inexperienced witnesses make is failing to wait for the entire question to be asked, before they try to answer it. This is problematic for a number of reasons. First, as noted above, only one person, at a time, is supposed to speak, in a courtroom. Since, you cannot answer the question, until it is asked, this means you are the one who must keep your powder dry, until it is your turn to talk.

If multiple people try to talk at the same time, even the most experienced court reporter will have difficulty understanding what is being said. That's because they cannot listen to two or more people, speaking simultaneously. You do not want a grumpy court reporter. Grumpy court reporters tend to make less than perfect records. And they tend to make judges grumpy. Judges like orderly courtrooms. I know I sure do. Do not upset this applecart.

Even if no court reporter is present, please wait until it's your turn to talk. If you do not listen to the entire question, you almost certainly will give an incorrect answer. So, do not speak, while someone else is speaking. This is particularly true, if there is a court reporter at work. So, please, just sit still, be quiet and listen to the entire question. Ditto for courtroom tape recorders.

As previously noted, reporters can only take down what one person is saying, at the same time. If they get annoyed, chances are the court will too, even if the judge is generally a patient person. Avoid doing this, by patiently waiting your turn. This is important enough for me to repeat this, for emphasis sake. Therefore, I am repeating it.

Unlike what people see on television, the art of asking questions, of witnesses, is an imperfect one. The practice of law is called, the practice of law, for a reason. An old joke reminds us mouthpieces it's called *practicing* law because lawyers keep doing it, until we get it right. For some folks that can take a lifetime. For others, even longer.

If you fail to wait for the question to be completely asked, you may answer *yes*, when you obviously meant to say *no*, had you waited, and listened, to the entire question. Doing so tends to make you appear unsure, at best, and untruthful, at worst, especially in front of juries. I can guarantee you it will result in a lecture, from the judge, every time you do it. So, please don't. Getting chewed out, by the judge, makes you look silly.

Lastly, if you answer too quickly, the opportunity for the prosecutor to object, to the form of the question, may be lost. You, and the prosecutor, have to work, as a team. If you do not work with them, obtaining justice will be far more difficult.

Never use the crystal ball approach to being a witness. In other words, do not guess, because you think you know, what the rest of the question, may be. Take your time, be patient, and be absolutely positive you understand the question. Make sure, you are the only one speaking, when you answer. If you wait, until the question is completed, you will.

2. Did You Understand the Question?

As noted immediately above, you need to wait for any question to be completely asked, before you try to answer it. However, it's more basic than that. Even though you wait for the question to be completely asked, does this mean you really understood it? Not necessarily.

If you did not understand the question, there is no way you can answer it, correctly and intelligently. So, if you do not understand any question, what should you do? For starters, never try to answer it. And, I mean *never*. What else? That's simple. Just tell the questioner, or the judge, you do not understand.

Then, ask to have the question repeated, or rephrased, depending on which applies. Should this happen, and trust me, it will, never allow yourself to be rushed. Although judges like to move things along in their courtrooms, because they almost always have some other case waiting to be heard, this is not your problem or concern.

You have a very important job, as a witness. First, you are under oath, and do not need to be accused of lying by some ignorant defendant, or overzealous lawyer. Therefore, be sure you understand any question, in order to testify competently. If you do not understand, that won't happen.

Never assume your failure to understand is because you did not comprehend. In truth and fact, it is almost always based, on the inability of the lawyer to pose a question you can, and should, reasonably understand, so you can answer it intelligently.

You are expected to do your job, by answering questions properly. Therefore, it is not asking too much for a lawyer to ask intelligible questions. That's their job. If you do not insist they do that, you are not doing yours. Stand your ground. Be polite, but firm. Never answer any question, unless you understand it completely, and are able to proficiently answer it. If you do not understand the question, you now know how to remedy this.

3. Be Articulate

Take the time to say what you mean. Do not speak too quickly, or too slowly. Keep your voice up, so everyone can hear you. Do not shout. Do not be uncomfortable, if it appears everyone in the courtroom is paying attention to what you are saying. They probably are. Get used to it. That's your turf now. You are its proud owner.

You need to be sure everyone connected with the case, can both hear and understand what you are saying. This includes the judge, prosecutor, defense counsel, defendant, court reporter, court clerk, and, if this is a jury trial, the jury. If you are unsure if everyone can hear you, a nice device I've seen employed is to ask the court reporter, or the judge, if you are speaking loudly enough.

There should be a microphone, right in front of you. Therefore, this should be a non-issue, as long as you are close enough to it, and are speaking distinctly enough, to be understood. Either way, if in doubt, always ask. Never forget to do this.

4. Be Responsive

Each question propounded to a witness, calls for a specific answer. Be sure you are being responsive, to each and every one of them. For example, if the question posed, asks you what time it is, state the time. Do not waste your time telling the questioner how you know that, what the time piece's brand name is, or where the watch factory is located.

What if you believe the prosecutor failed to ask you, a relevant and necessary question? Should you deviate from my instructions, and be *non-responsive*? No. Although the prosecutor may have simply forgotten to ask a particular question, it's more likely they decided to not ask it, for a tactical reason. Every prosecuting attorney is going to operate, a bit differently, than the next guy. Never give defense counsel unnecessary clues.

A prosecutor should always try to find time to talk with all witnesses, before they testify. In addition to learning what a witness is going to say, it's also an opportunity to explain why they choose to do, or not do, certain things, including how, and why they ask questions of witnesses, and even which ones they will ask.

Even if your prosecutor does not do this, it does not mean they are not taking care of business in the courtroom. Give them a chance. If you do not like the result, then you can talk to them, prior to the next case you share. See if you can politely suggest a different methodology. A good prosecutor should be open to new ideas.

If you can do so, during the case, in which this sort of issue arises, does time permit a discussion, with the prosecutor, during the next recess? Maybe they actually forgot to ask the question? If this happened, they can always ask the judge to allow them to reopen, and ask it out of order. If the answer is that important, the judge will do so.

5. Do Not be Argumentative

Be nice to defense counsel. And be nice to the defendant. I'm serious. You do not have to be combative to win. All you probably will do is convince some undecided jurors to not like you, and vote not guilty. I am not suggesting being buddy-buddy with the opposition. All I am saying is you will not score any points by scowling at everyone.

Do not waste energy fighting over minutiae. There's an old Latin expression: *de minimus non curat lex*, which translates to *the law does not deal with trifles*. If so, why should you? Let your evidence speak for itself. Do not be the guy who figuratively pounds counsel table. People do that because they do not have the facts, or the law, on their side. You do, or you would not be in court. Take comfort in that.

I remain convinced, to this very day, I lost a case a long time ago, in large part, because my case agent had a bad attitude. The bailiff actually had to tell him to shut up. Ironically, the reason he was sulking was because the defendant was a righteously chronic ne'er-do-well, and troublemaker. The LEO did not like him.

Neither did I but I sure did not waste my energy pouting. Do not get mad, get even. Present your case, and convict the bad guy. That is the best sort of revenge. The courtroom is not the place to compete, with a guy like that, and certainly not, down at his level. Cream always rises to the top of a container of milk. If there is anything we good guys should be doing, it's rising to the top.

Unfortunately, my investigating officer complained so much the jury began to hear what he was saying. Instead of paying attention to the evidence, and convicting a rather dedicated felon, some of the jurors were so turned off by my case agent's antics, they decided his behavior alone was the equivalent of reasonable doubt. Wrong move.

They deadlocked 9-3 for guilty, instead of easily convicting the bad guy like they should have. The evidence was certainly there in abundance. The really annoying part of this, for me, was the fact his sleazy defense attorney got a gift he was not entitled to receive. He would not have, but for what happened. It meant he won.

If you allow either the defendant, or defense counsel, to push your buttons, they will do so. The jury will see this. Remember, it's a defense attorney's job to make you look like a fool. If you give them an opening, they will be more than happy to oblige.

This is especially important to avoid, on cases, such as resisting arrest, or battery on a peace officer, like the one I just described. If you display a negative attitude for jurors to see, they may think you deserved what you got. So be sure you are thinking intelligently, on such issues. Remember to behave, appropriately.

6. Be Yourself

Yes, this may sound trite and cliché, at first blush. So stipulated. But, it is not. It's true, and it's axiomatic. What do I mean when I say *be yourself*? I mean exactly what that phrase implies. Allow your own unique personality to dictate, how you act, in the courtroom, and on the witness stand. If you are the serious type by nature, be yourself. If you are more jovial, be yourself. Just be sure to act appropriately for circumstances.

While all of us tend to have role models, we try to emulate, it does not mean you should trade yourself in, wholesale, in order to be someone you obviously are not. While it is helpful, to allow the examples of others, to be instructive, this should never mean we allow ourselves to be subjugated, by the more dominant personalities of other people.

If you try to come off, as someone, on the witness stand, other than the person you really are, you will not be comfortable with that role. I suspect the trier of fact will not, either, particularly, if that trier is twelve strangers in a jury box.

Focus your energy, on sharing relevant facts with them, whether they are the judge, or a jury. Interact with them, so they know you realize they are in the same courtroom, as you. If you center more on addressing the evidence, and sharing relevant facts with the folks, you have to convince you have met your burden of proof, you will not need to concern yourself, with how you are being perceived. Remember, the trier of fact needs to focus, on the story you are telling, not the story teller.

7. Be Prepared

Never go near any courtroom to give testimony, without bringing whatever document you need, to refresh your recollection, concerning the underlying facts of your case. This can include:

1. your copy of the citation
2. your incident report
3. any document prepared, by another officer, on the same case

A Superior Court judge I have known, since I began practicing law, has an expression that fits this issue, like a glove. He first used it, when he was still a prosecutor, during an argument with defense counsel. He bellowed "...if a wad of bubble gum, will refresh a witness' recollection, that alone is sufficient..." He won the debate. Now, that he's on the bench, hopefully, he has not forgotten that pearl of wisdom.

Before you enter any courtroom, always take the time to thoroughly review that document, regardless of whether it's a simple traffic citation, or a multi-page incident report. Know what is says. Never allow yourself to be rushed. Do not wait to review it, in the hallway of the courthouse. Find a hidey-hole, where no likelihood exists, anyone will interrupt your reading. It's been my experience, courthouses are just too busy. The prospect of someone who knows you, stopping by to chat, is too great to chance this.

Even though you believe you may have the relevant verbiage committed to memory, never approach any witness stand, without that document in your actual possession. The only exception? If this particular practice is prohibited in your jurisdiction, by the rules of court, or by your legislature. Otherwise, arm yourself.

If such a prohibition exists, that needs to change. Is there really a legitimate reason for this? Is the official concern, you may read from some document, at the witness stand, instead of just testifying from memory? That's easily remedied. The solution is to place any document, face down, on the witness stand, and be left that way, unless, and until, you need to refer to it, in order to refresh your recollection.

In other words, unless prohibited from doing so, take it with you. Do not read from it, as you testify. This will result in an objection from opposing counsel, and an admonition from the court. In case you are not familiar with *admonition*, in court, it's a polite way of saying you are getting chewed out.

What do you do, if you do not recall a salient point, and need to use a document, as a memory aid? That's simple. Just ask the judge, if you may refer to it. When permission is granted, take the time to read the relevant passage to yourself, you need to refresh your recollection. Do not allow anyone to rush you, as you do this. Always control the tempo.

If you need a brief recess to do this, do not be afraid to ask the judge. If the court grants your request, and the jury is excused from the courtroom, remember to stand, when the jury leaves, and when it reenters the courtroom. It's a sign of respect. Never forget to do this.

Remain at the witness stand, to read, and refresh your recollection. It's the perfect spot. You can do so, without interruption. However, before the judge retires to chambers, during the recess, ask, if you can stay at the witness stand. Otherwise, the bailiff may ask you to leave the courtroom, as they are generally cleared, at such times.

If doing this refreshes your recollection, you are ready to resume your testimony. If not, see if you can offer it, as past recollection recorded. I have never seen any peace officer witness, in any case I have ever touched, be refused a request, to refer to their report, so they can refresh their recollection.

If in doubt, ask. The worst you can be told is no. If your request is denied, expect the prosecutor to take exception to that. Why? Because they cannot do their job, if a key witness is unavailable, because they cannot remember what happened.

8. Do Not Volunteer

If you have been in the military, you should already know why I say this. If not, when I say *do not volunteer*, here is what I mean. Have you adequately answered the previous question? If you have, be patient. Wait for the next question. If you are an inexperienced witness, the temptation is great, to try to fill the void of discomforting silence, with words. This is not what you do, on the witness stand.

Avoid doing this. Avoid doing it at all costs. Just keep your hands folded, in front of you, if you are at the witness stand. Or, remain standing at counsel table. Take a sip of water, if need be. Look at the judge. Look at the defendant. Observe defense counsel. Smile at the clerk. Just be quiet, while you are taking all this in.

If no question is pending, and you try to speak, expect the prosecutor to quickly object, by saying "...no question pending..." This is your cue to shut up. Pardon my bluntness, but this is not the time for decorum. This is important enough that I would rather offend you, than not be assured this message is being thoroughly absorbed. So just sit, or stand, quietly, be placid, and wait for the next question, before you speak again.

9. Do Not Speculate

Do you know the difference between speculating and estimating? We talked about this earlier. Let's discuss it again. Here's the difference. If I ask you to tell me the length of my dining room table, and you have never been to my residence, asking you to do this is asking you to *guess*.

Why? That's true for a number of reasons. First, you do not know the length of my dining room table. Secondly, you do not even know, if I have one. Thirdly, you do not know, if I have a dining room. Lastly, you do not know, if I even have a residence. I could be living under a bush. I'm not, but you get the point.

Now, on the other hand, if you have been to my residence, you know the preliminary answers are all to be answered, in the affirmative, if:

1. you know I have a residence
2. you know I have a dining room
3. you know I have a dining room table
4. therefore, you know its approximate length.

By knowing the answers, to all the preliminary questions, your answer is not based, on speculation. Instead, your answer becomes an *estimate*. Providing estimates, from the witness stand, is standard, acceptable testimony. Guessing, on the other hand, is never acceptable. Be sure you know the difference, between the two. If you are basing your answer, on personal knowledge, you are estimating. If you have no personal knowledge, upon which to base your answer, you are speculating, or guessing. Do not do this! Know the difference between the two.

10. Tell the Truth

Under no circumstances should you refrain from telling the truth. In other words, without exception, *always tell the truth.* Granted, perjury is provable, only if you are testifying falsely, to a material fact. But, the object of the exercise, is not to avoid being prosecuted, whenever you testify. It's to convince the trier of fact, you are believable each and every time you testify, and with every single word, you utter.

Frankly, this should not be limited to, only when you are under oath. Build a professional reputation for consummate honesty. I am not suggesting you were not honest, before you became a LEO. In fact, my assumption is you already were, or you would not be one, in the first place. However, the fact you are already honest, does not mean the folks you are getting to know, such as prosecutors, judges, and defense counsel, know that yet. That's what I mean, when I say, you need to build your professional reputation for trustworthiness.

At the risk of sounding like an overgrown Boy Scout, if you are a cop, or a prosecutor, and are not used to telling the truth, you are in the wrong line of work. I cannot stress this enough. If I am being repetitious, I will not even say mea culpa. Not on this issue. So, if I sound like a Boy Scout? Oh well. Get used to it. Remember, if you damage your credibility, akin to virginity, it's gone forever.

It will only take one untruth to ruin a reputation, you have worked hard to build, your entire career. Guard it jealously. Safeguard it with your very life. In the end result, the only intangible, any of us have to sell, is our honesty and integrity.

One additional consideration. Telling the truth does not mean you cannot legally withhold information you possess, as a peace officer, from the court. Two examples that immediately come to mind are: (1) refusing to disclose the location of a confidential VIN, or, (2) refusing to disclose the identity of a confidential informant. You can do either, by invoking the section of your state's Evidence Code that authorizes you to do this. In California, rely on Evidence Code §1041, **et seq.**

Evidence Code §1041

"(a) Except as provided in this section, a public entity has a privilege to refuse to disclose the identity of a person who has furnished information as provided in subdivision (b) purporting to disclose a violation of a law of the United States or of this state or of a public entity in this state, and to prevent another from disclosing such identity, if the privilege is claimed by a person authorized by the public entity to do so and:

(1) Disclosure is forbidden by an act of the Congress of the United States or a statute of this state; or

(2) Disclosure of the identity of the informer is against the public interest because there is a necessity for preserving the confidentiality of his identity that outweighs the necessity for disclosure in the interest of justice; but no privilege may be claimed under this paragraph if any person authorized to do so has consented that the identity of the informer be disclosed in the proceeding. In determining whether disclosure of the identity of the informer is against the public interest, the interest of the public entity as a party in the outcome of the proceeding may not be considered.

(b) This section applies only if the information is furnished in confidence by the informer to:

(1) A law enforcement officer;

(2) A representative of an administrative agency charged with the administration or enforcement of the law alleged to be violated; or his identity."

In summation, if you follow the directions I have tried to share with you, in this book, you should be able to competently handle any courtroom situation you face, irrespective of whether it's an infraction, a misdemeanor, or a felony. It will not matter, if the fact finder is a judge, or a jury. Nor should it matter who defense counsel is.

The key to success? Do what you are supposed to do, in order to present a provable case. If you are doing your job, the attorney representing the defendant is simply not going to be that relevant. Once you grasp this, you are on your way to a fun, win-packed, and respectable career. Be well and stay safe, my stalwart brethren!

Appendix 1
Miscellaneous Laws

In this section you will find various laws. These include different state and federal appellate cases, U.S. constitutional provisions, civil and criminal jury instructions, and various state statutes.

Each referenced law will be keyed to the chapter in which it is described. The legal issue it covers, will be in the chapter itself. The legal citations for the appellate cases are listed, in the chapters, where they appear.

A legal citation is how an appellate court is listed. It is that particular case's legal address. For example, *Berkemer v. McCarty* is cited as (1984) 468 U.S. 420. The entry, in parentheses, is the year the case was decided. The volume is *#468*. The page where the opinion commences is *p. 420*. U.S. is short for *United States Supreme Court*. I also cover this issue earlier in this book.

Any reference, herein, is for illustrative purposes only, and is not meant to dissuade you from doing appropriate legal research, on any case you seek to prepare, for an appearance, in court. Each state has its own laws. If in doubt, ask your local prosecutor. It is my belief, the more clearly you digest relevant law, including knowing a defendant's constitutional rights, the more likely you will be, to prevail in any matter you handle.

Do you deal with any specific statutes you believe should be in a future edition of *Courtroom Survival for Traffic Officers*? Or are there other areas I should add to my planned *Courtroom Survival*™ series? If there are please E-mail me at mbrheljr@aol.com. Upon receipt, I will add such suggestions, to my pending research, for review and consideration.

To the best of my knowledge, none of the many convictions I worked hard to obtain, as a prosecutor, have ever been overturned on appeal. Ditto for any traffic trials I've presided over. My goal is to prepare you, so any conviction you obtain, also passes constitutional muster.

Work hard, be professional, and above all else, always remember to go home alive at the end of each shift. Be well and stay safe. Happy hunting, my brothers and sisters!

<u>CASES</u> (*California*)

- Bhatt v. Dept. of Health Services (Chapter 17)
- Carrington v. Superior Court (Chapter 18)
- Glage v. Hawes Firearms Co. (Chapter 18)
- In re Angelica P (Chapter 18)
- Williams v. Barnett (Chapter 18)
- People v. Ammons (Chapter 18)
- People v. Bravo (Chapter 18)
- People v. Burgener (Chapter 18)
- People v. Curley (Chapter 18)
- People v. Dennis (Chapter 18)
- People v. Farmer (Chapter 5)
- People v. Gonzales (Chapter 4/18)
- People v. Hill (Chapter 17)
- People v. Ingle (Chapter 4/18)
- People v. James (Chapter 18)
- People v. Lopez (Chapter 3)
- People v Lowe (Chapter 17)
- People v. Mason (Chapter 18)
- People v. Miller (Chapter 18)
- People v. Reyes (Chapter 18)
- People v. Sanchez (Chapter 18)
- People v. Scheib (Chapter 18)
- People v. Soldoff (Chapter 18)
- People v. Triggs (Chapter 4)
- Weiner v. Fleischman (Chapter 18)
- Williams v. Barnett (Chapter 18)

CASES (*Maryland*)

- Goode v. State (Chapter 3/6)
- Taylor v. State (Chapter 3/6)
- Cornish v. State (Chapter 3/6)
- Taylor v. Mayor of Baltimore (Chapter 3/6)

CASES (*New Jersey*)

- State v Bookbinder (Chapter 6)
- State v Dantonio (Chapter 6/7)
- State v Readding (Chapter 6)
- State v Wojtkowiak (Chapter 6)

CASES (*Federal*)

- Alabama v. White (Chapter 4/18)
- Beck v. Ohio (Chapter 4/18)
- Berkemer v. McCarty (Chapter 3/4/9/12)
- Borderkircher v. Hayes (Chapter 2)
- Brady v. Maryland (Chapter 8)
- California v. Beheler (Chapter 3)
- Carroll v. U.S. (Chapter 18)
- Chambers v. Maroney (Chapter 18)
- Connecticut Vs. Tomanelli (Chapter 7)
- Delaware vs. Moffitt (Chapter 7)
- Florida v. Meyers (Chapter 18)
- Gustafson v. Florida (Chapter 18)
- Herman & MacLean v. Huddleston (Chapter 18)
- Illinois v. Gates (Chapter 4/18)
- INS v. Delgado (Chapter 4/18)
- Kentucky vs. Honeycutt (Chapter 7)
- Mapp v. Ohio (Chapter 4)
- Michigan v. Thomas (Chapter 18)
- Miranda v. Arizona (Chapter 3)
- New Jersey vs. D'Antonio (Chapter 7)
- Ornelas v. U.S (Chapter 4/18)
- Schneckcloth v. Bustamonte (Chapter 18)
- Terry v. Ohio (Chapter 4/18)
- Texas v. White (Chapter 18)
- U.S. v. Arvizu (Chapter 4/18)
- U.S. v. Dreos (Chapter 5/6)
- U.S. v. Johns (Chapter 18)
- U.S. v. Murray (Chapter 3)
- U.S. v. Robinson (Chapter 18)
- U.S. v. Ross (Chapter 18)
- U.S. v. Sokolow (Chapter 4/18)
- U.S. v. Williams (Chapter 4/18)
- Wisconsin vs. Hanson (Chapter 7)
- Wong Sun v. U.S. (Chapter 4)

U.S. CONSTITUTIONAL PROVISIONS

- First Amendment (Chapter 1)
- Fourth Amendment (Chapter 1/4)
- Fifth Amendment (Chapter 1/12)
- Sixth Amendment (Chapter 1/10/12)

CODE OF FEDERAL REGULATIONS

- Chapter III–Part 392–Subpart G–Sec. 392.71 (Chapter 7)

- 13353 (Chapter 11)
- 13353.1 (Chapter 11)
- 13353.2 (Chapter 11)
- 13800 (Chapter 11/15)
- 13801 (Chapter 15)
- 22350 (Chapter 3/13)
- 22352 (Chapter 7)
- 22354 (Chapter 7)
- 22357 (Chapter 7)
- 22358 (Chapter 7)
- 22358.3 (Chapter 7)
- 23157 (Chapter 11)
- 12810.5 (Chapter 11)
- 40519(b) (Chapter 10)
- 40521 (Chapter 10)
- 40800 (Chapter 1, 7)
- 40801 (Chapter 1, 7)
- 40802 (Chapter 1, 7)
- 40804 (Chapter 1, 7)
- 40805 (Chapter 1, 7)
- 40806 (Chapter 1)
- 40807 (Chapter 1)
- 40902 (Chapter 10)
- 42005 (Chapter 10)

STATUTORY PROVISIONS *(states other than California)*

- AR Code Title 12 12-8-401 (Chapter 6)
- AR Code Title 27-51-201. (b) (1) (Chapter 6)
- AZ Revised Statutes 28-701.A (Chapter 1, 6)
- AZ Revised Statutes 28-703 (Chapter 6)
- Code of VA 18.2-266 (Chapter 14)
- MD Vehicle Law 10-301 (Chapter 6)
- MD Vehicle Law 16-112 (Chapter 6)
- MD Vehicle Law 21-106 (Chapter 6)
- MI Vehicle Code 257.628 (Chapter 6)
- MI Vehicle Code 257.633 (Chapter 6)
- MO Revised Statutes43.130.1 (Chapter 6)
- MO Revised Statutes 70.820 (Chapter 6)
- MO Revised Statutes 300.205 (Chapter 6)
- NJ Permanent Statutes 53.3-5 (Chapter 6)
- NY Crim. Pro. Law, §60.45 (Chapter 5)
- TX Code of Crim. Pro., Article 38.22(Chapter 5)

- TX Code of Crim. Pro., Article 38.23 (Chapter 5)
- TX Transportation Code 545.353 (Chapter 6)
- TX Transportation Code 545.355 (Chapter 6)
- TX Transportation Code 545.356 (Chapter 6)

New Jersey Office of the Attorney General; Department of Law & Public Safety

Radar Certification Requirements

- See www.state.nj.us/lps/dcj/njpdresources/radar.htm (Chapter 6)

Reference books

- Black's Law Dictionary (Chapter 19)
- Collision Investigation for the Patrol Officers (Chapter 8)
- The Traffic Accident Investigation Manual (Chapter 8)
- Traffic Investigation Manual for Police (Chapter 8)

Appendix 2
State-by-State Information

1. **Alabama**
Department of Public Safety
PO Box 1511
Montgomery, AL 36102-1511
www.dps.state.al.us

2. **Alaska**
Department of Administration
PO Box 110200
Juneau, AK 99811-0200
www.doa.alaska.gov

3. **Arizona**
Department of Transportation
PO Box 2100
Phoenix, AZ 85001
www.azdot.gov/mvd

4. **Arkansas**
Department of Finance & Administration
1509 W. 7th St.
Little Rock, AR 72201
www.dfa.arkansas.gov

5. **California**
Department of Motor Vehicles
PO Box 942890
Sacramento, CA 94890-0001
www.dmv.ca.gov

6. **Colorado**
Department of Revenue
1881 Pierce St.
Lakewood, CO 80214
www.colorado.gov/revenue/dmv

7. **Connecticut**
Department of Motor Vehicles
60 State St.
Wethersfield, CT 06101
www.ct.gov/dmv

8. **Delaware**
Division of Motor Vehicles
303 Transportation Circle
PO Box 698
Dover, DE 19903-0818
www.dmv.de.gov

9 **District of Columbia**
Department of Motor Vehicles
Government of the District of Columbia
PO Box 90120
Washington, DC 20090
www.dmv.dc.gov

10. **Florida**
Department of Highway Safety and Motor Vehicles
Neil Kirkman Bldg.
2900 Apalachee Pkwy
Tallahassee, FL 32399-0500
www.flhsmv.gov

11. **Georgia**
Department Driver Services
PO Box 456
Atlanta, GA 30334
www.dds.ga.gov

12. **Hawaii** *(Note: Hawaii is broken down county-by-county)*
Driver Licensing-Main Office
1119 Dillingham Blvd. Bay A-101
Honolulu, HI 96817
www.dmv.org/hi-hawaii/dmv-office-finder.php

13. **Idaho**
Transportation Department
Division of Motor Vehicles
3311 W. State St.
PO Box 7129
Boise, ID 83707
www.idaho.gov/dmv

14. **Illinois**
Office of the Secretary of State
Driver Services Dept
2701 So. Dirksen Pkwy
Springfield, IL 62723
www.dmv.org/il-illinois

15. **Indiana**
Bureau of Motor Vehicles
100 No. Senate Ave.
Room 440
Indianapolis, IN 46204
www.in.gov/bmv

16. **Iowa**
Dept. of Transportation
800 Lincoln Way
Ames, IA 50010
www.iowadot.gov/mvd

17. **Kansas**
Division of Motor Vehicles
915 S.W. Harrison St.
Topeka, KS 66626-0001
www.ksrevenue.org/vehicle

18. **Kentucky**
Transportation Cabinet
200 Mero St.
Frankfort, KY 40622
www.dmv-department-of-motor-vehicles.com/KY

19. **Louisiana**
Office of Motor Vehicles
PO Box 64886
Baton Rouge, LA 70896
http://omv.dps.state.la.us

20. **Maine**
29 State House Station
Augusta, ME 04333-0029
www.maine.gov/sos/bmv

21. **Maryland**
Motor Vehicle Administration
6601 Richie Hwy N.E.
Glen Burnie, MD 21062
www.mva.maryland.gov

22. **Massachusetts**
Registry of Motor Vehicles
PO Box 199100
Boston, MA 02119-9100
www.massdot.state.ma.us/rmv

23. **Michigan**
Secretary of State
Driver & Vehicle Records Bureau
430 West Allegan, 1st Fl.
Lansing, MI 48918
www.michigan.gov/sos

24. **Minnesota**
Public Safety Department
Driver & Vehicle Services
445 Minnesota St.
St. Paul, MN 55101-2128
www.dmv.org/mn-minnesota/dmv

25. **Mississippi**
Motor Vehicle Commission
PO Box 16873
Jackson, MS 39236-0873
www.mmvc.state.ms.us

26. **Missouri**
Department of Revenue
Harry S Truman State Office Bldg.
301 W. High St.
Jefferson City, MO 65101
www.dor.mo.gov/drivers

27. **Montana**
Motor Vehicle Division
303 No. Roberts
PO Box 201430
Helena, MT 59620-1430
www.doj.mt.gov/driving

28. **Nebraska**
Department of Motor Vehicles
PO Box 94789
Lincoln, NE 68509-4789
www.dmv.state.ne.us

29. **Nevada**
Department of Motor Vehicles
555 Wright Way
Carson City, NV 89711-0900
www.dmvnv.com

30. **New Hampshire**
Department of Safety
Division of Motor Vehicles
10 Hazen Dr.
Concord, NH 03305-0002
www.nh.gov/safety/divisions/dmv

31. **New Jersey**
Motor Vehicle Commission
PO Box 160
Trenton, NJ 08666
www.state.nj.us/mvc

32. **New Mexico**
Motor Vehicle Division
PO Box 1028
Santa Fe, NM 87504-1028
www.mvd.newmexico.gov

33. **New York**
Department of Motor Vehicles
6 Empire State Plaza
Albany, NY 12228
www.nydmv.state.ny.us

34. **North Carolina**
Division of Motor Vehicles
1100 New Bern Ave.
Raleigh, NC 27697-0001
www.ncdot.org/dmv

35. **North Dakota**
Department of Transportation
Driver & Vehicle Services Division
608 E. Boulevard Ave.
Bismarck, ND 58505-0700
www.dot.nd.gov/public/licensing.htm

36. **Ohio**
Bureau of Motor Vehicles
PO Box 16520
Columbus, OH 43266-0020
www.bmv.ohio.gov

37. **Oklahoma**
Motor Vehicle Commission
4334 NW Expressway, Ste. 183
Oklahoma City, OK 73116
www.ok.gov/omvc

38. **Oregon**
Driver & Motor Vehicle Services
1905 Lana Ave., NE
Salem, OR 97314
www.oregon.gov/ODOT/DMV

39. **Pennsylvania**
Department of Transportation
Bureau of Driver Licensing
1101 So. Front St.
Harrisburg, PA 17104
www.dmv.state.pa.us

40. **Rhode Island**
Division of Motor Vehicles
600 New London Ave.
Cranston RI 02920-3024
www.dmv.ri.gov

41. **South Carolina**
Department of Motor Vehicles
PO Box 1498
Blythewood, SC 29016
www.scdmvonline.com

42. **South Dakota**
Motor Vehicles Division
445 E. Capitol Ave.
Pierre, SD 57501-3185
www.state.sd.us/drr2/motorvehicle

43. **Tennessee**
Department of Motor Vehicles
PO BOX 945
Nashville, TN 37202
www.dmv-department-of-motor-vehicles.com/TN

44. **Texas**
Department of Motor Vehicles
4000 Jackson Ave.
Austin, TX 78731
www.txdmv.gov

45. **Utah**
Driver License Division
PO Box 144501
Salt Lake City, Utah 84129
www.driverlicense.utah.gov

46. **Vermont**
Department of Motor Vehicles
120 State St.
Montpelier, VT 05603-0001
www.dmv.vermont.gov

47. **Virginia**
Department of Motor Vehicle
PO Box 27412
Richmond, VA 23269
www.dmv.state.va.us

48. **Washington**
Department of Licensing
Driver Services Division
PO Box 9020
Olympia, WA 98507
www.dol.wa.gov

49. **West Virginia**
Division of Motor Vehicles
1800 Kanawha Blvd., E. Bldg. 3
Charleston, WV 25317
www.dmv.wv.gov

50. **Wisconsin**
Department of Transportation
Division of Motor Vehicles
PO Box 7910
Madison, WI 53707-7910
www.dot.state.wi.us

51. Wyoming

Department of Transportation
Driver Services Division
PO Box 1708
Cheyenne, WY 82003-1708
www.dot.state.wy.us

U.S. Territories

52. Puerto Rico

Department of Transportation & Public Works
PO Box 41243
Minillas Station
Santurce, PR 00940-1243
www.fta.dot.gov

53. Virgin Islands

Bureau of Motor Vehicles
Patrick Sweeney Police HQ
RR 02
St. Croix, VI 00851
www.usvibmv.org

Glossary

Admissible: Evidence, of such character, the court is bound to receive it.
Admission: Partial acknowledgement of wrongdoing; in the case of the accused, one that fails to address all the elements, of the crime alleged.
Arc: Two points on a curve.
Arraignment: The court appearance, when any defendant is officially informed of what they stand accused.
Authentication: Introducing sufficient evidence, to establish a document is what, its proponent claims it is.
Bail: Money, or security, posted with the court, by or, on behalf of, a defendant, in order to secure their release from custody, during the pendency of their case.
Bailiff: The uniformed peace officer who maintains order and security, in the courtroom.
Basic Speed: A reasonable and prudent speed, that does not endanger people, or property, having due regard for weather, visibility, traffic, and road conditions.
Bench: The wooden structure, at the front of the courtroom, behind which the judge sits; also used as a colloquialism, to describe a judicial officer, e.g., *bench* trial.
Best Evidence Rule: A requirement the original of a document must be offered, to prove its contents, unless otherwise permitted, by statute.
Burden of Proof: The duty, of a civil or criminal defendant, to prove, or disprove, a disputed fact. In criminal matters, the prosecution is constitutionally required to prove guilt, beyond a reasonable doubt; the defendant's burden is to create reasonable doubt.
Calibration: The act or process of fixing, checking, or correcting the graduations of an instrument, such as a speedometer, by a certified mechanic, or a radar tuning fork, by the officer, assigned to operate a radar unit; only the manufacturer calibrates radar devices.
Case: An action, or controversy, contested in a court of law, or comparable forum.

Certification: Confirmation of certain characteristics of an object, person, or organization; e.g., a certified copy is one attested to, by a government official, as a true and correct version of the original.
Charges: Violations of the law, allegedly committed by the accused, as set forth in court.
Chord: The straight line connecting the ends of an arc.
Citation: A document, prepared by a law enforcement officer, informing the accused of the violations allegedly committed; aka "traffic ticket." (See *Ticket*)
Clerk: The court officer, responsible for the court's clerical functions, such as maintaining its documents, entering judgments, and producing certified copies.
Closing Argument: Following the close of evidence, that portion of a contested proceeding, such as a trial, when the respective parties attempt to convince the trier of fact, what they believe the evidence has established.
Cold Shock: The phenomenon that occurs, when the coiled filament of a light bulb appears unaffected, but may be broken anywhere along the coil itself, thus indicating the bulb was off, at the moment of impact, during a traffic collision.
Collision: The act, or instance, of two objects, striking one another. (See *Traffic Collision*)
Commissioner: The court officer appointed, by a given jurisdiction's judges, or otherwise hired, to preside over assigned cases; rule on the admissibility of evidence, and decide the outcome of cases, but generally lacking authority to review search warrants. (See *Judge Pro Tempore*)
Complaint: A legal document filed, in a lower court of law, by the prosecuting attorney, accusing a named defendant of committing (a) misdemeanor and/or felony offense(s).
Confession: A complete declaration of guilt, by a criminal suspect, that includes each and every element, of every suspected crime.
Consensual Encounter: A professional encounter, between a peace officer and a civilian, not considered a seizure, within the meaning of the Fourth Amendment; the degree of criminal conduct required to justify such an event is zero.
Constitution: The fundamental law of a state, or a nation, agreed upon, by the People, through their elected representatives, as an absolute rule of action and decision, controlling, until it is changed by the People; rendering any governmental act done, in opposition to it, null and void.
Contact Patch: The area of contact, between a vehicle's tire and the roadway. (See *Skid Mark, Tire Friction Mark*)
Contempt: The willful disregard, or disobedience, of a public authority, such as a branch of government; e.g., contempt of court, or contempt of Congress.

Continuance: The judicially approved postponement of a legal action, until a specified future date.
Conviction: Imposition of judgment, or sentence, in a criminal case, thereby permanently, and conclusively, removing a defendant's presumption of innocence, in that matter.
Counsel: An attorney at law, licensed to make appearances, on behalf of clients, before all courts, of the jurisdiction of issuance of said license.
Counsel Table: The long table between the courtroom bar and the judge's bench, where counsel, investigators, and parties to an action, conduct business.
Corpus Delicti: Latin: *body of the crime*; combined elements of a crime (see *Elements*)
County Seat: Statutory situs of the main governmental offices, for a county.
Cross-Examination: That portion of a contested proceeding, such as a trial, where the opposing side's witnesses are examined, under oath, following their direct testimony.
Custodian of Records: One who prepares, and maintains, an entity's documents, in the ordinary course of business.
Declarant: One who makes a statement, or declaration, orally, or in writing, which may be offered, into evidence, as a state of mind exception to the hearsay rule.
Defendant: One accused of wrongdoing, in a civil or criminal matter; the latter may include infractions, misdemeanors, and felonies.
Demonstrative Evidence: Material objects presented to one's senses, offered to prove, or disprove, the existence of a material fact.
Denial of Motion: A ruling by the court, rejecting a party's request for relief; e.g., motion to exclude witnesses, or to suppress evidence.
Detention: Words, or actions, of a peace officer, which temporarily deprive someone of their liberty. (See *Investigative Detention*)
Direct-Examination: The act of questioning one's own witnesses, in any contested proceeding, such as court, or administrative tribunals.
Discovery: Requested review, by the prosecution or defendant, of any and all evidence the opposition plans to use, against them.
Dismissal: The discharge of a case, by the judge, at the request of a party, or when the court determines the moving party, has not met its burden of proof.
Disqualification: A determination, by a judicial officer, precluding that officer from presiding over a particular case, either at a party's request, or on the court's own motion.
Documentary Evidence: Documents offered into evidence, to prove, or disprove, the existence of a fact.

Driver: A person in actual physical control of a vehicle being operated. (See *Motorist, Operator*)
Driving Under the Influence: The act of operating a vehicle, while under the influence of an alcoholic beverage, drugs, or a combination thereof.
Due Process: A summarized constitutional guarantee, or respect for those immunities, so rooted in the traditions and conscience of a society, as to be fundamental, in the concept of ordered liberties.
Elements: The ultimate parts which unite anything. In a legal context, they combine, to comprise the totality, of an alleged crime.
Engineering and Traffic Survey (ETS): A survey of highway and traffic conditions, in accordance with methods, determined by a state's Department of Transportation, for use by that jurisdiction's statewide and local authorities; this includes reviewing prevailing speeds, accident records, and highway traffic and roadside conditions, not readily apparent to a motorist.
Equal Protection: A summarized constitutional guarantee that no person or class of persons shall be denied the same protections of the laws, enjoyed by other persons or classes, in like circumstances of their lives, liberties, and property.
Evidence: Testimony, writings, material objects, or other things presented to the senses, offered to prove, or disprove, the existence of a fact.
Failure to Appear: Not appearing for an official scheduled court proceeding, as directed on a document, such as a Notice to Appear, or as otherwise ordered by the court.
Failure to Pay Fine: Unexcused non-payment of a fine, by a convicted defendant.
Fatal Box: Traffic collision investigation tools. In smaller departments, this may include numerous tape measures, road crayons, roll-a-tapes, digital cameras, and hand tools, such as hammers, etching devices, and tee squares. In bigger departments, this will probably include computer-automated mapping devices, commonly known as *total stations.* (See *Total Station*)
Fine: The monetary amount defendants are required to remit to the court, following their conviction, pursuant to court order, and as authorized by law.
Foundation: The preliminary fact a party, seeking to introduce certain evidence, must establish, prior to the introduction of the evidence itself.
Freeway: A highway, in respect to which the owners of abutting lands have either limited, restricted, or no right of easement of, access to, or access from their abutting lands.
Granting of Motion: Relief granted by an official tribunal, such as a court of law.
Guilty Plea: A confession of guilt, either in open court, or in a judge's chambers.

Hearing: A proceeding conducted by a judicial officer, legally competent to swear witnesses to oaths, receive evidence, make legal rulings, and decide a case's outcome.

Hearing Officer: A governmental official, presiding over a hearing, authorized to administer oaths to witnesses, receive evidence, make legal rulings, and decide a case's outcome, based on proffered evidence, and applicable law.

Hearsay: Any out-of-court statement offered to prove the truth of the matter asserted.

Highway: A way, or place, including streets, publicly maintained, and open to the use of the public, for vehicular traffic.

Hot Shock: The phenomenon that occurs, if the coiled filament of a light bulb is stretched out, and still attached to the main arch of the bulb, indicating the bulb was on, at the moment of impact, during a traffic collision.

In Custody: The curtailing of a person's immediate liberty, by a peace officer's force, command, or a custodial facility, such as a jail or prison.

In Propria Persona: The act of representing oneself, in a courtroom, without benefit of counsel.

Intelligent: Endowed with understanding, reasoning, and comprehension.

Investigative Detention: A seizure, within the scope of the Fourth Amendment; detaining peace officers must set forth specific, articulable facts, supporting their reasonable suspicion the suspect has committed, or is committing a crime. (See *Detention*)

Judge: A judicial officer, either appointed by a state's governor to fill an unexpired term, or elected by the voters to preside over a court of law.

Judge Pro Tempore: The person appointed by one or more of a jurisdiction's judges to preside over assigned cases; rule on the admissibility of evidence, and decide the outcome of cases, but lacking the authority to review search warrants. (See *Commissioner*)

Judgment: The official decision, of a court of law, pertaining to the rights and claims of the involved parties.

Knowingly: With knowledge; consciously, or willfully.

Lawful: Legal, authorized, or warranted by law.

Lidar: Acronym for a modern form of radar, meaning *light detection and ranging*.

Magistrate: Judicial officer presiding over cases, in state and federal systems; this includes inferior state courts where Municipal Court has not consolidated with Superior Court; also the junior judicial officer in U.S District Court.

Marked Vehicle: A police patrol vehicle, sometimes assigned to traffic duties, generally bearing an agency's insignia, and painted in a distinctive fashion, as required by state law.

Maximum Speed: The fastest speed a motorist can travel, in a motor vehicle on any of that state's roadways, without exceeding the maximum posted speed limit.
Mid-ordinate: The center of the arc to a chord.
Miranda Rights: Requirement set forth in *Miranda v. Arizona* that a suspect, in police custody, must be advised of their right to remain silent, and be advised, by an attorney, before they can be asked questions that may lead to possible incriminating answers.
Motion: An application to a judicial officer, seeking relief, on any number of issues.
Motor Vehicle: A self-propelled vehicle.
Motorist: A person in actual physical control, of a vehicle being operated. (See *Driver*, *Operator*)
Municipal Court: An inferior state court, with territorial authority, generally confined to the jurisdiction, in which it is located, primarily where operations of Municipal and Superior courts have not yet been consolidated.
Negligent Operator: A motorist meeting, or exceeding, the permissible number of points that can be accumulated, over a given time frame, arising from too many convictions, for specified traffic offenses, or for being at fault, in too many traffic collisions. (See *Points*)
Night Court: Traffic court being conducted, during evening hours.
No Contest (aka Nolo Contendere): A plea of no contest, or nolo contendere, establishes guilt for a criminal proceeding, but cannot be used as an admission of wrongdoing, in any civil matter.
Not Guilty: A plea entered in criminal cases, which forces the prosecution to present evidence, at a jury trial, within a specific period of time, unless waived, to prove a defendant's guilt, beyond a reasonable doubt.
Notice to Appear: A court document informing a defendant of (an) alleged charge(s) they face, along with the date, time, and location of their required court appearance.
Objection: The act of objecting, to the presentation of evidence, in order to obtain a judicial ruling, intended to prevent its consideration, by the trier of fact.
Officer: As used in this context, a peace officer, assigned primarily to enforce traffic laws, generally, while wearing a departmental uniform, and operating a distinctively marked vehicle, depending on state law. (See *Traffic Officer*)
Opening Statement: Statement made at the beginning of trial, or at the start of a party's case, to inform those in attendance, what the evidence will establish.
Operator: A person, in actual physical control, of a vehicle being operated. (See *Driver*, *Motorist*)

Order: A court's ruling, following a party's request, for a judicial ruling, or a sua sponte decision, by the court.

Ordinance: A written law, generally passed, by a local governmental authority.

Overruling an Objection: An adverse judicial ruling that a witness answer, or not answer, a pending question.

Owner: As used in this context, a person with all the incidents of ownership, including legal title to personal property, such as motor vehicles.

Own Recognizance: Release from custody, of a defendant, upon promising to appear in court, as ordered, either orally, or in writing.

Pedestrian: Any person, generally on foot or, in some places, using a conveyance propelled by human power, such as a skateboard, or roller skates.

Photography: The art, or process, of producing images, by the action of radiant energy, and especially light, on a sensitive surface.

Plea: A defendant's response, to the filing of criminal charges; this can include a plea of guilty, not guilty, not guilty by reason of insanity, or nolo contendere, aka no contest.

Plea Bargaining: Negotiating the settlement of a criminal case, causing the defendant to admit guilt, and agree to a specified sentence.

Points: Statutory marks against one's driving record, based on convictions, or for being at fault, in too many traffic collisions, during a given time frame. (See *Negligent Operator*)

Post-Trial: Any relevant legal proceedings, occurring, subsequent to a trial.

Presumption of Innocence: The constitutional presumption, in favor of an accused, facing any criminal charge, requiring acquittal, unless guilt is proved, beyond a reasonable doubt.

Pre-Trial: Any relevant legal proceedings, occurring prior to a trial.

Prima Facie: Latin for *on the face of it*; e.g., prosecution must establish a *prima facie* case, before the court will permit a defendant's admission, or confession, into evidence.

Prima Facie Speed: The posted speed limit displayed on standard, official highway signs.

Probable Cause: The legal standard peace officers must meet with specific, articulable facts, supporting their belief a suspect has committed, or is committing, a crime, in order to conduct a lawful search, or make a lawful arrest; deemed to be a seizure, within the meaning of the Fourth Amendment.

Promise to Appear: An oral, or written, promise to appear in court, at a specified future date, time, and place.

Proof: Presentation of evidence, to establish a requisite degree of belief, of certain facts, in the mind of the trier of fact.

Proof of Completion: Establishing one has completed a legal requirement, such as traffic violator school, by presenting appropriate documentation, to the court, or your state's motor vehicle agency.

Proof of Correction: Establishing one has corrected any cited equipment violation, by presenting appropriate documentation, to the court, or an on duty peace officer.

Prosecutor: The attorney in the executive branch of government who works as a separate, but equal partner, with the judicial branch of government; dispensing justice, on a case-by-case basis, by making filing decisions, and representing their state's residents in court.

Radar: *Radio detection and ranging.*

Reasonable Suspicion: The legal standard of proof, required of a peace officer, who must state specific, articulable facts they believe a suspect either has committed, or is committing, a crime, in order to make a lawful detention; deemed to be a seizure, within the meaning of the Fourth Amendment.

Recess: A temporary cessation, of any court proceedings, ordered by the judge at the request of any participating attorneys, parties, or the court.

Relevant Evidence: Evidence having any tendency, in reason, to prove, or disprove, any disputed fact of consequence, to the determination of a given case.

Reversal: The act of a trial court setting aside, or overturning, its previous decision; the act of a higher court setting aside, or overturning, a lower court's decision.

Revocation: To recall something previously granted (e.g. a privilege to operate a motor vehicle).

Sentence: The judgment formally pronounced, by a court, upon a defendant, following the defendant's guilty or nolo contendere plea, or a guilty verdict, in any criminal proceeding, generally resulting in the imposition of certain penalties.

Sentence Bargaining: Negotiating the resolution of a criminal case, including the agreed-upon sentence to be imposed.

Service: The act of properly providing a person, court process, such as a subpoena.

Skid Mark: Rubber from a tire's contact patch, which remains on the roadway, as the result of a vehicle's wheels turning slower, than the vehicle's forward momentum. (See *Tire Friction Mark*)

Speeding: The act of exceeding the posted, basic, or maximum speed limit, by the operation of a motor vehicle.

Speed Trap: The act of estimating a vehicle's speed, by a peace officer, in violation of that state's vehicle code sections, specifying the definition of speed trap evidence; any evidence so gathered is normally deemed inadmissible, for any and all purposes.

Speedy Trial Rights: The absolute right to go to trial, by a date certain, unless a valid time waiver is provided the court, by the defendant.
State of Mind: Pertains to a declarant's state of mind, at the time of their out-of-court statement, in order to show bias, or any other factors normally relied upon, in order to impeach their testimony.
Statute: Laws, including treaties, and constitutional provisions.
Sua Sponte: By the court's own initiative.
Subpoena: Written process commanding a witness to appear, and give testimony, at a date, time, and place therein described.
Subpoena Duces Tecum: Written process, commanding a witness to appear, and give testimony, and/or produce specified documents, alleged to be in that person's possession, or under their control, at a date, time, and place therein described.
Suspension: A temporary cessation, or interruption, of some privilege or right.
Sustaining: A judicial act, upholding an objection, to proffered evidence.
Testimony: Oral evidence, offered by a witness, under oath, and subject to cross-examination.
Testing: The act, or process, of checking an instrument, such as a radar unit, by an officer assigned, and qualified to operate it, using properly calibrated tuning forks.
Ticket: A document which informs the accused of the charges they face; aka "traffic ticket." (See *Citation*)
Tire Friction Mark: Rubber from a tire's contact patch, which remains on the roadway, as the result of a vehicle's wheels turning slower, than the vehicle's forward momentum. (See *Skid Mark*)
Total Station: An optical instrument used in modern surveying, combining an electronic theodolite (transit), an electronic distance measuring device (EDM), and software running on an external computer. (See *Fatal Box*)
Traffic: Pedestrians, ridden animals, vehicles, street cars, and any other conveyances, using any street, freeway, or highway, for any purpose.
Traffic Collision: The act, or instance, of two objects striking one another. (See *Collision*)
Traffic Collision Investigation: The process of collecting, analyzing, and recording information, at the scene of a traffic collision.
Traffic Collision Reconstruction: The effort to determine, from whatever information is available, how a collision happened; *the process of actually going back in time and rebuilding, moment-by-moment and step-by-step, the events and circumstances that led to the collision.*
Traffic Court: A court of law, presided over by a judge, commissioner, or judge pro tempore that receives evidence, makes evidentiary rulings, and determines if a defendant's guilt has been proved, beyond a reasonable doubt.

Traffic Officer: A peace officer, assigned for the primary purpose of enforcing traffic laws, on duty, generally while wearing a departmental uniform, and operating a distinctively marked vehicle. (See *Officer*)

Traffic Violator School: A court-approved program which permits the dismissal of a traffic court defendant's case, upon completion of a legally authorized school.

Trial: A contested hearing, held in court, presided over by a judicial officer who receives evidence, makes evidentiary rulings, and determines if the defendant's guilt has been proved, beyond a reasonable doubt.

Trial by Declaration: A traffic court trial, where permitted by law, based on written declarations; if a conviction results, the defendant can normally request a trial de novo.

Trial De Novo: A second, or new, trial.

Vehicle: A device by which any person, or property, may be moved upon a highway.

Vehicle Code: The group of laws enacted by a state's legislature, for the purpose of regulating traffic, and promoting driver and pedestrian traffic.

Verification: An oath attached to any document, attesting to the truth of the facts contained therein.

Verified Complaint: A charging document, accusing a specific person of certain civil or criminal wrongs, attested to by the complaining party, under oath.

Voluntary: The voluntary relinquishment of privileges or rights.

Waiver of jury: When both prosecution and defense agree the judge or commissioner can hear their misdemeanor or felony matter, in lieu of a jury of one's peers.

Warrant: A judicial order, authorizing the arrest, search, or seizure of the person, or place, described therein.

Your Honor: The time-honored way of addressing the presiding judicial officer, in court.

Future Projects

Next planned Courtroom Survival book: *Courtroom Survival for DUI Cops*

1196-page *National Law Enforcement Directory* now being formatted. *NLED* contains contact info of every city, county and state law enforcement agency the **CBBC** team could find.

Current Print & Kindle versions

Biographies
America's Two Toughest Sheriffs: *President #44 On the Run?*

Novels
Deadly Duty - Joshua Travers, DA Adventure Series (Book One)

Courtroom Survival
Courtroom Survival for Traffic Officers

About the Author

Martin C. Brhel, Jr., is a man of many parts, as *Tombstone's* Doc Holliday might observe. Marty insists he's been there, done that so many times, in so many places, he feels more like Walter Mitty, than Walter Mitty.

Put another way? He's worn a few fedoras, during his adventurous journeys. Marty says he's blessed. Beautiful esposa and daughter. Wonderful friends. Life is good.

Here is probably the easiest way to check out his books. Just type **Brhel** into the search bar at Amazon.com. That will open a page with current print versions and Kindles for *Courtroom Survival for Traffic Officers*. Written reviews welcomed!

Once there, you will also find *Deadly Duty*, first novel in his *Joshua Travers, DA Adventure Series*, and *America's Two Toughest Sheriffs* (subtitle: *President #44 On the Run?*).

Soon, you will also find 1296-page *National Law Enforcement Directory*, as soon as it's formatted and published. Marty's game plan, now that he is in sole control of his books?

He will publish a new one every six months, give or take. These will include new novels, occasional bios/exposes, and some additional Courtroom Survival books. When time permits, he will also complete reconstruction of his website.

At www.CourtroomSurvival.com, his **Books & Law Enforcement Teaching** page will provide appropriate updates. And, as noted, you can also stay abreast of his new books at Amazon.com.

Beginning with *Deadly Duty*, every *Joshua Travers, DA Adventure* Series novel will be replete with clues. Some true. Some false. Which are which? Is there a key that unlocks these ambiguities?

Correct interpretation of the aforesaid intimations could allow you to discern the plot of the next tome the author is already writing. Or, is it plots? But, then again, maybe not. Perhaps, they are all false signs.

Truth Travers knows. But, does he know you well enough yet to share? It's not that Travers doesn't like you. He's just a cautious lad. His tours of duty as a USMC JAG Colonel, and as the Solita County DA, further restrains him.

Why did JPT Brhel write *Courtroom Survival for Traffic Officers*? That's simple. To the best of his knowledge, no one else has written a comprehensive courtroom tutorial for traffic officers. And, public safety demands just that.

During law school, Marty clerked for both public and private law firms. He guest-lectured Con Law I students on search & seizure issues, while he was still a Con Law II student. After taking the grueling California bar exam, he was sworn in. And, as a private attorney, he was soon representing accused criminals.

But, grasping his ethical duty to zealously represent his more dedicated felony clients, created increasing conflict with what he saw, as a higher calling, i.e., being a good neighbor. Thus, he joined the Riverside County District Attorney's office in 1987. He now has three reported appellate opinions on cases where he's been counsel.

Following a four-year stint, as Staff Counsel in charge of Department of Motor Vehicles Los Angeles legal office, he relocated to multi-city Coachella Valley, incorrectly labeled *Palm Springs* by tourists. Could he now dispense justice, in quantities proportional to proven wrongdoing? He could. And, he did.

During his fun run in the sun, *the drug czar of the desert* held many challenging positions: Deputy-in-Charge of Indio Municipal Court, Deputy-in-Charge of the Palm Springs office, Deputy-in-Charge of Misdemeanor Pre-Trials, and Deputy-in-Charge of Major Narcotic Violator Program for the county's seemingly infinite Eastern Division, eastward all the way to the California-Arizona border.

Following DA retirement, he got serious about writing books, and even created his own website. Brhel also accepted an invitation to teach cops at the academy level throughout southern California, doing that, from coast to coast. On a limited basis, he still does that.

His DA days brought him a talk radio show, *Crimefighters*, following creation of two non-profits: the Crime Control Education Foundation and the Crime Control Foundation of America. These allowed him to write public safety legislation, testify before the California Legislature, and educate the general public, by accepting invitations to speak to various groups.

Post-DA retirement included appearances in state and federal courts. Many of his civil rights clients were cops he served with, when he learned they were maltreated in the workplace. As Legal Defense Trust Administrator for the Riverside Sheriffs' Association, he oversaw legal representation, of more than 3,000 RSA members.

Next? A 3-year hitch with Board of Parole Hearings, conducting parole violator and life prisoner eligibility hearings, before joining their Strike Team. This team of experts implemented newly enacted Penal Code §3000.03, reviewing legislatively-mandated early release requests, of more 40,000 prison inmates and formal parolees.

Trying to pursue his writing, instead, he met yet another delay. In 2011, he was appointed to the San Diego Superior Court, as a Judge Pro Tem, continuing what he started in Riverside County courts back in 1978.

Even though he no longer practices law, he remains licensed to practice, before any California state court, U.S. District Courts in the Central, Eastern, & Southern Districts of California, and the U.S. Supreme Court.

He finally returned to Orange County last fall. His esposa, Mary, is a fellow writer, inventor, and very gifted photographer. *Columbo* displays her distinctive work at www.fineartamerica.com, while she edits her first novel. You can ask her about it, and her moniker, when she's free.

Meanwhile, Marty just accepted a 2-year appointment to the City of Laguna Niguel's Traffic & Transportation Commission. Who says you can't teach an old dog new tricks?

The award winning former DA's next escapade, you ask? Maybe Truth Travers knows. He claims it involves some Texas lawmakers and, apparently, a very bad 1888 Texas law. More later...

Copper Bible Book Company

Copper Bible Book Company is Marty Brhel's own publishing house. Care to learn some history? In 1987, as a brand new DA, he began two projects to guide peace officers in their professional duties.

First was his monthly practical advice column for cops, *Hey Doc Copper!*. Back then, *HDC!* was available by subscription, as a regular feature in a growing number of national law enforcement publications, and as a free public service to many Riverside County officers.

Marty also began writing Courtroom Survival books, primarily for cops. Unable to reach a meeting of the minds with a so-called mainstream publishing house, he decided to go it one better and create his own.

Thus, **Copper Bible Book Company** was born, publishing good books for cops, aka *copper bibles*. Ergo, the name. Between 1987 and 1990, **CBBC** published his first three books:

- *Catch 55: Courtroom Survival for Traffic Officers*
- *Catch 56: Courtroom Survival for DUI Cops*
- *Courtroom Survival for Small Claims Court Litigants*

Those books are now out of print. In their place are new ones. For reasons not relevant herein, events occurred, diverting his attention from writing projects. Although he planned to immediately begin writing books, too many post-DA-retirement adventures got in the way. Suffice it to say, in 2008, he returned to work on his books.

In 2014, after ending his relationship with his former literary agent, and former publisher, Brhel sensed it was time for **CBBC** to return to duty. Now, **CBBC** publishes any and all of Marty's books.

Amazon two amazing subsidiaries, CreateSpace and Kindle Direct Publishing, allow **CBBC** to publish top quality books, on demand. In large part, that is because of the awesome talents of longtime friend Bill Kasal.

Fellow author and **CBBC** Executive Editor, Bill Kasal was Palm Springs PD Reserve Captain, protecting and serving his community for ten years. He has also been a radio DJ, hosted his own TV show, now blogs, and is also a videographer.

Bill has formatted each of Brhel's current books, and created their beautiful covers. Analysis of Kasal's talents caused Marty to take this enterprise to the next logical place.

CBBC is now available for hire. If any authors believe the traditional publishing route is no longer viable, as do they, Marty's publishing house offers an ideal alternative, providing editing, proofing, and promptly produced high quality books.

Made in the USA
Monee, IL
04 November 2026

67378320R00177